Improvements in System Safety

T0142932

Related titles:

Towards System Safety
Proceedings of the Seventh Safety-critical Systems Symposium, Huntingdon, UK, 1999
Redmill and Anderson (Eds)
1-85233-064-3

Lessons in System Safety
Proceedings of the Eighth Safety-critical Systems Symposium, Southampton, UK, 2000
Redmill and Anderson (Eds)
1-85233-249-2

Aspects of Safety Management
Proceedings of the Ninth Safety-critical Systems Symposium, Bristol, UK, 2001
Redmill and Anderson (Eds)
1-85233-411-8

Components of System Safety
Proceedings of the Tenth Safety-critical Systems Symposium, Southampton, UK, 2002
Redmill and Anderson (Eds)
1-85233-561-0

Current Issues in Safety-critical Systems
Proceedings of the Eleventh Safety-critical Systems Symposium, Bristol, UK, 2003
Redmill and Anderson (Eds)
1-85233-696-X

Practical Elements of Safety
Proceedings of the Twelfth Safety-critical Systems Symposium, Birmingham, UK, 2004
Redmill and Anderson (Eds)
1-85233-800-8

Constituents of Modern System-safety Thinking
Proceedings of the Thirteenth Safety-critical Systems Symposium, Southampton, UK, 2005
Redmill and Anderson (Eds)
1-85233-952-7

Developments in Risk-based Approaches to Safety
Proceedings of the Fourteenth Safety-critical Systems Symposium, Bristol, UK, 2006
Redmill and Anderson (Eds)
1-84628-333-7

The Safety of Systems
Proceedings of the Fifteenth Safety-critical Systems Symposium, Bristol, UK, 2007
Redmill and Anderson (Eds)
978-1-84628-805-0

Felix Redmill   Tom Anderson
Editors

Improvements in System Safety

Proceedings of the Sixteenth Safety-critical Systems
Symposium, Bristol, UK, 5–7 February 2008

Safety-Critical
Systems Club

BAE SYSTEMS

 Springer

Felix Redmill
Redmill Consultancy
22 Onslow Gardens
London N10 3JU
UK

Tom Anderson
Centre for Software Reliability
University of Newcastle
Newcastle upon Tyne, NE1 7RU
UK

ISBN: 978-1-84800-099-5   e-ISBN: 978-1-84800-100-8
DOI 10.1007/978-1-84800-100-8

British Library Cataloguing in Publication Data
A catalogue record for this book is available from the British Library

Printed on acid-free paper

9 8 7 6 5 4 3 2 1

Springer Science+Business Media
springer.com

Preface

The Safety-critical Systems Symposium (SSS), held each February for sixteen consecutive years, offers a full-day tutorial followed by two days of presentations of papers. This book of Proceedings contains all the papers presented at SSS '08.

The first paper accompanies the tutorial, which is on the important topic of the safety case. In recent years, the emphasis of papers has shifted from defining and describing the safety case and its purposes to reporting on experiences of its use and developments in its theory. Two further papers in the book do this.

The Symposium is for engineers, managers, and academics in the field of safety, across all industry sectors, so its papers always cover a range of topics. Each year a number of papers address themes raised in the previous year, and the papers in the section on the safety case are examples of this. In addition, there is a section of individual papers, on the relationship between safety and security, safety process improvement, and software development.

Over the years, there has been increasing emphasis on the role of humans, not only in contributing to accidents but also in achieving safety. Thus, 'human factors' is a recurring topic at the Symposium. And the need to develop and maintain a good safety culture has also come to be recognised as an important topic. This year there are papers on both subjects.

In the final two sections, a number of papers address the key subjects of risk analysis and the achievement and assessment of overall safety. These topics are perennial, for they require both good process and methodical technique, and every year there are papers that make observations, present reports on informative experiences, and offer new ideas. This year is no exception, and the five papers in the two sections do all of these things.

Overall, the papers address many of the topics that are currently of special interest in the safety-critical-systems community, and we are grateful to the authors for their contributions. We also thank our sponsors for their valuable support, and the exhibitors at the Symposium's tools and services fair for their participation. And we thank Joan Atkinson and her team for laying the event's foundation with their planning and organisation.

FR & TA
October 2007

THE SAFETY-CRITICAL SYSTEMS CLUB
organiser of the
Safety-critical Systems Symposium

What is the Safety-Critical Systems Club?
This "Community" Club exists to support developers and operators of systems that may have an impact on safety, across all industry sectors. It is an independent, non-profit organisation that co-operates with all bodies involved with safety-critical systems.

Objectives
The Club's two principal objectives are to raise awareness of safety issues in the field of safety-critical systems and to facilitate the transfer of safety technology from wherever it exists.

History
The Club was inaugurated in 1991 under the sponsorship of the UK's Department of Trade and Industry (DTI) and the Engineering and Physical Sciences Research Council (EPSRC). Its secretariat is at the Centre for Software Reliability (CSR) in the University of Newcastle upon Tyne, and its Co-ordinator is Felix Redmill of Redmill Consultancy.

Since 1994 the Club has been self-sufficient, but it retains the active support of the DTI and EPSRC, as well as that of the Health and Safety Executive, the Institution of Engineering and Technology, and the British Computer Society. All of these bodies are represented on the Club's Steering Group.

The Club's activities
The Club achieves its goals of awareness-raising and technology transfer by focusing on current and emerging practices in safety engineering, software engineering, and standards that relate to safety in processes and products. Its activities include:
- Running the annual Safety-critical Systems Symposium each February (the first was in 1993), with Proceedings published by Springer-Verlag;
- Organising a number of 1- and 2-day seminars each year;
- Providing tutorials on relevant subjects;
- Publishing a newsletter, Safety Systems, three times annually (since 1991), in January, May and September.

Education and communication
The Club brings together technical and managerial personnel within all sectors of the safety-critical-systems community. Its events provide education and training in principles and techniques, and it facilitates the dissemination of lessons within and between industry sectors. It promotes an inter-disciplinary approach to the engineering and management of safety, and it provides a forum for experienced practitioners to meet each other and for the exposure of newcomers to the safety-critical systems industry.

Influence on research

The Club facilitates communication among researchers, the transfer of technology from researchers to users, feedback from users, and the communication of experience between users. It provides a meeting point for industry and academia, a forum for the presentation of the results of relevant projects, and a means of learning and keeping up-to-date in the field.

The Club thus helps to achieve more effective research, a more rapid and effective transfer and use of technology, the identification of best practice, the definition of requirements for education and training, and the dissemination of information. Importantly, it does this within a 'club' atmosphere rather than a commercial environment.

Membership

Members pay a reduced fee (well below the commercial level) for events and receive the newsletter and other mailed information. Not being sponsored, the Club depends on members' subscriptions, and these can be paid at the first meeting attended.

To join, please contact Mrs Joan Atkinson at: The Centre for Software Reliability, University of Newcastle upon Tyne, NE1 7RU; Telephone: 0191 221 2222; Fax: 0191 222 7995; Email: csr@newcastle.ac.uk

Contents List

Achieving and Improving System Safety

Safety and Risk Analysis

Tutorial Paper

Can Process-Based and Product-Based Approaches to Software Safety Certification be Reconciled?

T P Kelly

Department of Computer Science

University of York, York, YO10 5DD, UK.

tim.kelly@cs.york.ac.uk

Abstract

The certification of software for use in safety-critical systems is a requirement in many domains: defence, aerospace, rail, nuclear. However, there is still significant variance in the practice of software safety assurance across these different domains. This paper compares two quite different approaches (software safety case development under the UK Defence Standard 00-56, and software assurance under the civil aerospace guidance document DO-178B.) The paper highlights both the similarities and differences between these approaches. Ultimately, we consider whether there are any circumstances under which they can be considered to be compatible.

1   Introduction

Software certification is a common requirement across many safety-critical industries. A large number of software safety standards exist to define required software safety assurance practice. These standards vary in their requirements. Whilst some of this variance is in the detail (e.g. favoured verification methods), some large differences in philosophy remain. One such philosophical difference is between so-called *process assurance* based safety standards – such as DO-178B (RTCA, 1992) – and *product-based* safety standards – such as UK Defence Standard 00-56 Issue 4 (MoD, 2007). This paper examines this difference and discusses whether there are opportunities for reconciling these two approaches.

Sections 2 and 3 present a brief characterisation and overview of process-based and product-based approaches to software certification, including recognition of the problems that exist with both approaches. Section 4 discusses whether there are conditions under which it is possible to reconcile these two approaches. Section 5 presents some concluding remarks.

2   Process-Based Certification

A number of software assurance standards – such as DO-178B (RTCA, 1992) and IEC 61508 (IEC, 1999) – are described as being "process-based", in that they define a set of practices to be adhered to in the development, verification and validation of software. In such standards the software processes are typically prescribed according to the criticality of software failure. In the civil aerospace domain Development Assurance Levels (DALs) are used to define the level of rigour required. In the European Rail, Process Industry, and automotive domains Safety Integrity Levels (SILs) are used. SILs and DALs are similar concepts, but differ in the details of their allocation, requirements and application.

Both SILs and DALs define the level of risk reduction expected from a software system. The greater the criticality of a software-involved system, the greater the risk reduction is necessarily attributed to that system. SILs and DALs can also be thought of as specifying the required degree of freedom of the system from flaw. For software systems, this particularly relates to the degree of freedom from *systematic* errors in the design – introduced through failings in the software production process. Processes and techniques are specified for each SIL / DAL. The higher the SIL / DAL, the more demanding are the requirements on the software production process.

The following quote from the introduction to DO-178B summarises the philosophy behind the organisation of the standard:

> *"These guidelines are in the form of:*
>
> *- Objectives for software life cycle processes.*
>
> *- Descriptions of activities and design considerations for achieving those objectives.*
>
> *- Descriptions of the evidence that indicates that the objectives have been satisfied."*

DO-178B defines an outline software life-cycle. The main stages of this life-cycle are:

- Software Requirements (both High-Level and Low-Level)
- Software Design
- Software Coding
- Integration

Many of the requirements of DO-178B are expressed *over* this model of the process. For example, there are requirements (called 'objectives' in DO-178B) concerned with the consistency of the artefacts produced at each stage, and of the compliance between the artefacts of one stage (e.g. source code) and the artefacts of another (e.g. low-level requirements). DO-178B places a strong emphasis on traceability, and the human review of artefacts (such as requirements).   DO-178B also strongly favours testing as the primary means of verification.

The objectives of DO-178B vary according to DAL. At level D, the lowest level, 28 objectives are defined (covering aspects such as configuration management, tool qualification, and high-level requirements coverage. At level C, a further 29 objectives are added (covering aspects such as statement coverage, and testing of low-level requirements). At level B, a further 8 objectives are added (covering aspects such as decision coverage). Finally, at level A the requirement for MC/DC coverage is added, together with greater source code to object code traceability. In total, 66 objectives are defined for a Level A compliant software development.

2.1   Problems of Process-Based Certification

There are a number of well-established criticisms of process-based certification (Redmill, 2000).   Firstly, there is a lack of evidence that adherence to the prescribed processes leads to the achievement of a specific level of integrity. There is a poor correlation between prescribed techniques and the failure rate considered by many to be defined by a DAL – i.e. there is an implicit belief in the 'risk reducing' properties of the process that is not borne out in practice. Another criticism is that the prescription of processes can hinder the adoption of new process approaches that could improve the flexibility and predictability of software development (e.g. approaches such as Model Driven Development).   Finally, because of the differences in the detail of the requirements of SILs and DALs in different domains, DAL/SIL claims are not easily 'transferred' from one domain to another.   For example, a claim of achieving DO-178B Level A does not straightforwardly map across to the requirements of IEC 61508 SIL 4 (IEC, 1999).

The issue of whether adherence to a DAL/SIL can be used to support a failure rate claim relating to the systematic error in software remains widely debated. In concept, it is legitimate to talk of the probability of software failing (with respect to intent) due to a previously undisclosed systematic error. This can be considered to be the probability of revealing ('activating') the design flaw in a given operational environment. The now superseded UK Defence Standard 00-56 Issue 2 contained the concept of *Claim Limits* (MoD, 1996).   Claim limits were an attempt to acknowledge the potential for systematic error to contribute to overall system failure by limiting the minimum failure rate claimed based upon the achieved SIL. In concept, this is defensible. In the details, however, it becomes hard to defend as it relies upon an understanding of the correlation of software development processes to achieved failure rates – an understanding that is lacking in the majority of cases.   DO-178B takes a different line by stating that, *"Development of software to a software level does not imply the assignment of a failure rate for the software"*. Whilst this is strongly stated, it is still hard for many to "shake off" the belief that development to a DAL can be "reverse engineered" back to a corresponding (random) failure rate requirement.   For example, for a *catastrophic* failure condition, the DAL requirement is level A, the corresponding failure rate requirement is for the probability of failure to be less than 1×10^{-9} per flight hour (SAE, 1994). This does not imply, however, that the likelihood of a software (design error) contribution to a system-level hazard can be regarded as 1×10^{-9} per hour.

3   Product-based Certification

Product-based certification focuses on the construction of well-structured and reasoned safety arguments: Arguments are required to demonstrate the satisfaction of *product-specific* safety objectives derived from hazard analysis; justify the acceptability of safety, based upon product-specific and targeted evidence; and (potentially) justify the determination of the safety objectives and selection of evidence.   The arguments and evidence required to justify acceptable safety form the *safety case*, and are often summarised in a *safety case report* (Kelly, 2002).

For software, product-based certification demands that software level safety claims are *hazard-based* – i.e. they concern failures of the software that are believed to lead to system level hazards.   Ideally, these claims should be derived from a system-level safety case.   In a system-level safety case a claim relating to a specific behaviour of the software may be seen as a *contributing*, but *undeveloped* argument.   From the perspective of software safety, such claims are the starting point for the construction of the software safety case.   This is the intended relationship between system and software level safety cases under UK Defence Standard 00-56 Issue 4 (MoD, 2007).   This means that the focus in the software level safety arguments is on "*demonstrating the safety of ...*", rather than "*demonstrating the development of ...*" the software system.   Arguments and evidence about the development process followed are not of interest unless they can somehow be specifically related to the *product-specific* software safety claims.

3.1   Selecting Software Safety Evidence

Weaver (Weaver, 2002) has previously suggested how targeted software safety arguments can be constructed, based upon an understanding of the nature of the software failure mode being addressed (e.g. failure of omission, value failure, timing failure).   For example, a software failure mode of type *omission* could be argued to be absent if:

- All feasible paths through software functionality contain a unique output statement (the *primary* argument)

- Failure of other software functionality which could lead to a failure of primary software functionality does not occur (a *secondary* argument)

- All necessary resources exist to support correct operation of primary software functionality (another *secondary* argument)

- Primary software functionality is scheduled and allowed to run (at least) once (the *control* argument)

Evidence should then be selected to support the detail of these arguments. For example, Control Flow Analysis could be used to address the first bullet point above, whilst Schedulability Analysis could be used to support the last bullet point.

In addition to considering the *nature* of the claim being supported, evidence should be selected based upon the *required level of confidence* in that claim. The following guidance on this issue is given in Defence Standard 00-56 Issue 4:

> *"9.5.5.1 In general, arguments based on explicit, objective evidence are more compelling than those that appeal to judgement or custom and practice. It is therefore recommended that any argument should be developed in accordance with the following precedence:*
>
> - *Deductive, where the conclusion is implicit in the evidence used to support the argument.*
>
> - *Inductive, where the argument is firmly based on the evidence presented, but extrapolates beyond the available evidence.*
>
> - *Judgmental, where expert testimony, or appeal to custom and practice is necessary to support the conclusion."*

In addition, 00-56 recommends that the level of evidence ought to be chosen according to the level of risk associated with the system:

> *"The quantity and quality of the evidence shall be commensurate with the potential risk posed by the system and the complexity of the system."*

This can be seen as a generalisation of the SIL approach defined in previous issues of the defence standard.

3.2   Subjectivity in Safety Case Development

One of the principle difficulties faced when adopting a safety case based approach to software safety assurance is *subjectivity*. Typically, one party is responsible for preparing the safety case. Another party (the certification authority) is responsible for accepting the safety case. Safety cases are, by their nature, often subjective. The objective of safety case development, therefore, is to obtain mutual acceptance of this subjective position.

To address the question, "Is this safety case good enough?", it is important to recognise the distinction between inductive and deductive arguments (as this alters the nature of possible criticisms of the argument). A *deductive* argument is an argument that proceeds without any room for probability. An *inductive* argument is one that is based upon the estimation of the probable truth of the premises. In an inductive argument the probable truth of the premises is passed through the argument to the conclusion. Safety case arguments are rarely *provable* deductive arguments. Instead they are more commonly inductive.

For deductive arguments, it is possible to simply question the *validity* of the inference of the arguments in terms of truth or falsity.   For inductive arguments, the situation is more complicated.   The question in this case is of the overall *sufficiency* of the argument – i.e. are the premises of the argument "strong enough" to support the conclusions being drawn.   The sufficiency of the relationship between the premises and conclusion of the argument depends upon a number of attributes such as the coverage and robustness of the argument and evidence.

A major source of subjectivity in any software safety case is the perceived *trustworthiness* of the evidence presented as part of the case.   Uncertainty about the provenance of evidence in safety arguments can undermine confidence (Habli, 2007).   This is true even with supposedly 'deductive' evidence (e.g. formal proof). To address this issue, there is a requirement for additional arguments about the evidence generation process to be presented as part of the safety case.   These arguments could include those addressing the software development process where software artefacts are referred to directly as evidence within the safety case. Figure 1 illustrates this (ideal) relationship between process and product arguments.   Process arguments are used to argue about the derivation of evidence that is used as the basis of 'direct' (product-based) risk reduction arguments.   Such process arguments need to address issues such as the competency of the personnel producing evidence, the suitability and reliability of the methods used, and the qualification of tool support. A number of the objectives that exist in standards such as DO-178B already address these issues.   It should be recognised, therefore, that it is not these process requirements that are open to criticism.   Instead, it is the attempt to infer *direct* claims of integrity and safety from addressing these requirements that is questionable (as shown in Figure 2).

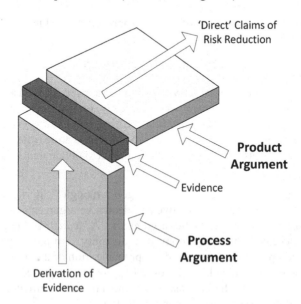

Figure 1 – Process Arguments Supporting Product Arguments

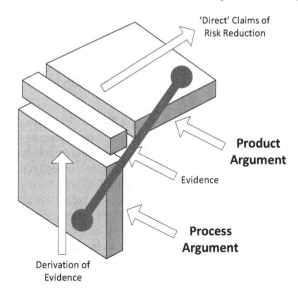

'Direct' Claims of
Risk Reduction

**Product
Argument**

Evidence

**Process
Argument**

Derivation of
Evidence

Figure 2 – Inferring Process Claims from Product Arguments

4   Incompatible Approaches?

Proponents of process prescription in software safety assurance often put forward the following arguments:

- "At least we know what we're supposed to do on this project"

- The use of a defined process facilitates costing, and planning (because of reduced variability in the process)

- It ensures a minimum baseline standard that "weeds out the cowboys"

Goal-based, product-oriented certification cuts standards and guidance back to undeniably true objectives such as the following (taken from Defence Standard 00-56 Issue 4):

> *"Safety is considered from the earliest stage in a programme and used to influence all activities and products"*

> *"Tasks that influence safety are carried out by individuals and organisations that are demonstrably competent to perform those tasks"*

> *"All credible hazards and accidents are identified, the associated accident sequences are defined and the risks associated with them are determined"*

Very few people would disagree with such statements. However, moving from the principles to practice can be hard for some developers. They ask, "But what do I do now?", and dislike that a "cover-all" answer cannot be given. Additional guidance is therefore required. (Indeed, additional guidance for the development of software safety cases against Defence Standard 00-56 is being prepared.) However, care will have to be taken to ensure that such guidance, when produced, does not simply become a *de facto* standard (thereby nullifying the benefit of the goal-based, and product-oriented, approach.)

There are circumstances under which adopting a DO-178B approach to software assurance could also be considered to satisfy the core requirements of an product-based approach. DO-178B places great emphasis on requirements handling within the software development lifecycle. For example, objectives are defined concerning requirements review, and the traceability of tests to requirements. If these requirements could be argued to include *all* safety requirements, then adopting a DO-178B process would encourage the production of (traceable) evidence against each one of these requirements (in the same way that the argument of a safety case provides a traceable structure from high level claims to evidence.) The strength of process-based standards such as DO-178B is that they provide guidance on how to develop and implement requirements in a trustworthy manner.

It is hard to establish a safety case purely from the satisfaction of positively expressed requirements that describe the desired behaviour of a software-involved system. Safety requirements often have a *negative* focus (Wu, 2007). They define properties that the software should *not* exhibit. This can create difficulties in assessing the completeness of any testing performed purely from a 'compliance' perspective. To provide assurance that all safety issues have been adequately reflected in the software requirements will require special attention. Whilst initially, software safety requirements can be derived from system-level safety analysis (as DO-178B suggests) other safety requirements will necessarily emerge as design commitments are made (i.e. safety requirements cannot simply be defined 'top-down'). This is where the DO-178B requirement for manual requirements review will almost certainly be insufficient. Safety-specific techniques (such as Hazard and Operability Studies and Functional Failure Analysis) must be applied as part of the software development process to capture new safety requirements alongside an evolving design.

As discussed in Section 3, in an product-based framework freedom is needed to choose arguments and evidence that address the specific nature of the software safety requirements. DO-178B currently over-emphasises testing as a verification method. However, in the revision of DO-178B (to produce DO-178C) proposals have been made to generalise the wording to call for verification instead of specific methods (Review, Analysis and Testing). This move "opens the door" for alternative forms of evidence to be selected without needing to be justified as a deviation from the defined verification approach.

Questions still remain, however, as to whether DO-178B/C is over prescribing the software development process and is ultimately asking for processes and evidence other that those truly required from a perspective of safety.

DO-178B is capable of producing evidence about the trustworthiness of the process. However, it does not provide guidance on how to produce product-based *claims* based on software 'hazard' and failure mode analysis. This is the key problem. DO-178B is therefore good for producing *backing* arguments about software development, verification and management rather than product-based arguments about the safety-related aspects of the software itself.

5   Summary

Many perceive that the trend in software safety assurance is towards product-based certification (such as that required by UK Defence Standard 00-56 Issue 4). However, process-based standards such as DO-178B are still in widespread use. An product-based approach often places more emphasis on 'direct' product arguments, with a targeted (rather than 'scatter-gun') approach to evidence selection. DO-178B offers a prescribed approach to software development that *will* result in product evidence (largely test-based) being produced, and *implicitly* establishes a software safety case based upon the traceability of requirements into implementation.   However, it is the absence of explicit justification of the approach adopted, concern over the completeness of safety issues being captured in requirements, and the lack of freedom to choose appropriate evidence that sets it apart from that of a true software safety case approach. Most importantly, the distinction that exists between *assuring the process* and *assuring the products that result from the process* must be recognised.

6   Acknowledgements

The author would like to acknowledge the contribution of Ibrahim Habli in reviewing and commenting on this paper.

7   References

Habli, I., Kelly, T., *Achieving Integrated Process and Product Safety Arguments* in *The Safety of Systems*: Proceedings of the Fifteenth Safety-critical Systems Symposium, Anderson, T., Redmill, F. (ed.s), Bristol, UK, Springer, 2007

IEC (1999) IEC61508 - Functional Safety of Electrical / Electronic / Programmable Electronic Safety-Related Systems, International Electrotechnical Commission (IEC), 1999

Kelly, T. P. *(2004) A Systematic Approach to Safety Case Management,* in *CAE Methods for Vehicle Crashworthiness and Occupant Safety, and Safety-Critical Systems,* Document Number 2004-01-1779, Society of Automotive Engineers, March 2004

MoD (1996) Defence Standard 00-56 Safety Management Requirements for Defence Systems, UK Ministry of Defence, Issue 2, 1996

MoD (2007) Defence Standard 00-56 Safety Management Requirements for Defence Systems, UK Ministry of Defence, Issue 4, 2007

Redmill, F. (2000), Safety Integrity Levels – Theory and Problems, in *Lessons in System Safety*: Proceedings of the Eighth Safety-Critical Systems Symposium, Anderson, T., Redmill, F. (ed.s), Southampton, UK, Springer, 2000

RTCA (1992) *Software Considerations in Airborne Systems and Equipment Certification,* Radio Technical Commission for Aeronautics RTCA DO-178B/EUROCAE ED-12B, 1992

SAE (1994), *ARP 4754 - Certification Considerations for Highly-Integrated or Complex Aircraft Systems*, The Society for Automotive Engineers December 1994.

Weaver, R. A., McDermid, J. A., Kelly, T. P. (2002), *Software Safety Arguments: Towards a Systematic Categorisation of Evidence,* in proceedings of the 20th International System Safety Conference (ISSC 2002), Denver, Colorado, USA, System Safety Society, 2002

Wu, W, Kelly, T. P. (2007) *Towards Evidence-Based Architectural Design for Safety-Critical Software Applications,* in *Architecting Dependable Systems IV*, Lecture Notes in Computer Science , Vol. 4615, Lemos, Rogério de; Gacek, Cristina; Romanovsky, Alexander (Eds.), Springer, 2007

Themes Reprised from SSS '07

Making Safe Software Secure

Odd Nordland
SINTEF ICT
Trondheim, Norway

Abstract

Safety and security are traditionally treated separately, particular with respect to software. The increasing demand for remote access to computer controlled industrial systems requires merging the two fields. Some possible methods are described and possibilities for improving both safety and security related standards are presented.

1   Introduction

Nowadays it is almost unthinkable to control a complex technical process without using computers. They are used in nuclear power stations, chemical plants, rail and air traffic control and a vast number of industrial applications. In the past decades, extensive experience has been gathered in developing software that can perform the control tasks in a safe and reliable way; indeed, it is usually considered safer to let a computer perform a complex control task, rather than relying on fallible humans: the computer is faster, doesn't get tired, never forgets or overlooks anything and doesn't get distracted by its surroundings.

Unfortunately, the increasing reliance on computer systems for technical control makes us increasingly dependent on the computer's software, which in turn makes us vulnerable if the software gets modified in an undesirable way. Indeed, simply misusing otherwise correct software can become a threat.

The internet has shown how easy and effective it can be to connect to remote computers. Salespeople can access their company's data bases and place orders without having to return from their business trip first and home banking is widespread. On the other hand, the internet has also brought us the problems of hackers, viruses and spyware.

There is now a growing demand to use remote access not only to monitor but also to control processes in e.g. oil platforms, albeit not necessarily by the internet. But however it is done, remote access opens the door for hackers, virus programmers or terrorists who want to interfere with the process control; a possibility they didn't have earlier. So now it is not enough to have safe software in industrial control; it has to be secure too.

2   Safety and security

The terms safety and security are often mixed and there is a multitude of definitions for each of them. Meine van der Meulen (van der Meulen 2000) collected four different definitions of "safety" and six different definitions of "security" from various standards, guidelines etc. Some standards even operate with multiple definitions, an indication that even the authors of the standard could not reach an agreement. The Internet lists a larger number of definitions for security than for safety, so there is apparently a greater consensus on the meaning of the word safety than on the meaning of the word security. However, a glance at those definitions reveals a considerable overlap, and very often the terms are even considered to be synonymous!

The problem is not specific to the English language. The Germanic languages have one word for both safety and security and a certain degree of difficulty in expressing the differences: it is widespread use the English words to indicate which meaning is intended, but that certainly doesn't contribute to clarification, more the opposite.

The problem is that a definition should be concise, complete and comprehensible. For the complexity of the concepts behind safety and security, this is almost impossible to achieve. The result is that somebody will always find an aspect that isn't covered by the definition. So rather than trying to produce yet another set of definitions, we shall use a somewhat more verbatim explanation of what is meant here.

We start by considering a technical system that we want to control. This means that the system can have an effect on its environment (i.e. the rest of the world), but it can also be affected by its environment. If the effects are undesired, we will try to prevent them from occurring.

The word "undesired" is important here: the effect of a bomb is to blow up a building, which is usually undesirable, particularly if you happen to be in that building. But it's but not undesired: the undesired effect is blowing up the <u>wrong</u> building!

The <u>in</u>ability of the system to affect its environment in an undesired way is usually referred to as safety; the <u>in</u>ability of the environment to affect the system in an undesired way is usually called security. Alternatively, safety and security are used to express attributes that are based on measures that aim at preventing the system from having an undesired effect on its environment respectively vice versa.

Now these explanations are intentionally kept very generic. Particularly with respect to security there is a tendency to limit the concept to e.g. protection against terrorism or other malicious acts. This is a too narrow view: an earthquake is not a malicious act, but it can certainly damage or destroy power plants, buildings or roads. Constructing buildings or roads to survive an earthquake is in fact a typical security measure, because it is protecting the building or road from being damaged by its environment. But it's also a safety measure, because by protecting a building from being damaged by an earthquake, we are also protecting the inhabitants of that building from being harmed by the building.

At this stage we see that safety and security are strongly coupled. Nancy Leveson (Leveson 1995, p.182) argued for keeping safety and security segregated, stating *"Although there are some commonalities and interactions, safety is a distinct quality and should be treated separately from other qualities, or the tradeoffs, which are often required, will be hidden from view."* As we will see in the next section, the connection between safety and security has become so much stronger that segregating the two can have the effect that mutual aspects can get completely overlooked, because neither side feels responsible.

3   Scenarios

Part of the problem is that it is possible to misuse a perfectly correct function of a technical system to achieve a totally undesired effect. A typical example is a Denial-of-Service attack against an internet service provider. The perfectly legitimate function of transferring data, e.g. by e-mail, is misused to flood the service provider's machines so that they are unable to provide their services to genuine customers.

Now such attacks will cause some economical damage to the service provider, and probably also to some of his customers, but human life will not usually be endangered. But there are other possibilities.

3.1   Rail Traffic Control

Nowadays railway networks make extensive use of computer systems to control and monitor rail traffic. A central element of such systems is the network of interconnected computers that control traffic and trackside equipment at stations and junctions. Trains that run on such networks are equipped with on-board computer systems that send data to, and receive and process data from, the interlocking computers. The information sent to the train includes data about the maximum permissible speed, the distance to the next signal, its status and so on. The on-board computer transmits data back to the interlocking computers, such as the train number, the train's position, speed and travelling direction etc.

The data transfer is achieved by radio signals: there are transponders, so called "balises", placed between the tracks at strategic positions. The trains have a transceiver on board, and when they pass over a balise they transmit their data to it. The energy they transmit is sufficient to activate the circuits of the transponder, which then transmits its data back to the train.

In such a situation, falsified data can have a catastrophic effect. If the train's on-board computer can be tricked into allowing maximum speed in a sharp curve or an area where construction works are going on, the result could be as terrible as the Eschede accident in Germany in 1998.

A lot of effort is invested in making the software capable of recognising and either correcting, or at least ignoring erroneous data, but the complexity of the communication mechanisms is usually considered sufficient to prevent intentional generation of bogus messages. However, terrorists or other criminals have plenty of money and technical facilities available, and an insider with sufficient knowledge of the system could possibly succeed in creating bogus messages with the aid of a sufficiently determined criminal organisation.

3.2   Remote maintenance

For systems in a hostile, or at least difficult to access environment, there is a growing demand to perform not only control, but also maintenance activities using remote control. An example is the oil platforms in the North Sea. It is an expensive exercise to send maintenance staff out to each and every platform in order to update the software running on the computers. How much easier would it be to send the latest software update by radio link and do a remote installation? It would be faster too, since all platforms could be upgraded simultaneously.

But if the software gets modified during transmission, the result could be that once safe software becomes unsafe or even dangerous. We could end up with a complete loss of control with catastrophic effects for the people on board the platforms and for the environment. So preventing falsification of transmitted software becomes just as important as making sure that the transmitted software is safe.

3.3   Telemedicine

In sparsely populated areas, such as the far North of Norway, doctors are few and far between. Those that are available are, of necessity, general practitioners. For patients who need specialist treatment, the distance to the nearest specialist can be prohibitive. A possible solution is to use a specialist, located far away in a big hospital, as an online supervisor for the general practitioner. A video connection is needed, so that the specialist can see what his colleague is doing, and the data that is typically monitored electronically (such as pulse rate, blood pressure etc.) can be transmitted directly to the specialist. He, in turn, may remotely control some of the equipment, such as infusion pumps for example.

If the data that is exchanged gets tampered with, the remotely controlled equipment might start executing completely wrong treatment, possibly with a fatal effect. So the safe data, which is also part of the software on such equipment, must be protected.

4   Methods

The above scenarios are simple examples that illustrate that safe software must itself be protected. In the past, enormous efforts have been made to ensure that software that controls a technical process is safe. Now it's time to make it secure.

Security is an attribute that should be built in to the software from the outset. Many of the methods that have been developed in order to achieve safety can be adapted to security. Line et al. (Line 2006) discussed the similarities and differences between safety and security methods and argue "... *the analysis techniques and tools that are used to determine and classify hazards can easily be adapted to threats, and the techniques for analyzing threats can be adapted to hazards...*" Saglietti (Saglietti 2005) has also pointed out the potential in adapting safety techniques to incorporate security and states "... *it is felt that this question is becoming increasingly important and should be handled in a unified, systematic way by means of an extended fault tree analysis, capable of integrating security incidents as sub-events possibly leading to safety-related failures.*"

There is still a lot of work to be done before we get unified analysis techniques, and we cannot afford to wait for them. There is safe software in use today that needs to be protected in an ever changing and increasingly networked environment.

And that protection can be achieved by a combination of hardware, software and administrative procedures. Some possibilities are sketched below.

4.1   Hardware

Software can be protected by hardware! Obviously, segregating the machine from any form of network will also protect the software running on it. Where this is possible it should be done. Modifications to the software will then necessitate a data transfer by some form of removable data carrier, which in turn requires a conscious and controllable human activity. Falsification of the software will still be possible, but at a much higher risk for the person doing it. In addition, administrative procedures can contribute to preventing such acts of sabotage.

The use of "dongles" to prevent software piracy was never particularly popular, because it was and is inconvenient for the users and not least because a dongle cannot be downloaded: the hardware has to be delivered to the customer and physically connected to the computer that the software is running on.

For commercial off-the-shelf software that is intended for a mass market, dongles are probably more of a drawback than a benefit. But for dedicated safety critical software that is not subject to mass distribution, the technology could provide a high degree of protection against falsification of the executable code in a flexible and reliable way. The fact that a dongle is removable means that it can easily be replaced when the software is updated; it can also be used to make sure that only compatible versions of different programs are installed on the machine.

4.2   Software

The software security community has developed a multitude of technologies to protect data, albeit not necessarily with the protection of safe software in mind. But methods that have been developed to protect data integrity will also protect code integrity, so the task is not really new.

Line et al. (Line 2006) argue *"The techniques used in software safety have been around for quite some time and are well established and tested. Some of these techniques may be useful also for security people who may thus benefit from the experiences of the safety community. On the other hand, there are also security techniques that will become significant for the safety community. For example, in the near future we will see more use of open communication networks for remote control of industrial and transportation applications. When vitally important commands are transmitted through such open networks, security techniques such as encryption and authorization control will become indispensable for safety. Security techniques will have to become an integral part of safety thinking."*

One challenge can be the timing aspects. Safety related software must often react rapidly and cannot afford to be slowed down by lengthy, time consuming verification, authentication or decryption procedures. A possible solution is to encapsulate the safety critical software in a secure shell.

Jaatun et al. (Jaatun 2007) describe an "onion model" to protect safety critical software in an offshore application. Basically, the system uses several layers of software surrounding the safety critical kernel; each layer has specific access options so that the further in a layer is, the more strongly it is protected. The safe kernel can then perform its tasks without having to include security related activities.

4.3   Administrative procedures

Administrative procedures are often overlooked as a safety measure, whilst they are often considered for security. Typically, users will be required to use passwords that are changed regularly and are sufficiently long to make them difficult to crack. Requiring controlled authorisation should be a must for modifying safety critical software, but the fact is that it is not usually done. At best the computer should be put into maintenance mode or switched offline before the software is modified, but the technician who has to do the job does not normally need a password to start. And certainly not a set of passwords, depending on the kind of maintenance he has to do.

Even with a password controlled access, the technician will assume that the data he has been given is correct. One way of ensuring that the new data is correct could be to get it installed twice by two different technicians at two different times. If the two installations are not identical, the data has been modified.

5   Assessment

For both safety and security there are certification schemes based on independent third party assessments. However, the schemes are substantially different: for safety the standards identify requirements to be fulfilled in order to achieve a defined safety integrity level; for security the standards describe assessment methods to be applied in order to achieve a certain level of confidence, but they don't define the security requirements to be fulfilled.

5.1   Safety assessments

Depending on the application area there are often sector specific safety standards with sector specific safety requirements, but as far as software is concerned, IEC 61508 can be regarded as the "mother" of the safety standards. Indeed, IEC 61508 explicitly states that it "...*provides general requirements for ... safety-related systems where no application sector standards exist...*" One consequence of this is that many sectors, for example offshore, don't even try to develop sector specific standards and simply apply IEC 61508 directly. In those cases where sector specific standards have been developed, such as the railways, they at least claim to be a sector specific implementation of IEC 61508, albeit without providing any form for evidence! Nevertheless, the requirements from IEC 61508 for software can be used as a suitable example.

It should be noted that IEC 61508 also explicitly states that it "... *does not cover the precautions that may be necessary to prevent unauthorised persons damaging, and/or otherwise adversely affecting, the functional safety of ... safety-related systems.*" In other words, security is explicitly excluded.

The standard uses the concept of Safety Integrity Levels ("SIL") which was first introduced by the British Defence Standard 00-56 (MOD 1996). In spite of being over twenty years old, the concept is still poorly understood. The important thing to understand is that SILs are related to safety critical <u>functions</u>, not to the components or equipment that are used to implement those functions. In particular, the failure rates that are used to define the different safety integrity levels refer to failures of the safety critical function, not to failure rates of the equipment.

Let us take a very simple example: a motor car has a hydraulic and a mechanical braking system. A failure of either the hydraulic or the mechanical braking system alone does not mean one has lost the braking function, so the failure rate of the braking <u>function</u> will be lower than the individual failure rates of either the hydraulic or the mechanical braking system.

For software the concept becomes somewhat more complicated. Software may possibly be the sole way of implementing a safety critical function, and it is virtually impossible to determine a failure rate for software. Ideally software - if it is perfectly correct - can never fail. But of course software is seldom, if ever, perfectly correct, so it can fail. Ultimately, the probability of the software containing faults that can lead to a failure is determined by the techniques and methods that have been applied when the software was being developed and throughout its entire life cycle. The standard identifies a variety of techniques and measures to be applied during the software life cycle, and it is then the task of an independent assessor to determine if and to what extent this has been done.

This process is independent of the safety integrity level, since the SIL is regarded as a property of the system being assessed, not of the assessment procedure. It is therefore not correct to say "a system is certified to SIL 3"; it IS a SIL 3 system in that it must fulfil the safety integrity requirements that are defined for SIL 3. The assessor can certify that the corresponding requirements either are or are not fulfilled, but a SIL 3 system cannot become a SIL 4 system without being modified, in which case the whole safety certification process has to be repeated.

5.2   Security assessments

For security, and in particular software security, criteria for assessing the software have been defined in the so-called Common Criteria. Together with the Common Evaluation Methodology they form a toolset for evaluation and certification of both software and hardware with respect to security.

The Common Criteria consist of three parts: part 1 is an introduction giving an overview of the standard, part 2 contains a listing of possible security functions and part 3 defines the Evaluation Assurance Levels (EAL). Although seven different EALs are defined, there are only guidelines on how to evaluate according to EALs 1 to 4, because the international community has not yet agreed upon the process and techniques for evaluation according to the higher EALs.

There are attempts to define some kind of correspondence between SILs and EALs. This simply reveals how poorly the concepts are understood. EALs say something about the degree of confidence one can have in the results of an assessment, and it is no problem to "upgrade" a system's EAL by simply re-assessing it. That hasn't made the system more secure, it has only increased our confidence in its security. Whether a SIL 4 system that is certified to EAL 1 is better than a SIL 3 system that is certified to EAL 4 is currently not determinable.

6   Future work

There is a lot to do before we can claim that safe software is secure. Certainly existing safety related software can and should be given improved protection, and the foregoing text has given some examples of how this can be done. It is important to note that making already existing safe software secure does not have to compromise the safe functionality of that software in any way. And when suitable standards have been agreed upon, it will be possible to certify that safe software is also secure.

As mentioned earlier, there are both safety and security standards for software. The safety standards define safety integrity requirements, but leave it entirely up to the assessor to determine how to evaluate whether those requirements are adequately fulfilled or not. For security the opposite is the case: the standards define how to evaluate a system, but they don't define "security integrity levels". Clearly, there is room for synergy here!

As a first step, the safety community should look at the security standards and agree on assessment methods for safety. There are already several guidelines, such as (HSE 1992, MOD 1996, Pygott et al. 1999 or HSE 2003), so the work has, in fact, been begun. Now the community has to agree on a set of common evaluation criteria for safety related software.

At the same time, security levels should be defined for safety related software. Clearly, we will have different demands for the security of e.g. banking software and simple internet browsers, so there is already a degree of implicit categorisation. Here again, the international community must agree on how to assign security functions to well defined categories and how to allocate a security category for a given application.

When those two tasks have been done, it will be possible to start merging the safety and security standards. The result could still be two standards, but this time one standard would be defining safety and security requirements while the other would be defining assessment methods and criteria. And then the speakers of Germanic languages will be able to retain their single word for safety and security.

7   References

HSE (1992). Safety Assessment Principles for Nuclear Plants. HSE Books, Sudbury, 1992.

HSE (2003). Safety Case Assessment Manual. HSE Books, Sudbury, 2003.

Jaatun M G, Grøtan T O, Line M B (2007). Secure Safety: Good Practice for Secure Remote Access to Critical Safety Systems In Offshore Installations. Private communication to be published later.

Leveson N (1995). Safeware: system safety and computers. Addison-Wesley, Reading, Massachusetts, 1995

Line M B, Nordland O, Røstad L, Tøndel I A (2006). Safety vs. Security? In: Stamatelatos M G and Blackman H S (Eds.) Proceedings of the Eighth International Conference on Probabilistic Safety Assessment and management - PSAM 8. ASME Press, New York, 2006, ../pdfs/track-10/PSAM-0148.pdf

Ministry of Defence (1996). Defence Standard 00-56: Safety Management Requirements for Defence Systems. Her Majesty's Stationary Office, London, 1996

Pygott C, Furze R, Thompson I and Kelly C (1999). WP5 Final Report, Safety Case Assessment Approach for Air Traffic Management (ATM). ATM System Criticality Raises Issues in Balancing Actors' Responsibility (ARIBA). DERA, 1999

Saglietti F (2005). Assessing Software Safety and Security for Critical Infrastructures. European CIIP Newsletter 2005 Vol. 1 No. 2, pp 30-33

van der Meulen M J P (2000). Definitions for Hardware and Software Safety Engineers. Springer Verlag, London, 2000

Safety Process Improvement with POSE and Alloy

Derek Mannering
General Dynamics UK Limited,
St. Leonards-On_Sea, UK,

Jon G. Hall, Lucia Rapanotti
Centre for Research in Computing, The Open University,
Milton Keynes, UK.

Abstract

Safety Standards demand that industrial applications demonstrate they have the required safety integrity and this starts with the initial requirements phase. This paper shows how the Problem Oriented Software Engineering (POSE) framework, in conjunction with the Alloy formal method, supports this task through its ability to elaborate, transform and analyse the project requirements and thus develop a solution for an avionics case study. In particular, this work reports on how the POSE/Alloy combination was used in conjunction with the POSE safety pattern to improve the requirements analysis capabilities of an existing, successful safety critical development process.

1 Introduction

Most modern safety standards are based on the principle of reducing risk to acceptable levels (Bate and Conmy 2005), accepting the fact that absolute safety (zero risk) cannot be achieved (Redmill 1999). For example, IEC 61508 (Redmill 1999) requires the identification of the risks posed by the system under development - and that any such risks will be reduced to tolerable levels by including safety functions in the design responsible for providing the necessary risk reduction. Therefore risk management is an integral part of modern safety system development.

Safety standards also require hazard identification and preliminary hazard analysis to occur in the early phases of the development process (Martino and Muniak 2002). This is consistent with studies that have shown that a large proportion of anomalies occur at the requirements and specification stages of a system development (Ellis 1995; Leveson 1995). A study by Lutz concluded that safety-related software errors arose most often from inadequate or misunderstood requirements (Lutz 1993). Indicating the need for a more careful analysis of the requirements to ensure their adequate assimilation and comprehension. Further, other work has highlighted the need to conduct a safety analysis of the requirements (de Lemos et al. 1998; Gerstinger et al. 2002). These factors all support the notion that safety must be built into the design, and that the evolving design representations analysed to demonstrate that they have the desired safety properties (Leveson 2000a) as early as possible in the life cycle - preferably during the requirements phase.

An important goal of this paper is to show that the Problem Oriented Software Engineering (POSE) framework (Hall et al. 2007b) can be used to address these issues by supporting (a) risk reduction at the requirements phase, (b) requirements comprehension and assimilation, and (c) safety analysis of the requirements. POSE and the structuring of the requirements it provides, in conjunction with the POSE safety pattern (Mannering et al. 2007c), can be used to address the early analysis of the requirements issue by directly supporting the assimilation of information about the requirements, and the process of formulating a requirements model that can be validated. This model can then undergo hazard identification and preliminary hazard analysis - called Preliminary Safety Analysis (PSA) in this paper - as required by the safety standards (e.g. (UK-MoD 2004)). The successful result is a revised requirements model that is known to be able to satisfy its identified safety requirements and thus forms a good basis for the remainder of the development process. If the analysis indicates problems, then the process is iterated.   This provides a suitable degree of risk reduction, such that the development process is only continued if the requirements model has been shown to be capable of satisfying its safety requirements. Thus addressing the issue of providing sufficient risk reduction early in the development process.

Analysis is further supported by the fact that the POSE framework provides an efficient and effective development vehicle. For example, an advantage of the POSE safety pattern is that its PSA uses the same information and models as used for the development tasks. This is efficient, because it means that the overhead of having to validate specific safety analysis models is avoided.

Another goal of the work is to demonstrate the flexibility of using the POSE/Alloy combination for safety critical development, through its ability to transform, model, simulate and prove requirements properties. In addition the requirements modelling work resulted in the development of enhancements to the standard Alloy trace models in (Jackson 2006) to allow finer control over the simulation function.

The paper is organised as follows: a summary of the POSE framework and its application to safety is described in Section 2. Section 3 discusses the background of the current study, with the case study itself presented in Section 4. Section 5 contains discussion and related work, while Section 6 concludes the paper.

2 POSE and Safety

Problem Oriented Software Engineering (POSE) (Hall et al. 2007b) is an extension and generalisation of Jackson's Problem Frame approach (Jackson 2001). In POSE, software development is viewed as solving a problem, the solution being a machine - that is, a program running in a computer - that will ensure satisfaction of the requirement in the given problem world consisting of real-world domains. Typically the requirement concerns properties and behaviours that are located in the problem world at some distance from its interface with the machine. Like Problem Frames, POSE views the problem world as a collections of domains described in terms of their known, or *indicative*, properties, which interact through their sharing of phenomena, i.e. events, commands, states, etc..

POSE is defined as a transformational system, akin to a Gentzen-style sequent calculus (Kleene 1964) that allows problems to be transformed into problems that are easier to solve, or that will lead to other problems that are easier to solve. A set of transformation rule schema capture (atomic) discrete steps in development. Each requires a justification of application in order for the transformation to be solution preserving - simplifying only slightly, this means that a solution to a transformed problem is also a solution to the original problem - although justifications need not be formal. The combination of the justifications is an argument that the solution is adequate as a solution to the original problem. The interested reader is referred to (Hall et al. 2007b) for a complete presentation of POSE.

Although POSE is suitable for developing a wide range of software-based systems and is applicable throughout the development life-cycle, here we are only concerned with work on applying POSE to the requirements analysis of embedded avionics systems. This follows from the first author's area of interest, particularly the goal of improving the front-end of an existing, successful safety critical development process. A series of published papers chart the development of POSE to support this goal, and it is worth summarising the progress made.

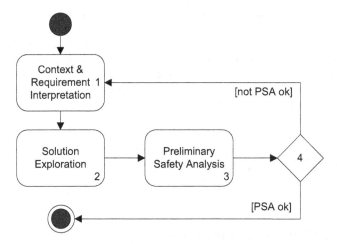

Figure 1 POSE Safety Pattern

The first paper, (Mannering et al. 2007c) showed that POSE transformations can be combined to form a re-usable process template or 'pattern' for safety-critical development. One such process is shown in Figure 1 as a UML activity diagram. The POSE activities in the figure include (a) *Context and Requirement Interpretation* used to capture increasing knowledge and detail in the context (i.e., the environment into which the solution will be introduced) and requirement of the problem - briefly, detail is added to a problem's context as knowledge of it grows; (b) *Solution Exploration* briefly, an architecture (logical and/or physical) for the solution is chosen, and used to transform the problem; (c) *Preliminary Safety Analysis (PSA)* a combination of problem simplification and traditional safety analysis conducted to ensure a feasible solution structure has been chosen. The choice point (labelled 4) uses the outcome of the PSA to determine whether:

- the current architecture is viable as the basis of a solution; or
- whether backtracking and (re-)development of the problem (activity 1) and/or another candidate architecture (activity 2) should be chosen.

The pattern is iterative, ending when an architecture suitable for solution development is found. POSE allows the capture of many important artefacts of the process, including a record of the choices that have been made and the rational for the revision of requirements statements. The case study in (Mannering et al. 2007c) demonstrated the utility of the POSE safety pattern and also how POSE is consistent with and complements Normal Design ideas (Vincenti 1990).

The next paper, (Mannering et al. 2007a), provides some early evidence that POSE (and the POSE safety pattern) in conjunction with Alloy could be used to improve an existing safety process. This work showed that the POSE/Alloy combination was capable of detecting anomalies early in the development process, that were discovered by much later (and hence more costly) validation work in the original process. This paper extends that work by addressing requirements proof and consistency issues.

Parallel work, reported in (Mannering et al. 2007b), showed how POSE, and the POSE safety pattern, could be used to develop a requirements model of an audio message warning system. The work showed how the PSA identified that the original selected architecture was not capable of satisfying its safety targets and sketched out how POSE could be used to develop a compliant solution. This work demonstrated the utility of the domain removal transformations and the corresponding justification structure – which provides a trace of the decision making process in selecting and modelling an architecture.

Finally, another strand of work, reported in (Hall et al. 2007a) looked at how the POSE notion of transformation and related justification obligation can be exploited for the co-development of both safety case and design, always within the context of the application of the POSE safety pattern.

3 Current Study and its Background

The case study work presented in this paper is based on a multi-level safety analysis process typical of many industries. For example, commercial airborne systems are governed by ARP4761 (SAE 1996) that defines a process incorporating Aircraft FHA (Functional Hazard Analysis), followed by System FHA, followed by PSSA (Preliminary System Safety Assessment, which analyses the proposed architecture). In this paper we use PSA in place of PSSA.

In this work requirements follow the fundamental clarification work of Jackson (Zave and Jackson 1997) and Parnas (Courtois and Parnas 1997) which distinguishes between the given domain properties of the environment and the desired behaviour covered by the requirements. This work also distinguishes between requirements that are presented in terms of the stakeholder(s) and the specification of the solution which is formulated in terms of objects manipulated by software (van Lamsweerde 2000). Therefore there is a large semantic gap between the system level requirements and the specification of the machine solution. One of the goals of applying POSE is to bridge this gap by transforming the system level requirements into requirements that apply more directly to the solution. However, there is a need to check that the transformed requirements can satisfy their safety obligations - hence the POSE safety pattern (Figure 1) was developed to include PSA as a "continue or iterate back" gateway in the development process.

The first author is a member of his company's Mission Systems group, which has a successful safety critical development process. Formal specification in Z (Spivey 1992) and formal code proof using SPARK (Barnes 1996) are an integral part of this process. The system safety properties are defined in Z and are then transcribed (rather than refined) into the detailed Z design specification. The code proof is performed against the Z design specification. An important validation step is the formal proof of conformance of the Z design specification against the formal Z safety properties. This process provides a formal path from the high level safety properties down to the code that implements them. Late validation that uncovers anomalies reduces confidence, lengthens development schedules and so adds cost. The problem is that the safety analysis occurs too late in the development life cycle which results in a required improvement being identified for the safety critical process which was to perform a meaningful safety analysis early in the life cycle on the safety properties. The combination of POSE and Alloy were selected to provide this improvement.

The industrial development team has extensive experience in using the Z formal method, so this suggested that the modelling notation used should be closely allied to Z, but must have support for animation and proof. Two possible contenders were one of the B-tool family (Schneider 2001) or Alloy (Jackson 2006) - Alloy was selected for this work as the tool is freely available. Alloy is a lightweight formal method developed from the goal of combining the power of a SAT (Boolean satisfiability) solver with the descriptive power of the Z language. A "lightweight" notation is desirable as it supports a fast and efficient analysis of the requirements which integrates well with the POSE philosophy. Further, Alloy has an active and growing user community and is continuously being developed and enhanced. It has strong animation and proof capabilities within well-defined limits, and allows complex behaviour to be modelled using clear, simple constructs. As such, it fits well as the modelling tool for the POSE safety pattern.

Formulating the requirements model is a non-trivial exercise with many important issues requiring resolution. These include the question of what form should the requirements model take? At what level should the model be pitched? What are the interfaces and how is the functionality to be distributed? What are the characteristics of the environment that are significant to the model? Fortunately the

POSE safety pattern provides much of the information and structuring that allows these issues to be addressed. As discussed, Alloy is used for modelling in this work because it fits well with the existing process, but in general there are other suitable candidates, some of which are described in Section 5.

The POSE safety pattern used on earlier case studies (Mannering et al. 2007c; Mannering et al. 2007b), worked with structured textual requirements which were formalised into a Parnas Table-like form (Courtois and Parnas 1997) for the safety analysis. This was considered adequate for safety related applications, but for safety critical applications a higher integrity approach is desirable. For this reason Alloy was selected to formalise the requirements in this paper.

4 The Failure Annunciation System Case Study

The case study in this paper uses the audio warning system introduced in (Mannering et al. 2007b) to develop further the notion that the POSE safety pattern provides powerful and useful capabilities for use as a front-end requirements modelling and analysis approach. In particular, this work shows how the POSE/Alloy combination allows requirements to be formally modelled, transformed, simulated and proved. The work also shows the important impact of derived requirements and the need to resolve the issues that they cause.

4.1 Summary of the POSE Safety Pattern Applied to the FAS

The case study concerns the design of a Failure Annunciation System (FAS) that is part of the warning system on a military aircraft. The FAS provides audio warnings to the pilot if certain critical monitored systems have failed. A detailed explanation of the application of the POSE safety pattern process is contained in (Mannering et al. 2007b), but a summary is provided in the following text to provide a context for the ensuing work. A first representation of the FAS problem is given as $P_{Initial}$:

$$P_{Initial} : CS^{cat}, SYS^{sys}, Pilot_{audio}, Speaker_{message}^{audio}, FAS_{cat,sys}^{message} \vdash R_{cat,sys}^{audio}$$

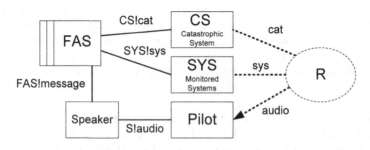

Figure 2 The FAS Problem $P_{Initial}$

Figure 2 presents this FAS problem in the related Problem Frames graphical notation for convenience, in which event and other phenomena sharing - the superscripts and subscripts in $P_{Initial}$ – correspond to the annotated lines between the domains in Figure 2. Note that the requirements model being developed is based on the POSE topography, i.e. it uses the domains and phenomena from POSE.

The FAS can be seen to monitor directly the status of the Catastrophic System (CS) using a discrete input cat - shown as CS!cat to show that the input originates from the CS. It also monitors the status of the other critical aircraft systems (SYS) which is represented by the generic SYS!sys status message from SYS to the FAS. The FAS issues warning audio messages (shown as FAS!message) to the pilot via the pilot's headphones – represented by the speaker in Figure 2. The overall system requirements, R, consist of the functional requirements Ra to Rd and the safety requirement RS as follows:

Ra: When a monitored system has failed, the FAS system shall play the correct audio message to the pilot.

Rb: Message levels shall be comfortably heard by the Pilot.

Rc: If more than one system has failed messages shall be selected for play in the order: Cat fail, Sys fail.

Rd: If no system failures are detected, then no message shall be played.

RS: For hazards H1 and H2, their respective safety targets (Critical/10^{-7} failures per flight hour (fpfh) and Related/10^{-5} fpfh) shall be satisfied.

Where H1 is "Inadvertent indication of the Catastrophic message" and H2 is "Failure to indicate the Catastrophic message". Therefore, R is represented by Ra & Rb & Rc & Rd & RS, and is indicated in the dotted ellipse in Figure 2. A complete statement of R should also include requirements that cover space, weight, interfaces, maintenance and so on, but these are beyond the scope of this work.

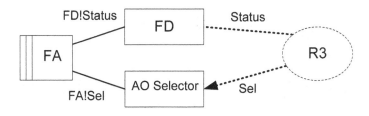

Figure 3 The Progressed FA Problem P_{Prog}

The POSE safety pattern was then applied to this problem, and a trial solution architecture was instantiated during the Solution Exploration step (see Figure 1). The problem was simplified using Problem Progression transformations and then PSA was applied (step 3 in Figure 1). The resulting simplified problem, P_{Prog}, is shown in Figure 3 and the transformed requirements are shown in Table 1. However, the PSA, detailed in (Mannering et al. 2007b), identified that the architecture could not satisfy the system safety requirement (RS) and an alternative architecture was developed to overcome these identified limitations. This involved introducing a derived requirement DR as follows:

"Each message will have a unique identifier and if the selected message identifier does not correspond to that of the currently playing message, then audio must be inhibited, audio otherwise being allowed".

R	Requirement Text
R3a	When a monitored system has failed, then AO Selector shall generate a sequence of bytes that corresponds to the selected system fail message.
R3c	If more than one system has failed messages shall be selected for play in the order: Cat fail, Sys fail.
R3d	If no system failure is detected then the AO Selector block shall generate no message.
RS'	For hazards H1 and H2, their respective safety targets (Critical/10^{-7}fpfh and Related/10^{-5}fpfh) shall be satisfied.

Table 1 Requirements after POSE Safety Pattern Applied

Incorporating DR resulted in the development of a modified FPGA AO Selector component to: (a) include sending back the message identifier (id) of the currently playing message to the FA in a status message; and (b) add a mute input to the FA control that allows the FA to mute audio output if the message identifier does not tally with the required message to be played. The changes to the AO Selector (AOS') are shown in Figure 4(a). As noted in (Mannering et al. 2007b) the POSE development sequence must backtrack to $P_{Initial}$ to allow the introduction of the new architecture. The POSE transformation sequence was then repeated, and this results in P'$_{Prog}$ shown in Figure 4(b). The POSE representation is as follows.

$$P'_{Prog} : FD^{Status}, AOS'^{id}_{Sel,Mute}, FAS^{Sel,Mute}_{Status,id} \vdash R3'^{Sel,Mute}_{Status,id}$$

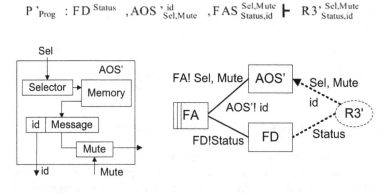

Figure4 (a) Modified AO Selector (AOS')   (b) Modified P'$_{Prog}$

Each POSE transformation has a justification associated with it. The sequence of steps from $P_{Initial}$ to P'$_{Prog}$ have the justifications J'$_1$ to J'$_{34}$ as shown in Figure 5. The justification (J'$_1$) for the revised architecture is that "the original POSE development sequence was infeasible because it did not satisfy the safety requirements; the revised architecture can satisfy both the functional and safety requirements". That is, the revised justification includes the original failed sequence and its shortcomings, as a rationale for selecting the revised architecture. The other justifications map directly to those used for the original POSE transformation sequence (J$_2$ to J$_{34}$) as detailed in (Mannering et al. 2007b).

Figure 5 Modified POSE Development Sequence

4.2 Formal Requirements Analysis

In earlier work, (Mannering et al. 2007b), requirements validation was performed using Parnas Tables (Courtois and Parnas 1997) to formalise the requirements, and manual proof was used to show that the systematic safety targets were satisfied. In this work Alloy is used to formalise the process. This has two advantages (a) the requirements model can be simulated to show that it has the desired behaviour, and (b) the individual requirements (e.g. R3a, R3c) can be encoded as predicates which can then be proved against the requirements model using Alloy's check predicate facility. The first step is to build the requirements models and these are based on the model examples presented in Chapter 6 of (Jackson 2006).

The first model to be produced was the original P$_{Prog}$ shown in Figure 3 and this is shown in Figure 6. In the following text a reference to "#n" identifies the part of Figure 6 being discussed. Time is modelled as a single linear ordering using the supplied utility `ordering`. The interface phenomena (e.g. FA!Sel and FD!Status) are modelled as types. For example Status defined at #1 in Figure 6, consists of `catnon` meaning only the CS system has failed, `sysnon` meaning only a SYS has failed, `catsys` meaning both the CS and SYS indicate failures and `non` meaning no failures detected. The Sel (#2) and Mess (#3) phenomena can be modelled similarly. The domains are defined as data types shown in #4 in Figure 6. The behaviour of these domains is defined using predicates which define the changes from the current time (`t`) to the next time (`t'`). For example FDBehave – refer to #5 in Figure 6.

The function `extract[]` (#7) defines how the FA interprets the status information from the FD. The function `decode[]` (#8) translates the message selection given by Sel into the appropriate message. There are two models for the FD behaviour. The first as shown in Figure 6, is the generic one as used in (Jackson 2006). This model is good for the proof work, but is problematic for the simulation work since the user has little control over which trace behaviour is selected. To overcome this limitation a second model was introduced which allows control over the time range when phenomena were selected. This second model is shown below.

```
pred FDBehave (t,t' : Time) { trange[t, 0, 1] => FDSame[t,t']
    else trange[t, 2, 4]  => (FD.status.t' = catnon )
        else trange[t, 5, 6] => (FD.status.t' = non )
            else trange[t,7,9] => (FD.status.t' = sysnon )
                else trange[t,10,11] => (FD.status.t' = catsys )
                    else trange[t,12,16] => (FD.status.t' = catnon)}
```

The function `trange[]` (#6 in Figure 6) uses the fact that time is modelled as a linear ordering, so the function `prevs[]` can be used to effectively "count" the previous time instants via the cardinality function #. This allows the range of values to be set up as required, e.g. `trange[t,2,4]` is true if `t` is in the range from 2 to 4.

The trace behaviour (#9) is defined using the function `init[]` and the fact `traces{}` and follows the model presented in (Jackson 2006). The simulation is run by invoking the predicate `show1` (#10) which runs through this trace behaviour. The simulation results validated that the model did satisfy the requirement R3.

The next step was to encode the individual requirements R3a, R3c and R3d as predicates, and to prove that these predicates were consistent with the requirements model over an adequately large range of values, e.g. the predicate for R3a follows.

```
assert R3a {all t1,t2: Time | (t1 in prevs[t2] &&
FD.status.t1=catnon && t1=prev[prev[t2]] => AOS.mes.t2 = mes1)
&&
### Similar terms for catsys, sysnon and non ### }

check R3a for 16 but 5 int
```

The results provided strong evidence that the Alloy requirements model of Figure 6 does satisfy its functional requirement (R3a, R3c & R3d).

4.3 Requirements Consistency and Resolution

Establishing the consistency of a system's requirements is an extremely important task, since from inconsistent requirements any system can be shown to be adequate. Establishing their consistency early in the life cycle is also desirable as part of the risk reduction exercise. Although previous development work relied on manual consistency checks, stronger and more compelling evidence can be gained from using a formal model such as the Alloy model presented in Figure 6.

The modified architecture of Figure 4(b) was also modelled in Alloy. This required a more complex model to deal with the additional id and mute phenomena. The main changes occurred to the behaviour of FA and the AO Selector (AOS') as follows.

```
pred FABehave(t,t':Time) {FA.sel.t' = extract[FD.status.t]
                          && FA.mute.t' = checkid[t,t'] }

fun checkid[t,t':Time]: OK {AOS.id.t'=decode[FA.sel.t] => noo
                            else yes}
```

```
//### Problem PPROG ###
open util/ordering[Time] as Ti
sig Time {}

// ### Define Phenomena ###
sig OK {}
one sig  yes, noo extends OK {}

sig Status {}
one sig  catnon, sysnon , catsys, non extends Status {} //#1

sig Sel {}
one sig  m1, m2, m3, ni extends Sel {}                    //#2

sig Mess {}
one sig  mes1, mes2, mes3, noni extends Mess {}           //#3

// ### Define Domains ###                                     #4
one sig FA { sel : Sel -> Time } {}
one sig FD {status : Status -> Time} {}
one sig AOS {mes : Mess -> Time} {}

// ### DEFINE OPERATIONS ###                                   #5
pred FABehave(t,t':Time) { FA.sel.t' = extract[FD.status.t] }

pred FDBehave (t,t':Time) {FD.status.t' = catnon or
                           FD.status.t' = catsys or
                 FD.status.t' = sysnon or FD.status.t' = non}

pred AOSBehave  (t,t': Time) { AOS.mes.t' = decode[FA.sel.t] }


pred trange [t: Time, ts,tf: Int] {#prevs[t] >= ts &&    //#6
                                   #prevs[t] =< tf}

fun extract[st: Status] : Sel {(st=catnon or st=catsys)  //#7
             => m1 else  st = sysnon => m2 else ni}

fun decode[s: Sel] : Mess { s = m1 => mes1               //#8
             else  s = m2 => mes2 else noni}

// ### Define the Trace Model ###                             #9
pred init [t : Time] {FD.status.t  = non && FA.sel.t = ni &&
AOS.mes.t = noni}

fact traces { init[Ti/first[]]
   all t  : Time - Ti/last[] | let t' = Ti/next[t] |
       FDBehave[t,t'] && FABehave[t,t']  && AOSBehave[t,t'] }

// ##### PROPERTIES #####
pred show1() {}                                              #10
run show1 for 16 but 5 int //Set bit width to cover -16 to +15
```

Figure 6 Alloy Definition for Problem P$_{PROG}$

```
pred AOSBehave (t,t':Time) {AOS.mes.t' = (FA.mute.t = noo =>
                                 decode[FA.sel.t] else noni) &&
      (AOS.id.t' = decode[FA.sel.t] or AOS.id.t' = mes3) }
```

The function `checkid[]` returns "noo" if the selected message agrees with the id returned from the AOS'. If the result is "yes", then audio is muted as required. The revised model was simulated and the results showed it had the desired behaviour.

The next step was to try to formally prove that the revised model satisfied its functional requirements (R3a, R3c, R3d and DR) and to demonstrate their consistency. The check for R3a produced a counter example (i.e. the proof failed).

The fact that the failure was expected follows from inspection of R3a (Table 1) and DR. R3a requires the correct operation of the selection mechanism, whilst DR ensures safe operation by muting audio if there is a discrepancy between the selection and the message output functions. Therefore, when the R3a predicate is applied to the modified architecture it produces a counterexample at the point where a message should be output but the mute is in operation due to an identified problem with the message id. The resolution requires R3a to take due account of the derived requirement DR. This can be achieved by modifying R3a to become:

R3aM: When a monitored system has failed, then AO Selector shall generate a sequence of bytes that corresponds to the selected system fail message except when a discrepancy is identified with the message identifier.

With this modification R3aM and DR are consistent. This is demonstrated by proving that the modified predicate corresponding to R3aM (shown below) does not produce a counterexample.

```
assert R3aM {all t1, t2, t3 : Time | (t3 = prev[t2] &&
FA.mute.t1 = noo && FA.mute.t3 = noo && FA.mute.t2 = noo &&
t1 in prevs[t2] && FD.status.t1 = catnon  &&
t1 = prev[prev[t2]] => AOS.mes.t2 = mes1)
&&
### Similar terms for catsys, sysnon and non ### }
```

The proof work was extended to the other requirements to demonstrate that the requirements model satisfied them, and that they were consistent.

In POSE terms the requirements resolution and consistency checks constitute a transformation that will affect the requirements description, but may also affect the domains if the resolution requires modifications to the architecture. For the FAS design, the consistency resolution just affected the requirements as shown in the POSE representation below. The justification for the transformation is that after it the requirements are known to be consistent.

$$\frac{FD^{Status}, AOS^{\;id}_{Sel,Mute}, FA^{Sel,Mute}_{Status,id} \vdash R3'R^{Sel,Mute}_{Status,id}}{FD^{Status}, AOS^{\;id}_{Sel,Mute}, FA^{Sel,Mute}_{Status,id} \vdash R3'^{Sel,Mute}_{Status,id}} \qquad [ReqC\,\&R]$$

4.4 Revisiting the PSA

The preliminary safety analysis work is based on knowledge about the domains and their shared interfaces – especially the phenomena, since it is through these that the information and control data flows. This is why the first step in the POSE safety pattern, "Context and Requirement Interpretation", is so important. Information not collected or collected incorrectly will adversely impact on the efficacy of the resulting requirements model and thus the safety analysis based on it. As noted earlier, the requirements model is based on the structuring provided by POSE and uses the POSE phenomena as its interface data. The hazard identification work, e.g. the Functional Failure Analysis (FFA) (SAE 1996) reported in (Mannering et al. 2007b), is based on the interface data and the knowledge gained about the domains. Further, earlier work in (Mannering et al. 2007c) has shown that the POSE model provides the basis for the functional fault tree analysis (FTA) (Vesely et al. 1981) work used to investigate any issues identified by the FFA.

The availability of a formal model allows additional safety analysis work to be undertaken. For example, the impact of failures or errors in behaviour can be investigated. The sensitivity of the model to different anomalies can be simulated, thus allowing the robustness of the requirements model to be evaluated. The sensitivity of the formal FAS requirements model was investigated by introducing anomalies into the behaviour of the various components. An obvious case was the Mute phenomenon stuck active so that no messages were output. This is fine for the hazard H1, since an inadvertent Catastrophic message cannot occur in this scenario. However it causes issues for H2, since obviously this scenario means the Catastrophic message cannot be played when required. This problem was investigated using functional FTA on the AOS' (Figure 4(b)). The analysis showed that the proposed AOS' design was capable of satisfying the required systematic and hardware failure rate targets to meet H2. Hence the design represented by P'_{Prog} is considered feasible with respect to this issue. The analysis of other safety issues is reported in (Mannering et al. 2007b), and this also reports the adequacy of the P'_{Prog} design. Therefore, from a safety perspective, the P'_{Prog} design is considered feasible.

5 Discussion and Related Work

The POSE notion of problem used in this work fits well with the Parnas 4-Variable model, which has been used by Parnas et al, as part of a table driven approach (Courtois and Parnas 1997). This model and table-based approach is particularly well suited to defining embedded critical applications. This is demonstrated by the fact that they form the basis for the SCR (Heitmeyer and Jeffords 2007), and the SpecTRM (Leveson 2000a) methods, which form part of a human centred, safety-driven process which is supported by an artefact called an Intent specification (Leveson 2000b). The work in this paper is located in the area of the second-level System Design Principles of the Intent specification, and thus may be complementary to the third, Blackbox level provided by SpecTRM. It is feasible to go directly from the POSE transformed model into SpecTRM or SCR. However, the ``lightweight'' characteristics of Alloy which allows requirements models to be produced and analysed very quickly, is of benefit for investigating the behaviour of the requirements. For example, this would be a useful precursor and check before using the comprehensive SCR tool suite that covers the rest of the development process.

Recent work in developing AMBERS (da Cruz and Raistrick 2007), also uses the 4-Variable model (based on the SCR variant), tables for the requirements phase and targets the SCADE system for the subsequent development. AMBERS has similar goals to and is also compatible with POSE, but it does not include the specific high level PSA feasibility check.

The work of Anderson, de Lemos, and Saeed (de Lemos et al. 1998) share many of the principles and concepts that have driven the development of this work. Particularly the notions that safety is a system attribute and the need to apply a detailed safety analysis to the requirements specifications. The main advantages of the POSE approach over that work are: (a) it provides a framework for transforming requirements; (b) it is rich in traceability; and (c) the models it uses are suitable for the safety analysis. The latter means it is efficient because there is no need to develop `new' models (with all its attendant validation problems) just to perform the PSA. Further, the traceability makes it particularly suited for use with standards such as DS 00-56 (UK-MoD 2004) and the DO-178B (RTCA/DO-178B) software guidelines.

An important consideration is how the POSE/Alloy combination copes with change. It was found that evaluating the impact of changes was assisted by the traceability inherent in POSE, supplemented by the use of labelling in the POSE transformations and the Alloy modelling. That is, a representative label was used to indicate where a requirement was transformed (POSE) or implemented (Alloy). This allowed the impact of changes to be quickly located and assessed.

The sequence of justifications for the POSE transformations was also found to be useful, since the strength of the justification was directly related to confidence in the ultimate success of the transformation. That is, where confidence was strong then the development after transformation was found to be straightforward. In contrast, weaker justifications were more problematic and ultimately required more effort to strengthen them. The conclusion is that the ability to see the strengths and weaknesses of an argument thread are very useful, and a good indicator of where extra effort will be required.

6 Conclusions

The case study work agrees with the results obtained from the earlier papers (Mannering et al. 2007c; Mannering et al. 2007a; Mannering et al. 2007b) and further demonstrates that the POSE safety pattern successfully allows the safety feasibility of a system's requirements to be analysed early in the development life cycle. As in the earlier case work, the analysis was found to be quick and efficient since it uses the same information and models that are produced to support the development work. Not having to produce and validate a special model for the safety work was a significant advantage.

These earlier papers have shown that POSE is flexible enough to work well with a variety of common development approaches. The results of this case study further confirm this finding by showing that the POSE/Alloy combination works well and is suitable for supporting the front-end work of a safety critical process. The case study demonstrates that the use of the POSE safety pattern improves the existing safety critical process by allowing formal proof of properties and requirements resolution to occur. Further, overall, risk reduction is achieved via the requirements consistency checks, and the PSA - the development only continues if the PSA is successful in showing that the requirements model is capable of satisfying its safety obligations.

The POSE/Alloy combination was found to be effective for producing requirements models, with POSE providing the context (especially the interface information) that facilitated the quick development of models in Alloy. Further, making the modification to the trace models to allow control of the (simulation) time when inputs to the model were changed allowed the behaviour of the model to be explored more quickly and effectively than originally encountered. This allowed problem areas to be explored more thoroughly and also allowed the proposed solutions to be successfully validated. Further, encoding the requirements as predicates allowed a proof to be made that the requirements model satisfied its requirements. Providing strong evidence to support the efficacy of the model.

The analysis results demonstrate that a formal model is a major benefit. The formal model allows simulation to validate the behaviour of the model is as required, it allows proof that the model satisfies its requirements and it allows the consistency of the requirements to be established. In addition, the formal model also allows the effect of failures to be evaluated from a safety view point, and thus allows the robustness of the architecture to be evaluated.

The success of the case study work also supports the suggestion that the knowledge elements gained from each study from this sequence of case studies can be combined to form a coherent and comprehensive front end requirements analysis technique for embedded systems development. Future effort needs to extend the work to cover additional formal description techniques such as using the B-method in place of Alloy. Further, interfacing to other critical development techniques such as SCR and SpecTRM would be useful. However, the POSE/Alloy combination has demonstrated its merit for use with the existing safety critical process and a more comprehensive case study development is planned to further strengthen the knowledge about how to effectively apply the technique.

Acknowledgements

We are pleased to acknowledge the financial support of IBM, under the Eclipse Innovation Grants. Thanks also go to our colleagues in The Open University, especially Michael Jackson.

References

Barnes, J. (1996). High Integrity Ada; The SPARK Approach, Addison-Wesley.

Bate, I. and P. Conmy (2005). Safe composition of real time software. HASE'05, Heidelberg, Germany.

Courtois, P.-J. and D. L. Parnas (1997). Documentation for Safety Critical Software. 15th International Conference on Software Engineering, Baltimore, USA.

da Cruz, M. F. and P. Raistrick (2007). AMBERS: Improving Requirements Specification Through Assertive Models and SCADE/DOORS Integration. Safety Critical Systems Symposium, Bristol, UK.

de Lemos, R., A. Saeed and T. Anderson (1998). On the Integration of Requirements Analysis and Safety Analysis for Safety-Critical Systems, University of Newcastle upon Tyne, UK.

Ellis, A. (1995). Achieving Safety in Complex Control Systems. Safety Critical Systems Symposium, Brighton, United Kingdom, Springer-Verlag.

Gerstinger, A., G. Schedl and W. Winkelbauer (2002). Safety versus Reliability: Different or Equal. 20th International System Safety Conference, Denver, Colorado, USA, System Safety Society.

Hall, J. G., D. Mannering and L. Rapanotti (2007a). Arguing safety with Problem Oriented Software Engineering. 10th IEEE Int. Sym. on High Assurance Systems Engineering (HASE 2007), Dallas, Texas.

Hall, J. G., L. Rapanotti and M. Jackson (2007b). Problem Oriented Software Engineering: A design-theoretic framework for software engineering. 5th IEEE Int. Conference on Software Engineering and Formal Methods (SEFM 2007), London, UK.

Heitmeyer, C. and R. Jeffords (2007). Applying a formal requirements method to three NASA systems: Lessons learned. IEEE Aerospace Conference, Big Sky, MT.

Jackson, D. (2006). Software Abstractions Logic, Language, and Analysis, The MIT Press.

Jackson, M. A. (2001). Problem frames : analysing and structuring software development problems. Harlow, Addison-Wesley.

Kleene, S. (1964). Introduction to Metamathematics, Van Nostrand, Princeton.

Leveson, N. (1995). Safeware : system safety and computers. Reading, Mass. ; Wokingham, Addison-Wesley.

Leveson, N. G. (2000a). "Completeness in formal specification language design for process-control systems." Proceedings of the third workshop on Formal methods in software practice 2000, Portland, Oregon. ACM Press: 2000.

Leveson, N. G. (2000b). "Intent Specifications: An Approach to Building Human-Centered Specifications." IEEE Transactions on Software Engineering Vol. 26(No. 1): pp. 15-35.

Lutz, R. R. (1993). Analysing Software Requirements Errors in Safety-Critical Embedded Systems. IEEE International Symposium Requirements Engineering, San Diego, California.

Mannering, D., J. G. Hall and L. Rapanotti (2007a). Relating Safety Requirements and System Design through Problem Oriented Software Engineering. SAFECOMP 07, Nuremburg, Germany.

Mannering, D., J. G. Hall and L. Rapanotti (2007b). Safety Process Improvement: Early Analysis and Justification. IET Safety 07, London, England.

Mannering, D., J. G. Hall and L. Rapanotti (2007c). Towards Normal Design for Safety Critical Systems. FASE 07, Braga, Portugal.

Martino, P. A. and C. Muniak (2002). The Role of System Safety Engineering in Product Safety. 20th International System Safety Conference, Denver, Colorado, USA, System Safety Society.

Redmill, F. (1999). "An introduction to the safety standard IEC61508." System Safety Society **35**(1).

RTCA/DO-178B Software Considerations in Airborne Systems and Equipment Certification.

SAE (1996). ARP4761: Guidelines and Methods for Conducting the Safety Assessment Process on Civil Airborne Systems and Equipment.

Schneider, S. (2001). The B-method: An Introduction, Palgrave.

Spivey, J. M. (1992). The Z-Notation – A Reference Manual, Prentice Hall.

UK-MoD (2004). Safety Management Requirements for Defence Systems Part 1 Requirements, MoD: 44.

van Lamsweerde, A. (2000). Requirements Engineering in the Year 00: A Research Perspective. ICSE'00, 22nd International Conference on Software Engineering, Limerick.

Vesely, W., F. Goldberg, N. Roberts and D. Haasl (1981). Fault Tree Handbook, U.S. Nuclear Regulatory Commission.

Vincenti, W. G. (1990). What Engineers Know and How They Know It: Analytical Studies from Aeronautical History, The Johns Hopkins University Press.

Zave, P. and M. Jackson (1997). "Four Dark Corners of Requirements Engineering." ACM Transactions on Software Engineering and Methodology **VI**((1)): 1-30.

How to Select a Programming Language Subset to Maximise Software Quality

Wojciech Basalaj
Programming Research, 9-11 Queens Road, Hersham, Surrey KT12 5LU, UK
Wojciech_Basalaj@programmingresearch.com

Abstract

Safety standards usually require a programming language subset to be in place, but leave this up to the project or certifying authority to define it. Typically, language subsets are put together on a theoretical basis, i.e. picking and choosing from or extending existing coding standards, or analysing language vulnerabilities. We advocate a different and perhaps complementary approach based on the ISO 9126 standard.

ISO 9126 provides a framework for measuring quality, and correlating system quality (e.g. safety) with the underlying quality of source code. In this paper we offer a methodology to maximise this correlation stipulated by ISO 9126. We document a case study in which this methodology has been applied to construct a language subset, with the following empirically demonstrable properties:
- when followed on past projects resulted in better quality
- when not followed on past project resulted in worse quality

This approach is equally applicable to mission-critical as well as safety-critical systems.

This methodology can also be applied to software complexity metrics (e.g. Cyclomatic Complexity), which coupled with a threshold will constitute a language sub-setting rule. However, in this case study we were unable to demonstrate that any source code metrics had an impact on the overall system quality.

Keywords: safety-critical, software quality, language subsets, coding standards, software metrics.

1 Requirements for a Language Subset Definition

It is a well known fact that commercial programming languages such as C, C++ and ADA have features which can result in unpredictable behaviour. This is undesirable in any software system, and cannot be tolerated in a system with a high cost of failure. The language constructs that fall within this unpredictable category can readily be identified from the language specification [ISO1990, ISO 2003a]. Prohibiting use of such language constructs will remove barriers to adopting the language to develop a safety- or mission-critical system. This practice is commonly known as language sub-setting, and well known examples are SPARK ADA [Bar2003], MISRA-C [MIR1998, MIR2004a] and JSF++ [LMC2005], see Section 2 for more details. A language subset can be complemented by restricting language constructs that are well defined and predictable but in practice have been shown to be error prone.

One can also go beyond ensuring program predictability and correctness to address other quality concerns, such as maintainability and reusability. Typically, this takes the form of source file layout and naming conventions. This can be combined with language independent techniques, e.g. calculating and limiting software complexity metrics. Such additional restrictions combined with a language subset constitute comprehensive coding guidelines, commonly referred to as a *coding standard*.

All prevalent safety standards mandate that only a safe subset of a programming language is used. In the following sub-sections we review 3 commonly used standards from different industries in terms of their provisions for: language sub-setting, coding standards, and analysis of in-service data. As these safety standards aim to be generic and non-prescriptive as much as possible, they do not define or mandate any particular language subset. An organisation seeking compliance to one of these safety standards needs to show that their chosen programming language and its subset address all the specified requirements and recommendations.

It should be noted that another aspect of defining a language subset is its expressiveness. If the language is overly constrained, for example by blanket restriction on certain language features, the programmer may not be able to express the design easily, resulting in less maintainable or efficient code. There is even scope for introducing additional defects as more source code may need to be written to work around the 'missing' language features. For a given language and application the quest is to find a sweet spot - a minimal language subset certifiable at the desired level of system safety.

In this paper we will focus on a C++ case study for finding such a minimal subset. However, this technique is applicable to any programming language and any quality criteria, as outlined in Section 3. To put this approach in perspective Reinhardt [Rei2004] identifies 438 unique sub-setting rules. As this predates the most recent coding guidelines [LMC2005, Sut2004], the actual state-of-the-art set of C++ rules is even larger. Adopting such a large set of rules as a language subset is problematic:
-    expressiveness may be adversely affected
-    comprehensive enforcement (e.g. required for safety certification) will be burdensome
-    unavoidably some rules will be mutually exclusive

In Section 4 we propose a solution that scores individual rules based on their effect on the overall system quality. Note that historic quality measurements need to be available if an existing system is being extended. In the case of a green field project, data for a similar system can be used instead, providing they are based on the same programming language and quality criteria (e.g. safety as defined by a given safety standard). There are 2 main drawbacks with this approach:

- if too few data points for comparison are available, the results may not be reliable,
- if a particular rule has never been broken, there is no evidence to support or reject its inclusion in the language subset.

These can be mitigated by making more quality data available, e.g. by increasing the granularity of measurements to individual sub-systems, or modules. Also, the set of rules identified by this empirical technique can be complemented with a traditional subset selection approach - review and extension of existing rule sets [LMC2005, PRG2004, Rei2004].

1.1 IEC 61508

IEC 61508 [IEC1998] is an international standard addressing the lifecycle of electrical, electronic and programmable electronic, safety-related systems. It is widely used in the industrial automation and control fields [Bar2007], but is not industry specific. In this standard a Safety-Related System (SRS) is defined as a system that "implements the required safety functions necessary to achieve or maintain a safe state for the Equipment Under Control". This potentially restricts the scope quite considerably as compared to other safety standards (Sections 1.2 and 1.3), which would cover all of the software used in the equipment/system, as long as it could impact safety.

Part 3 of the standard [IEC1998] covers the software component of SRS specifically, and Section 7.4.4 addresses requirements for programming languages. It states that at higher levels of safety integrity, the programming language used shall be completely and unambiguously defined or restricted to a subset with these properties. Additionally it states that a coding standard is to be used for development of all safety-related software, covering the following aspects:

- good programming practice
- exclusion of unsafe language features (e.g. undefined features, or unstructured constructs)
- source code documentation

Paragraph 7.9.2.3 identifies software complexity metrics as a suitable method of software verification, and recommends them at all safety integrity levels.

In the context of software operation and modification procedures, Section 7.8 stipulates that authorised software modification requests need to be raised for any changes to the system. An integral part of a change request is its rationale, and one of the examples given is systematic fault experience.

1.2 Def Stan 00-56 & 00-55

The latest Defence Standard 00-56 Issue 4 [MoD2007], places no specific requirements on programming language selection, except that "evidence of selection of good practice methods, tools, technology etc (... specific software language ...)" needs to be provided. However, it refers to the superseded Def Stan 00-55 as "equivalent guidance".

The final Defence Standard 00-55 Part 1 Issue 2 [MoD1997] contains Section 28 dedicated to programming language selection. It states that Safety Related Software needs to be implemented in a high-level language or a subset of such a language with the following characteristics:
- strongly typed
- block structured
- formally-defined syntax
- predictable program execution

Additionally, for a subset its definition and means of enforcement need to be provided.

Section 36 mandates use of a coding standard, with the additional required properties that source code compliant to this coding standard will be susceptible to static analysis and formal methods.

Both Def Stan 00-56 (Section 11.3) and 00-55 (Section 42) require that in-service history is maintained for SRS, and in particular any anomalies in the system are reported and analysed.

1.3 RTCA/DO-178B

RTCA/DO-178B [RTC1992] Section 11.8 "Software Code Standards" contains specific restrictions on programming languages or their subsets to be used for software in airborne systems - unambiguously defined:
- syntax
- control behaviour
- data behaviour
- side-effects

There is additional guidance on defining naming and layout conventions, and complexity metrics.

Section 11 discusses software life cycle data, and in particular sub-section 11.20 stipulates that change history needs to be maintained, with special attention to changes resulting from failures affecting safety. Additionally, sub-section 11.17 discusses "problem reports" as means of identifying and recording the resolution of anomalous behaviour of a software system.

2 Publicly Available Language Subsets

The most popular subset of the C language [ISO1990] is MISRA-C [MIR2004a]. Originally, it was developed specifically for the automotive industry, but it has since been adopted in other industries, e.g. defence, aerospace, rail and medical [MIR2004b], often in conjunction with common safety standards (Section 1.1, 1.2 and 1.3). The rules in this subset are either classified into required or advisory, and within either category rules are considered to be of equal importance. Except for any documented and signed off deviations, compliant source code cannot have any violations of required rules. There is no requirement to comply with or track deviations to advisory rules.

There are 3 main contenders to the title of the most popular, publicly available, C++ language subset. High Integrity C++ [PRG2004] was developed first, and is positioned as a best practice coding standard rather than specifically addressing safety. However, with suitable additions it can be applied in a safety-critical setting [Rei2004]. The origin of many rules can be traced to existing C++ guidelines [Hen1997, Mey2005, Sut1999], which tend to focus on specific programming aspects. Similar to MISRA-C, rules are organised into (mandatory) Rules and Guidelines.

JSF++ [LMC2005] has been designed from the outset as a safety-critical subset of C++, and is being used on the F-35 Joint Strike Fighter programme. It includes rules to address undefined, unspecified, indeterminate and implementation-defined behaviour in C++ [ISO2003a], best practice rules, and some MISRA-C:2004 rules deemed applicable to coding in C++. Its authors point out that it is a superset of a subset: where certain language features are prohibited completely, e.g. function parameters of array type, it defines and mandates use of a custom library alternative – superset of ISO C++. The main rationale is that programmers will not be required to 'reinvent the wheel', and likely introduce implementation errors, but instead will use a well tested library (also see Section 1). The rules are classified into 3 categories:
-    shall - compliance is mandatory and needs to be verified
-    will - mandatory, but verification is not necessary, as these rules do not concern safety
-    should - advisory rules

The most recent development in the arena of C++ subsets is MISRA-C++, which at the time of writing this paper is undergoing a public review. This language subset is based on previous work in this area, as well as contributing unique guidance.

Compliance to a language subset is often treated as a pass/fail test, i.e. all mandatory rules need to be complied with, except for signed off deviations. However, a more generalised approach is possible, where the level of compliance is measured, either as the absolute number of violations for a particular source file, module or component, or normalised by the size of the entity, e.g. number of lines of code. This would allow correlating compliance with measurements of other aspects of the product, e.g. run time behaviour or user experience.

3 ISO 9126 Quality Model

The ISO 9126-1 standard [ISO2001] has been introduced to formalise the notion of Quality of a Software System. 3 distinct aspects are considered:
- Internal Quality measured for a non-executable form of the Software System, e.g. its source code.
- External Quality, which pertains to the run-time behaviour of the system, as experienced during dynamic test.
- Quality in use, which addresses the degree to which user goals and requirements are fulfilled.

Internal and External Quality can be further categorised into 6 separate characteristics:
- Functionality
- Reliability
- Usability
- Efficiency
- Maintainability
- Portability

Each of these 6 characteristics can be further subdivided, and there are 27 sub-characteristics in total.

Quality in Use has been divided into 4 characteristics:
- Effectiveness
- Productivity
- Safety
- Satisfaction

ISO 9126-1 advocates measuring each of these characteristics, but does not specify how. Examples of suitable metrics are given in Technical Reports: 9126-2 [ISO2003b], 9126-3 [ISO2003c], 9126-4 [ISO2004]. The standard stipulates that with suitable choices of metrics Internal Quality should predict, or in other words correlate with External Quality, which in turn should predict Quality in Use.

In this study we will be focusing on the Satisfaction Quality in Use characteristic. We will attempt to demonstrate that this characteristic can indeed be predicted by measuring Internal Quality of a software system, see Section 4.1. Similar principles can be applied to other Quality in Use characteristics, notably Safety.

Prior to conducting such a study we needed to settle on suitable metrics for Internal Quality. ISO 9126-3 [ISO2003c] is a Technical Report that proposes such metrics.

The vast majority of them are measured in terms of the percentage of items (functions, variables, etc.) meeting a specific requirement. There are a number of problems with such a definition of metrics. Their calculation cannot be easily automated, and their value needs to be determined by comparing implementation and design documents with specification. These metrics indicate how much work on the project has been completed, rather than the underlying quality of the implementation. Such metrics represent good project management practice for green-field projects, but cannot be applied easily when part of the system is re-engineered. Lastly, quality or lack thereof is not seen as an attribute of source code, as none of the proposed metrics are based on direct measurements on source code. This is against the guidance of ISO 9126-1 [ISO2001] page 15.

Prior to ISO 9126 there has been a vast amount of research devoted to software complexity metrics [Fen1998]. These traditional metrics, such as Cyclomatic Complexity or Estimated Static Path Count, are concerned with the structure of a function, vocabulary of a source file, etc. Therefore, they may yield the same values for drastically different versions or stages of a Software Product, e.g. Cyclomatic Complexity for pseudo code stage may be the same as for the final implementation. Moreover, there is no well-defined and substantiated way of mapping these metrics to ISO 9126 characteristics. We examine possible correlations of such software metrics with Quality in Use metrics in Section 4.2.

The rules of a language subset (see Section 1) represent common pitfalls associated with a particular programming language, and have been derived either from experience or on theoretical grounds, by examining the language specification [ISO1990, ISO 2003a]. Therefore, counting the number of violations of such rules in a Software Product appears well founded, and intuitively corresponds to a measure of its Internal Quality. This proposition is rigorously evaluated in Section 4.1.

4 Quantitative Results

Company A has an ongoing programme for improving customer satisfaction. To this end they are tracking software faults discovered in the field. The incidence of critical software faults tends to vary across their products, and the intention is to identify measurements on source code, i.e. Internal Quality metrics, that would correlate with these fault data, i.e. Quality in Use: Satisfaction metric. Once such source code factors are identified, it will be possible to re-engineer the software to minimise their value and thereby minimise the incidence of critical faults in future software releases.

Company A's customers view operation of these products as mission-critical; however, the same principles can be applied to safety-critical or safety-related software. Tracking occurrences of software failures is a common safety certification requirement (see Sections 1.1, 1.2 and 1.3), hence a Quality in Use: Safety metric can readily be derived.

Together with Company A we have collected code metrics for a number of their software products, and correlated them with the corresponding critical fault data. These code metrics fall into two categories:

incidence of language subset rule violations,

software complexity metrics [Fen1998].

The results are documented in Sections 4.1 and 4.2 respectively.

4.1 Language Subset Rule Correlation

As a pilot study we focused on 18 software products written in C++, and owned by a single business unit. Critical fault data for each of the products was available, covering a period of the last 12 months. In order not to disadvantage large projects, we normalised these measurements of Quality in Use: Satisfaction by the size of the corresponding code base, i.e. amount of Kilo Lines of Code (KLOC).

Rather than narrowing the study to a specific subset of the C++ language (see Section 2), we decided to include as many coding rules as possible, in our search for those that exhibited correlation with the fault data. QA C++, a static analyser for C++ from Programming Research, includes over 1000 rules (messages) ranging from ISO Compliance and Undefined Behaviour [ISO2003a], Best Practice [Hen1997, Mey2005, PRG2004, Sut1999, Sut2004], to code layout conventions. This includes rules pertaining to individual source files as well as issues occurring across files, see Table 1 for examples.

confidence	msg#	QA C++ message text
99.5%	1512	'%1s' has external linkage and is declared in more than one file.
99%	1508	The typedef '%1s' is declared in more than one file.
99%	2085	For loop declaration of '%1s' is hiding existing declaration.
99%	4239	Class type control loop variable '%1s' modified in loop block.
97.5%	4217	Variable '%1s' is not accessed after this initialisation before it is next modified.
97.5%	4237	Class type control variable '%1s' not declared here.
97.5%	3600	This 'int' literal is an octal number.
95%	1505	The function '%1s' is only referenced in one translation unit.
95%	4243	Multiple class type loop control variables found: '%1s'.
95%	4325	Variable '%1s' is not accessed further.
95%	4004	Continue statement found.
95%	4208	Variable '%1s' is never used.
0%	2015	This function may be called with default arguments.

Table 1. Message correlation with critical fault data for a sample of QA C++ messages

For every software product we recorded the frequency of occurrence of each QA C++ message, and normalised the measurements by the size of the product in KLOC.

While we could look for correlations between these raw measurements for fault data and message frequencies, this would make an unnecessary assumption that both of these populations of measurements were distributed similarly. Instead, we decided to use ranks of the measurements only. If we were to order the software products according to fault data frequency, and for a given QA C++ message according to its frequency of occurrence, similarity between these two orderings would imply a positive correlation between the message and fault data. Considering that we are dealing with a large number of products, from a statistical standpoint it is not necessary that these orderings are identical, for there to be a significant correlation. Given that the number of permutations of 18 entities: 18! = 18*17*...*2 = 6,402,373,705,728,000 is a staggeringly large number, if a pair of orderings is within the 5% group that are the most similar, we can say with 95% confidence that they are correlated. 95% confidence interval is usually considered the minimum level to achieve statistical significance.

This leaves the question of how we are going to judge similarity between two given orderings of 18 products. Spearman's Rank Correlation Coefficient R_s [Sie1965] is a non-parametric statistical test, meaning that it works on the ranks of measurements. It evaluates to 1.0 if the orderings are exactly the same and -1.0 if they are exactly opposite, i.e. one is an inversion of the other sequence. The closer the value of R_s to 0 the less similar both orderings are. In this study we are only interested in positive correlations between Quality in Use and Internal Quality metrics: $R_s > 0$. Given that we are dealing with 18 products, in order to have 95% confidence of a positive correlation between QA C++ message and fault data, the value of R_s needs to be no smaller than 0.401. Table 2 documents critical values of R_s for higher confidence intervals.

Confidence	95%	97.5%	99%	99.5%	99.9%
Critical Value of R_s	0.401	0.472	0.550	0.600	0.692

Table 2. Critical Values of Spearman's Rank Correlation Coefficient R_s for 18 entities

The first 12 rows of Table 1 list QA C++ messages that are positively correlated with critical fault data for the 18 software products under consideration, with at least 95% confidence. As an illustration the last row contains the message that has the value of R_s closest to 0. Figures 1-5, which can be found at the end of this paper, display the correlation between the ranks of fault and message frequencies for each software product as a scatter plot, for a representative selection of messages from Table 1. Dots (software products) that lie on the $y=x$ (diagonal) line represent complete agreement between the ranks. In Figure 1 dots are much closer to the diagonal line than in Figure 5, which visually confirms the accuracy of the Spearman's Rank Correlation Coefficient. Figure 6 corresponds to the message with the smallest value of R_s; for convenience both positive $y=x$ and negative $y=19-x$ correlation lines are drawn. As can be seen dots are equally distant from both diagonal lines.

This result can be interpreted as follows: there is at least 95% likelihood that 12 QA C++ messages detailed in Table 1 are positively correlated with critical faults in 18 software products under consideration. This allows us to assume that by re-engineering these products to reduce the incidence of these messages, future occurrence of critical faults may also be reduced. As the organisation is interested in improving customer satisfaction, targeting these messages and monitoring their frequency can supplement the existing quality procedures.

It is worth pointing out that these 12 recommended messages are Best Practice rules, rather than rules targeting Undefined Behaviour, e.g. array access out of bounds, or division by 0. Such rules targeting potential 'bugs' are unlikely to occur frequently in the code. If for 18 products most frequencies are 0, the Spearman's Rank Correlation Coefficient will rarely exceed the critical value, and so the corresponding QA C++ message will not be flagged up as correlated with critical fault data. Therefore, it is necessary to supplement rules/messages identified by this statistical procedure with rules targeting unpredictable behaviour, portability issues, and other priorities identified for the software products in question.

4.2 Metrics Correlation

Apart from looking for correlations between critical faults and QA C++ messages, we were interested in examining whether software complexity metrics [Fen1998] could be of use. QA C++ calculates several function, file and class based metrics. We have recorded the average, maximum and standard deviation value of every metric for each of the 18 software products. We then calculated the values of Spearman's Rank Correlation Coefficient R_s between the critical fault data and these metric data across the 18 products. The results are shown in Table 3. Critical value of R_s at 95% confidence level is 0.401, and none of the metrics meet that for either average measurement, maximum or standard deviation. Therefore, we could not recommend any of these software metrics to be included in the quality initiative.

5 Summary

The traditional process of defining a programming language subset is based on identifying unsafe constructs, and creating rules that restrict language use, such that these constructs are avoided. Typically, a number of mandatory rules will be identified, without any reference to their relative severity. A particular rule may address an unsafe construct by banning it altogether, without any consideration to usage context, or the fact that the programmer may have to write extra code to work around the absent feature, possibly eliminating any benefit. A successful subset needs to be safe but at the same time as minimal as possible to retain sufficient expressiveness.

metric	avg	max	Std dev
Class metrics			
Coupling to other classes	0.041	0.005	0.043
Deepest inheritance	0.083	0.166	0.100
Lack of cohesion within class	-0.012	-0.061	-0.046
Number of methods declared in class	-0.098	-0.020	-0.023
Number of immediate children	0.055	0.025	0.061
Number of immediate parents	0.055	0.034	0.055
Response for class	-0.031	-0.057	-0.031
Weighted methods in class	-0.017	-0.034	-0.069
Function metrics			
Cyclomatic complexity	0.087	-0.141	-0.234
Number of GOTO's	-0.153	-0.238	-0.154
Number of code lines	-0.061	-0.068	-0.256
Deepest level of nesting	0.103	0.234	0.087
Number of parameters	0.129	0.192	0.122
Estimated static program paths	-0.362	n/a*	0.084
Number of function calls	-0.102	-0.019	-0.239
Number of executable lines	0.017	0.018	0.009
File metrics			
Comment to code ratio	0.283	0.153	0.287
Number of distinct operands	-0.220	-0.239	-0.304
Number of distinct operators	-0.035	0.260	0.124
Total preprocessed code lines	-0.074	0.142	-0.087
Total number of tokens used	-0.144	0.040	-0.138
Total unpreprocessed code lines	-0.073	0.077	-0.117
Total number of variables	-0.187	-0.044	-0.261

Table 3. Metrics correlation with fault data
Critical value of *Rs* at 95% confidence level is 0.401

An alternative approach proposed and scrutinised in this paper is to use in-service data already mandated or at least recommended by safety standards or process standards. This data may cover for example failures attributed to a given version of a software system or a given sub-system. A statistical technique is used to reveal which sub-setting rules are in agreement with the in-service data. For example if incidence of failures is positively correlated with non-compliance to a particular

---

*For technical reasons we were not able to accurately calculate this value.

rule, it makes sense to mandate this rule in the future. Conversely, if a rule has very low or negative correlation with in-service data, it can be excluded from the subset, enhancing its expressiveness. Finally, for some rules the in-service data may be inconclusive and their merit needs to be decided using the traditional approaches to subset selection.

For a brand new software system of its kind, initially there will not be any in-service data to base this technique on. In this case an off-the-shelf language subset could be used to start with. As in-service data becomes available rules can be added to the subset if a positive correlation is established. As the system matures so will the language subset used to create it. The assumption is that if a rule is added to the subset, the code base will be retrospectively updated to comply with the new rule. A fully enforced rule will never be considered for removal in the future, as there will not be any statistical evidence to back this up[†]. However, if a rule has previously been excluded from the subset, it may later be added if there is new evidence to support this. This may happen for example if a new programming technique is adopted part way through the project. As the rule selection process is objective with this technique, there is scope to discover domain specific rules, which will address causes of specific, reported failures.

References

[Bar2003]   J. Barnes. *High Integrity Software: The SPARK Approach to Safety and Security.* Addison-Wesley, 2003.

[Bar2007]   R Barry. *Solid project lifecycle planning with IEC 61508 software development.*   www.embedded-control-europe.com/know-how?kid=91, 2007.

[Fen1998]   N.E. Fenton, S.L. Pfleeger. *Software Metrics: A Rigorous Approach.* 2nd edition. PWS, Boston, 1998.

[Hen1997]   M. Henricson, E. Nyquist, N. Erik. *Industrial Strength C++: Rules and Regulations.* Prentice Hall, 1997.

[IEC1998]   IEC 61508-3:1998. *Functional safety of E/E/PE safety-related systems – Part 3: Software requirements.*

[ISO1990]   ISO/IEC 9899:1990. *Programming languages – C.*

[ISO2001]   ISO/IEC 9126-1:2001. *Software engineering – Product quality – Part 1: Quality model.*

[ISO2003a]   ISO/IEC 14882:2003. *Programming languages – C++.*

[ISO2003b]   ISO/IEC TR 9126-2:2003. *Software engineering – Product quality – Part 2: External metrics.*

[ISO2003c]   ISO/IEC TR 9126-3:2003. *Software engineering – Product quality – Part 3: Internal Metrics.*

[ISO2004]   ISO/IEC TR 9126-4:2004. *Software engineering – Product quality – Part 4: Quality in use metrics.*

---

† value of the Spearman's Rank Correlation Coefficient is undefined if all entries are 0

[LMC2005]   Lockheed Martin Corporation. *Joint Strike Fighter Air Vehicle C++ Coding Standards*. www.jsf.mil, December 2005.

[Mey2005]   S. Meyers. *Effective C++: 55 Specific Ways to Improve Your Programs and Designs*. 2nd edition. Addison Wesley, Boston, 2005.

[MIR1998]   MIRA. *MISRA-C:1998 - Guidelines for the Use of the C Language in Vehicle Based Software*. www.misra-c.com, 1998.

[MIR2004a] MIRA. *MISRA-C:2004 - Guidelines for the use of the C language in critical systems*. www.misra-c2.com, 2004.

[MIR2004b] MIRA. *MISRA-C:2004 Press Release*. http://www.misra-c.com/downloads/MISRAC2004press.pdf, 2004.

[MoD1997]   Defence Standard 00-55. *Requirements for Safety Related Software in Defence Equipment*. Issue 2. UK Ministry of Defence, 1997.

[MoD2007]   Defence Standard 00-56. *Safety Management Requirements for Defence Systems*. Issue 4. UK Ministry of Defence, 2007.

[PRG2004]   Programming Research. *High Integrity C++ Coding Standard Manual*. www.codingstandard.com, 2004.

[Rei2004]   D. W. Reinhardt. *Use of the C++ Programming Language in Safety Critical Systems*. MSc Thesis, University of York, 2004.

[RTC1992]   RTCA/DO-178B. *Software Considerations in Airborne Systems and Equipment Certification*. RTCA Inc, 1992.

[Sie1965]   S. Siegel. *Nonparametric Statistics for the Behavioral Sciences*. McGraw-Hill Book Company, Berkshire, 1956.

[Sut1999]   H. Sutter. *Exceptional C++*. Addison Wesley, Boston, 1999.

[Sut2004]   H. Sutter, A.. Alexandrescu. *C++ Coding Standards: 101 Rules, Guidelines, and Best Practices*. Addison Wesley, Boston, 2004.

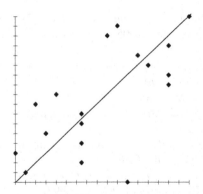

Figure 1. correlation for message 1512
R_s=0.649, confidence interval 99.5%

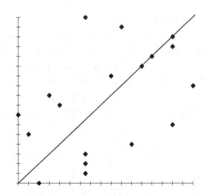

Figure 4. correlation for message 1505
R_s=0.466, confidence interval 95%

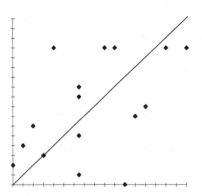

Figure 2. correlation for message 1508
R_s=0.568, confidence interval 99%

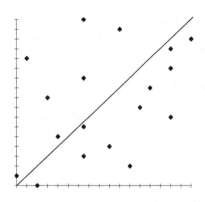

Figure 5. correlation for message 4208
R_s=0.403, confidence interval 95%

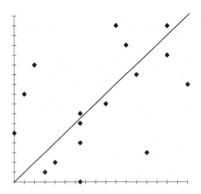

Figure 3. correlation for message 4217
R_s=0.533, confidence interval 97.5%

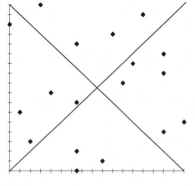

Figure 6. correlation for message 2015
R_s=0.001, i.e. no correlation

The Safety Case

Safety Case Development
How can I continue the work?

Tadeusz Cichocki
Dr Tadeusz Cichocki Konsulting
Chorzów, Poland
tadeusz.cichocki@tckon.eu

Abstract

This paper concerns the meaning of "safe" and current practice regarding safety analysis, safety case and safety assessment. The intention is to state some *diagnosis,* i.e. to identify an illness or problem from its signs and symptoms and to conclude from such an act. Safety engineering practice and the way of conceptualizing the problem is alarming the author when he is trying to be clear as far as possible in saying what we are doing and assuring. Some work in progress is mentioned.

1. Introduction

In the context of general uncertainty which concerns the state of the world, the effects of our actions, or others' actions, we engineer systems and safety justification of their application. The justification is presented (under technical term *safety proof, safety case* or *trust case*) as a documentation of a phenomenon that can announce achievement of requirements defined. Relying on patterns we know it guides and composes final results of all other safety engineering activities by the development project.

A *system* in engineering (developers) mind may just be a collection of statements intended to describe it sufficiently but it is expected that their justification provides a complete explanation of the engineering problems and solutions against stated requirements, including *a justified statement about some exhaustive list of fatalities being avoided*. The main questions to be answered include the following:

- Who (what element of the system environment) may be injured or lost while the system is put into operation?
- What is the possible scope of this undesired influence?
- What acceptance (safety) criteria for his influence are identified?

- If / how the acceptance criteria are satisfied by the change proposed?
- What are the procedures and roles responsible for the system properties maintenance?

On a more detailed level this list develops into a hierarchy of technical questions which depends on the system structure and its development and technology applied context. Thorough answers compose the safety argumentation needed, but then they are to be supported (see Fig. 1) by an understanding of uncertainty related to it (*formally a parameter associated to a result of some measurement; an indication of soundness of the engineering statements above*). In general uncertainty is caused by (Radhakrishna Rao C. 1989):

- lack of information,
- unknown degree of inaccuracy of the information available.

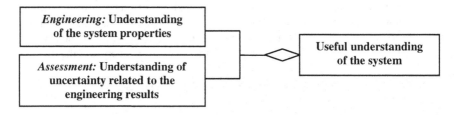

Figure. 1. Useful understanding "structure".

In order to manage the safety justification issues an objective measure (a relevant model to compare to) is needed and its existence is assumed. Using this measure one could be able to state that in the specific system engineering process *the risk* is sufficiently reduced.

While models approach us to the essence of the matter, *safety engineering* domain lacks certainty of what the models should be. We are quite often not sure of what knowledge collected (acquired through experience or independent of experience) is sufficient. Multiple partial models (which influence the actual factors considered in any safety analysis) and an *independent safety assessment process* are used to confirm that *all* doubts were investigated and successfully resolved. The doubts in general may include the following:

a) some model is found showing possible scenario to some lose,
b) an available model does not represent (adequately) the reality under investigation,
c) there is no analysis regarding confidence to the models used,
d) some traditional, expected or normative models are not considered.

In addition, there are "out of the art" problems, which appear quite often when time or other resources constraints imply management pressure issue, as represented by the following quotations from real Development Projects:

„They (competition) do not use the rules of Cenelec norms*, so we will not too."

„Should I use clear terminology? I do not care ..."

„This measure does not prevent hazards at all or in 95% of all cases."

"Systemic approach is an academic one; we are doing what our customers expect us to do."

"We should avoid this new and so much popular now management and human factors staff; we are engineers."

Experience, possessing appropriate information and skills for those involved in the development and acceptance process becomes a crucial quality requirement.

This paper is written to stress the difficulty of defining the framework for systems safety engineering and assessment by exploring some of the elements of the engineering and assessment processes and use this as a general diagnosis of the current practice in the context of the Cenelec railway norms. In addition two tools are shortly discussed in sections 4 and 5 which, based on the author experience, help in the safety argumentation development.

2. Safety Analysis - Generic Pattern

Accidents are seen as a result of inadequate control actions not enforcing necessary constraints on the system design and operation (Leveson N.G. 2005). In the case of railway systems, to overcome the inertia of a train some means of signalling to indicate in advance the state of the railroad and conditions ahead are necessary. Developers of the evolving systems are to assure:

- The system's accident free logic,
- Reliability of the information provided, including cases when some components of the system fail,
- Ability to use the information adequately to avoid accidents.

Development of such systems is currently supported by a number of Cenelec norms which postulate some general, more or less clear, complete and consistent techniques and methods. The specific development project is to present their meaning in the project context and therefore to find the way the system under development (its properties) will be understood.

2.1. The notion of *risk* problem

Demand for measurability and calculations introduced a notion of *risk*, which is to play a fundamental role in the approach according to Cenelec. Risk is a forecast in terms of probability/frequency for a future accident of certain severity. Some hazards are decided to be acceptable due to its possibly minor consequences or rare appearance. Safety then is the freedom from unacceptable risk level.

---

* In this paper these are norms: EN 50126, EN 50128, EN 50129 and related to them.

The risk definition appears to be very simplistic there: *"it is a combination of the frequency, or probability, and the consequence of a specified hazardous event"*.

The 'combination' is interpreted to be 'multiplication' if the two intuitive parameters used may be multiplied and their values are reasonably found. Also the 'probability' notion there is used in an intuitive, not being precise, way only: it is an indication of 'our intensity of conviction' or 'the likelihood of an expected event occurring'. It has nothing to do with the mathematical approach to probability, where (after Kolmogorov) to avoid paradoxes and confusions probability is seen as a function which satisfies some axioms. Different concerns regarding these axioms inspire to investigations of alternative generalizations like Bayesian view or Dempster-Shafer belief functions. E.g. in the Bayesian view, probabilities are subjective values (experts' opinions, some background information while there is no direct previous data) and Bayes' law is a mechanism for "changing one's mind" (see (Singpurwalla N.D. 2006) for an extended discussion).

In addition to the problem of how the risk measure should be defined, there are others around:

(1) Obtaining accurate estimates of probabilities of specific events may be problematic and therefore the use of such quantitative techniques for the decision making is controversial.

(2) Risk perception and estimate is dependent on (Redmill F. 2001):
  • Techniques applied – mostly understood on a general and intuitive level,
  • Human factors – concentration, skills, group work, management, values, education, experience, current information, comfort or discomfort.

(3) The scope and will to manage, control or decide on something depends on personal interests, life views and state of mind.

2.2. Effective control of safety

Essentially the questions to be answered in the safety engineering process are:

1. Should one prevent or mitigate results of all possible catastrophic scenarios one knows? All credible failure modes are to be covered by the analyses, particularly including *accidents*. Can one identify rare events?

2. How can one measure what remains after systematic application of known solutions? What is the size of 'out of control margin'? How can one deal with one-of-a-kind situations?

The only, but not completely satisfactory approach in practice is to:

1. Address all of the system stakeholders' requirements,
2. Follow known experience regarding systems safety engineering, and
3. Observe the results during the system operation.

The safety engineering process is naturally based on the following major steps to (Leveson N.G. 1995), (Leveson N.G. 2005), (Zalewski J. and all 2003):

1. model the basic technical and human processes of the system - specific system behavior, process or operations of some organization within the context of its operation,

2. identify the system safety constraints - solutions necessary to maintain acceptable status of the system and to be introduced during the system design and operation; control measures and strategies,

3. identify the hierarchical control structure in place to enforce the constraints,

4. identify key events that can impact the above, particularly the system *hazards* (system component failures or the interactions among the components and its environment that can lead to accidents); locate accident scenarios in the system,

5. identify key consequences that arise from the events (e.g. inability to complete a particular step in the process),

6. identify ability of controllers to ascertain the state of the system from information about the system state received,

7. design effective management systems to ensure those controls are put in place, maintained and improved.

8. understand slow variation or degradation of the models and conditions over time, particularly in the physical system, human operator behaviour, or the environment.

Such explicit models of safety and risk control, including explicit and auditable safety management systems are needed for the transport industries in particular.

Analysis can only compare artifacts (e.g. code against specifications). Therefore what can be achieved is limited by precision of descriptions and notation used. Due to the rare events, completeness and accuracy of models, patterns and efforts in the development project are of critical concern.

Complexity of control systems behaviour is a source of design faults. Lack of software continuity complicates testing. To find out what constitutes an architecture of software, what are the arrangements of elements and structures, we have to look at the basic principles (van Katwijk J. and all 2003), (Zalewski J. 2003). That the results obtained by one risk analyst are unlikely to be obtained by others starting with the same information, is not unusual situation (Redmill F. 2001).

Further explanation is required regarding design or organizational solutions minimizing risk which are likely to be *reasonably practicable*. In the UK it is a legal term and it is used in the context of railway applications. In deciding what is reasonably practicable one needs to consider (what is quite subjective):

1. comparison of measures with good practice and expert judgment,

2. the level of risk (i.e. how dangerous a situation is) and

3. degree of effort (in time and expense) needed to put in place measures that are appropriate to.

It is clear that the ALARP principle (that all practicable risk reduction has been done) should be applied with appropriate effort but the practice requires that cost of investment should be lower than the monetary value of injuries expected to avoid if the measures are in implemented.

However there are many risks where that which is good practice is not yet agreed, particularly in the modern railway industry with an increasing technological change. In such cases the decision must be made from *first principles.*

3. Underlying Activities of the Analysis

3.1. Appropriate representation of the problem

Whenever a system is described, there are always made assumptions on the context in which that system or its development project will operate.

To minimize subjectivity of safety judgments, information about the required behaviour of the system under construction and the project and its context itself is to be collected. The broad picture should include: designers' competence, tools efficiency, criteria of acceptance of their work, their responsibilities and dependence, or how data about the past are indicative of future trends and what the risks we are willing to accept in the future, agreements on 'best practice' or limitations of knowledge and technology; accepted patterns to specific problems and discussions concerning overconfidence in specific solutions.

The actual system is to be seen in the context of its actual application and based on clearly defined operational profile. Also regulations are always to be seen in the context of their intended use (*how can we apply the UK criteria for Japanese systems which are adapted in Dubai?*).

It is to be noted that domain or government committees are source of some of the measures used in safety engineering while some of the concepts used are problematic, e.g. SIL (Safety Integrity Level) .

3.2. Traceability Analysis

With the lack of keys to perfect link between actions and outcomes we are to improve our consideration of factors including identification of those which are out of our control. In the safety assessment process it is important to examine the decision process itself and the resulting outcome, not just one of the separated issues.

Requirements traceability is the system description which binds requirements with their sources and with components and properties of artifacts created during the development process. When an implicit assumption turns out to be wrong, it is potentially very difficult to identify those parts of the system which were dependent on that assumption. A relationship (*trace*) is established between two or more products of the development process, especially products having a predecessor-successor or master-subordinate relationship to one another. *Traceability* information can be used to support:

1. explanation of aspects of the design which need to be considered during impact analysis when a requirement changes;

2. the maintenance and evolution of software systems and documentation;

3. the reuse of software systems and their components; and

4. the inspection and testing of software systems.

Change propagation is a central aspect of software development: as developers modify software entities such as functions or variables to introduce new features or fix bugs, they must ensure that other entities in the software system are updated to be consistent with these new changes. Change may introduce new forms of failure. Various approaches to control the amount of change propagation and to avoid hidden dependencies were proposed, e.g. the Object Oriented paradigm.

The traceability, a resources consuming task, should ideally be supported by some automation. For understanding of an interactive complexity of object-oriented systems, the OF-FMEA method was developed (compare section 4 of this paper).

3.3. Project management and Safety Culture

Implementation of a minimal process (e.g. including project scheduling, resource planning, configuration management) and reliance on staff expertise as postulated by the Cenelec norms is not sufficient.

Traditional accident models were explaining losses caused by failures of physical devices (chain or tree of failure events) in relatively simple systems. They are less useful for explaining accidents in software-intensive systems and for non-technical aspects of safety such as organizational culture and human decision-making. A so called *safety culture* for a development company and processes associated with routine tasks there, in general, is now identified (but not by Cenelec norms) as an area of root cause of accidents and that there is the greatest and most fundamental potential for improvement (Cooper M.D. 2000), (Sorensen J.N. 2002), (Speirs F. and Johnson C.W. 2002), (Braband J. 2004). Safety culture refers to a shared set of understood knowledge and values in a particular group. It is recognized that the organization's structure may have limitations in providing the 'glue' that holds organizations together and act according to its mission (compare particularly (Senge P.M. 1990)). The Safety Culture enables organization members to close the gap between their values, intentions, and actual behavior. Fundamental values promoted by the culture should be:

• Group approach,
• Trust,
• Open communication.

Two of the Safety Culture questions are:

(1) How is *independence* of opinion of safety personnel assured?

(2) If (and how) the development management is willing to consider the views on nonconformity issues to be closed properly? What are the relevant procedures?

Roles and goals give structure and organized direction to our personal mission. Expectations around roles and goals may be conflicting or ambiguous and should be clearly understood and to be shared by other people. Clear identification of areas of activity and strategies give a sense of direction and trust. The paradigm that one person's success is not achieved at the expense or exclusion of the success of others is to be applied (Robson M. 2002).

4. OF-FMEA Method

Software failures are in general the result of flaws possibly introduced in the logic of the software design, or in the code-implementation of that logic. These may produce an actual functional failure, in case they are "performed" on an execution path activated according to the specific inputs to the software. It is known that standard testing approaches are not suitable for determining failure rates in regions defined for safety-critical systems (Littlewood B. 2004).

To model and predict the characteristics and properties of these designs accurately new tools and approaches are needed. Consideration of all possible behaviours of the system could be valuable evidence. Since "all possible" behaviours may be too many to examine for traditional techniques, two complementary approaches have evolved that attempt to reduce the number of behaviours that must be considered. One way tries to show that the system always does the right thing, the other tries to show that it never does a seriously wrong thing.

One of the ideas under investigation concerns a reasonable use of formal methods. Experience of using the "formal" way of systems development, verification and its quality assurance is extending. Formal methods, in general, are used for:

1. terminology clarification (including domain objects and structures: net topology, stations, …),

2. methodology clarification,

3. patterns for technical solutions,

4. development and analysis support (to reason about properties of systems) in the phases of specification, design refinement and verification, software code and tests generation.

The general way followed during a formal system development is to start from a description of some specific domain. Then one is to state the requirements and answer the question: *Can the description tolerate abnormal situations?* Finally, introduce the tolerance of abnormal situations and argue on the relation of the description to the reality and accepted models.

In formal verification, we verify that a system is correct with respect to a specification. When verification succeeds and the system is proven to be correct, there is still a question of how complete the specification is, and whether it really covers all the behaviours of the system.

Automated examination of scenarios can be taken still further using model checking. In model checking, the case explosion problem is transformed into one of *state explosion*, meaning that the time and space required to run the model checker grows rapidly and eventually becomes infeasible as the size of the model grows, so that abstraction, or consideration of only limited numbers of fault cases and real-time delays, must be employed.

Beyond being fully automatic, an additional attraction of model-checking tools is their ability to accompany a negative answer to the correctness query by a counterexample to the satisfaction of the specification in the system. Thus, together with a negative answer, the model checker returns some erroneous execution of the system. These counterexamples are very important and they can be essential in detecting subtle errors in complex designs.

To support understanding an Interactive complexity of the systems, the OF-FMEA method was developed (Cichocki T. and Górski J. 2000), (Cichocki T. and Górski J. 2001), (Cichocki T. and Górski J. 2002). The UML (*Unified Modelling Language*) and CSP (*Communication Sequential Processes*) specification languages and FDR (*Failures Divergence Refinement*) tool are used. The method may address component failures and system failures (the individual components are operating as planned but the problems arose in the unplanned effects of these component behaviour on the system).

4.1. OF-FMEA background

Failure Modes and Effects Analysis (FMEA) and its variants have been widely used in safety analyses for more than thirty years. With the increase of application domain of software intensive systems there was a natural tendency to extend the use of (originally developed for hardware systems) safety analysis methods to software based systems.

FMEA is focused on safety consequences of component failures. Identified failure modes of a component are analysed case by case. The analysis process results in an explicit and documented decisions that take into account the risk associated with a given failure mode. The decision can be just the acceptance (supported by a convincing justification) of the consequences of the failure or it can suggest necessary design changes to remove (or mitigate) the consequences or causes of the failures. Documentation is an important output of FMEA. This documentation can be then referred to by a safety case for the considered system.

The work that aims at extending the FMEA to make it suitable to analyze object-oriented software designs is presented in (Cichocki T. and Górski J. 2000), (Cichocki T. and Górski J. 2001), (Cichocki T. and Górski J. 2002), compare also

(Zalewski J. and all 2003). It is assumed that to analyse failure mode consequences formal methods are being used. The approach called OF-FMEA (*Object-oriented Formal FMEA*) follows the 'classical' FMEA process while analysing system designs and aims at analysing the dependence of system behaviour on possible failures of its components. OF-FMEA extends FMEA in three aspects:

- assumes that the analysed system is being developed using the object-oriented approach,
- assumes that the object-oriented models of the system are supplemented with their formal specifications,
- assumes that the analysis of failure consequences is based on the formal specifications and is supported by an automatic tool.

4.2. Overview of OF-FMEA

Object models are general enough to represent systems (people, software and hardware) and can then be specialised towards representation of software components. As the consequence, system development can proceed without a major switch of the modelling approach while changing the attention from the system to software aspects. This is an important advantage during the analysis as we can pass the borders between heterogeneous components of the system (both, hierarchically and horizontally) without being forced to work with heterogeneous models.

In OF-FMEA CSP (*Communication Sequential Processes*) was chosen as a formal base for object-oriented models. The motivation behind this choice was that CSP is well suited to modelling co-operating components that interact by passing messages along communication lines. And it was exactly the situation we were facing during our case studies (related to railway switching). The system we were working with is composed of components with a relatively little state information. The components exchange messages with their environment through defined communication channels. A natural way of specifying such components is by describing their possible interactions with the surrounding world. This way of viewing interfaces is well suited to the way FMEA considers the system components: it concentrates on failures, i.e. on what is visible to the environment and to much extend disregards the mechanism (the component's interior) that led to the failure.

It is assumed that before we start OF-FMEA an adequate environment to support the work has been set up. Part of this environment is object-oriented models of the system of interest. Of particular interest are two categories of models:

- The *object model* that presents the system in terms of its constituent objects and relationships among them; of particular interest is the *decomposition* relationship as it shows how the system decomposes into its components.
- The *object collaboration diagrams* showing how objects interact through communication channels; the channels may model the actual

communication links (if the objects are already designed and implemented) or show the designers' intentions concerning the further development of the system.

We assume that the models have been checked against relevant consistency and correctness criteria (e.g. by checking them against documentation standards and by passing them through an inspection process).

Failure checklists are based on experience, producer recommendations, sectoral norms and engineering judgement and support identification of component failure modes. To support modelling of the identified failure modes we provide a set of patterns. Each pattern suggests how to modify the specification of a "normal" behaviour of the component (and possibly of some co-operating components) in order to model a given failure mode. An application of a pattern to represent a given failure mode in the specification of a component is called *failure mode injection*. The specifications with injected failure modes are then verified against safety properties to check for possible failure consequences.

Each analysis is different and demands careful and innovative thought.

It is helpful, however, to have a standard sequence of steps to follow.

This provides consistency from one analysis to another, which is useful to both the analysts doing the study and the managers reading the report.

The OF-FMEA method comprises the following steps:

- Choosing the scope of the analysis.
- Formal modelling of the system.
- Analysis of component failures.
- Failure mode injection campaign.
- Interpretation of the results.

The steps are presented in more detail in the subsequent sections.

4.3. Choosing the scope of the analysis

While applying OF-FMEA we concentrate on the decomposition hierarchy of the object model. This hierarchy shows how the higher level components are built out of the lower level ones. On top of this we can see the whole system as a single component. Its required properties specify what is considered important concerning the mutual influence of the system and its environment, e.g. for a critical system we postulate that the system should be safe. The lower level decomposition shows the system components and explains how they interact. In our case study the system of interest is LBS – the Line Block System. It controls the traffic of trains between adjacent railway stations. The related decomposition structure is shown in Fig. 2 (see the next page). At Level 0 we have a generic railway system and its only attribute represents our (the public) concern that the system should be safe. Level 1 shows the signaling system and its relevant co-operating components. The next Level 2 shows the place of LBS within the signaling system. This is the level with respect to which we interpret the railway signaling rules derived from the railway regulations. The rules impose safety constraints on the model.

With respect to the hierarchy objects the rules can be understood as the explanation of what "safe" of Level 0 means in terms of levels 1 and 2 of our decomposition. Levels 3 down to 6 represent design decisions (explain the structure of LBS in terms of its components and their interactions).

We chose Level 2 as the reference level during our analysis that means that by "safe" we understand that the system is compliant with the railway safety regulations. And we chose Level 6 as the lowest component level (we did not consider further decomposition levels). Our goal was to analyse how possible failure modes of the components can affect the safety properties expressed with respect to Level 2.

Object models represent the structural aspects of the system design. Communication among objects is represented by collaboration diagrams that belong to the suite of models recommended by UML. An example collaboration diagram is shown in Fig. 2. It explains how components of Level 4 co-operate to implement the i-th Local Control Point object.

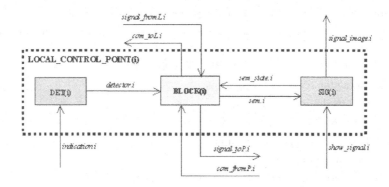

Figure. 2. Collaboration diagram of the components of the i-th Local Control Point object.

4.4. Formal modelling of the system

The object and collaboration diagrams are input to the OF-FMEA method. From this input we develop formal specification of component interactions. For this purpose we use CSP. Each component of the collaboration diagram becomes a CSP process with input and output channels as shown in the diagram. In addition to this we develop formal models of safety requirements of the system. The requirements are derived from the railway safety regulations. Each requirement is modelled as a CSP process and imposes some restrictions on the ordering of events in the system. The requirements refer to the events that are visible on Level 4 of our decomposition.

We can verify consistency of the formal specifications using the FDR tool. During verification we compare the specification of the system (seen as composition of its components) with the specification of the safety requirements. During verification we check for each safety requirement if the following relation holds:

$$TS \subseteq TSR,$$

where TS denotes the set of event traces of the system (restricted to events visible on Level 4) and TSR denotes the set of event traces of the process modelling a safety requirement. This verification process can follow the design process (in a sense that after we design the next decomposition level we can verify it against the specification of the safety requirements).

Formal specifications that were positively verified against the safety requirements are the input to the next step, the analysis of component failures.

4.5. Analysis of component failures

Failures are modelled as deviations from the "normal" behaviour of a component (observed on the component's interface). The modelling is achieved by altering the specification of a component and its interaction with other components. To provide for completeness of failure modes we follow a systematic procedure of failure mode identification. The problem is to formulate hypotheses about potential failure modes of a component X and to decide which of them are included in further analyses (by accepting or rejecting the failure hypotheses).

The results of the fault injection campaign are interpreted by undertaking the following decisions: failure mode acceptance, failure mode handling or failure mode elimination.

The choice between the above interpretations depends on the judgement of the analysts/designer and is beyond the OF-FMEA method. The criteria used to support such decision include availability of the resources for redesign, availability of candidate components to replace a given one, and the assessment of the credibility of the considered failure mode.

5. Safety Assessment Activity

Many standards (e.g. the Cenelec railway norms) require development of a Safety Case to demonstrate the acceptability of safety critical systems. The Safety Case must provide confidence that the system is deemed safe enough to operate. A state of *belief* or *trust* of the system users must be achieved, that state of the mind by which it assents to propositions because of some qualities of the source. People quite often realize that they *know* more than they can explain. This is probably the case of Safety Case. It is to represent a clear, comprehensive, definable and auditable argument that a system or installation will be acceptably safe throughout its life (including decommissioning) within a defined environment (Bishop P.G. and Bloomfield R.E. 1998), (Weinstock Ch. B. and all 2004). In parallel, an Independent Safety Assessment develops its Safety Assessment Report based on evidence found during the assessment activities, and an independent Safety Claim Structure (where the evidence and assumptions used are linked by the explicit arguments to support a decision) is included there as well. Viewpoints of stakeholders (or safety goals) are proposed as a means of managing the analytical complexity of safety critical systems (McDermid J. 2000). Each of the viewpoints is a declarative statement of intent to be achieved by the *system* (i.e. the software-to-be together with its environment) under consideration. It is represented by models of the system and its process of development. The representation forms a justified strategy or means of compliance.

An independent study is conducted by the author of this presentation in the context of safety assessment of a railway interlocking application and relevant Cenelec railway norms. The assessment is based on the following program:

- establish a common understanding amongst internal and external stakeholders as to what the railway is expected to deliver with regards to safety,
- develop a trusted framework of processes and criteria for safety decision makers to apply,
- achieve clarity and stability in the safety governance of the railway.

An independent assessment is not to mandate any ideas, approaches or technologies. However it is always based on ideas, approaches or technologies of choice. The first choice is based on the physical and statutory environment of use of the system under assessment and on our state-of-the-art (generic) knowledge about how systems safety engineering is to be conducted today. Based on the choices a consistent structure of assessment criteria are developed and used in the investigation. An assessment is successful (i.e. *states conformance and therefore recommends acceptance*) if all the assessment criteria are satisfied. Due to doubts investigation during the process the project could improve its own argumentation and make its stronger.

Pragmatic and easier way to produce the justification is to address questions raised by different stakeholders (e.g. users, certifiers or standards). If the list of the questions and answers is complete (from the specific point of view of each stakeholder, e.g. see Table 1), then the justification is complete and valid. The documentation should provide an adequate information (a pattern) to be understood by the stakeholders' representatives.

The first principles approach is shown in the example in Table 2.

Table 1. The first example of top level safety claims

	The system is acceptably safe to operate from a hazard control perspective
C1	Hazards, risk tolerability criteria and use conditions of the application domain are identified
C2	The *System Requirements Specification* (related to C1) is adequate, i.e. sufficient to control risk, and implemented
C3	Effectiveness of the solution (to C2) proposed is proved
C4	Conformity of the solution implemented (related to C3) is proved
C5	Operational usage of the system developed is postulated

Table 2. The second example of top level safety claims

	First principles - Generic rule or criteria
1	*Safety* is a property of a complete system in a given context.
2	Safety targets (*safety requirements and risks acceptance criteria*) are to be set for the application to achieve an acceptable level of risk and implemented.
3	Quality of the project is the quality of its processes – systematic use of proper methods to proper tasks – while customer is not left out of the picture.
4	Where demonstration of safety is fundamental for the Project acceptance, it is essential that the test method, and the conditions under which it is to be carried out, are fully described. Safety verification, validation and certification strategy is established in accordance to the level of safety risks.
5	In a risk based approach to safety engineering, an identification of hazards and risks is to be guided by the specific domain relevant data and qualified safety engineering resources.

A complete Claim Breakdown Structure, the goal decomposition, based on the norms and domain guidelines is represented as a tree. *Argumentation tables* are developed and maintained for each of the claims to collect argumentation based on sub-claims, facts, assumptions, context information, references, comments, models. They are all finally included into the Safety Assessment Report to the complete assessment argumentation.

6. Conclusions

This paper is written to stress the difficulty of defining the framework for systems safety engineering and assessment by exploring some of the elements of the engineering and assessment argumentation and use this as a general diagnosis of the current practice in the context of the Cenelec railway norms. As such the goal is too difficult to be properly completed in the paper form and in time available to the author. However the effort to prepare the paper was a very good reason to formulate some of the problems again and continue their consideration in the new projects.

What we do is an attempt to rationalize the very intuitive world. The author was not able to answer the question how all of this should be precisely defined but what is important for him is to care about strong intuitions and to make them stronger project by project. In parallel, it is to be reminded that our "fluency" in tools and real application problems is to be maintained as well. The two tools shortly discussed in sections 4 and 5 (and described more completely in earlier papers), based on the authors experience, help in the safety argumentation development and need further attention in the specific projects context.

7. References

Bishop P.G. and Bloomfield R.E. (1998). *A Methodology for Safety Case Development.* Safety-critical Systems Symposium, Birmingham, UK, 1998.

Blechinger Ch. (2004). *ProCEN – A tool to manage the CENELEC RAMS Process.* SIGNAL + DRAHT (96) 4/2004, 15-16.

Braband J. (2004). *The importance of a safety culture in railway signaling.* SIGNAL + DRAHT (96) 5/2004, 33-36.

Cichocki T. and Górski J. (2000). *Failure Mode and Effect Analysis for Safety-Critical Systems with Software Components*, in: Floor Koornneef, Meine van der Meulen (Eds.) *Computer Safety, Reliability and Security*, Proceedings of 19th International Conference SAFECOMP 2000, Rotterdam (The Netherlands), October 24-27, 2000, Springer Lecture Notes in Computer Science 1943, p. 382-394.

Cichocki T. and Górski J. (2001). *Formal Support for Fault Modelling and Analysis*, in: Udo Voges (ed.), Proceedings of *Computer Safety, Reliability and Security*, 20th International Conference SAFECOMP 2001, Budapest (Hungary), September 26-28, 2001, Springer Lecture Notes in Computer Science 2187, p. 190-199.

Cichocki T. and Górski J. (2002). *OF-FMEA - an approach to safety analysis of object oriented software intensive system.* The 9th International Conference on Advanced Computer Systems (ACS'2002), Miedzyzdroje (Poland), October 23-25, 2002 (published *in* The Kuwer International Series in Engineering and Computer Science – 752, ISBN: 1-4020-7396-8, September 2003, p. 271-280).

Cichocki T. (2004). *Safety Analysis Methods - software development questions*, Proc. of NATO Advanced Research Workshop, "Cyberspace Security and Defence: Research Issues", September 6-9, 2004, Gdańsk, Poland, Kluwer Academic Publishers B.V., p.101-124.

Cooper M.D. (2000). *Towards a Model of Safety Culture*. Safety Science (2000): vol. 36, p.111-136 (http://behavioural-safety.com/articles/Towards_A_Model_Of_Safety_Culture/).

Edmonds B. (1999). *Syntactic Measures of Complexity*. PhD thesis, The University of Manchester, 1999, (245 pp.).

van Katwijk J. and all (2003). *An Approach to Evaluate Real-Time Software Architectures for Safety-Critical Systems*. 2003, Proc. Workshop on Critical Systems Development with UML San Francisco, Calif., October 21, 2003, 121-128 (http://www.eg3.com/real/safety.htm).

Leveson N.G. (1995). *Safeware: System Safety and Computers*. Addison-Wesley Publishing Company, 1995, ISBN 0-201-11972-2, (680 pp.).

Leveson N.G. (2005). *A Systems-Theoretic Approach to Safety in Software-Intensive Systems*. IEEE Transactions on Dependable and Secure Computing 1, 1 (January-March 2004): 66-86.

Littlewood B. (2004) *Assessing the dependability of Software-based systems: the importance role of confidence*. KKIO 2004, Software Engineering Conference, Gdańsk, 5-8 October, 2004, p. 13-14.

Maguire R. (2006) *Safety Cases and Safety Reports. Meaning, Motivation and Management*, Ashgate Publishing, 2006, pp.176.

McDermid J. and all (2000) *Managing Analytical Complexity of Safety Critical Systems using Viewpoints*. Department of Computer Science, University of York, UK.

PMI (2003). Project Management Institute, *A Guide to the Project Management Body of Knowledge* (*PMBOK® Guide*), November 2003, (257 pp.).

Radhakrishna Rao C. (1989) *Statistics and Truth. Putting Chance to Work*. Council of Scientific and Industrial Research, New Delhi, India, 1989.

Redmill F. (2001) *Subjectivity in Risk Analysis*. Risk Analysis and Safety Management of Technical Systems, Conference and Workshops, Gdansk- Gdynia, 25-27, June 2001, p. 75-89.

Redmill F. (2004). *Risk-based test planning during system development*. KKIO 2004, Software Engineering Conference, Gdańsk, 5-8 October, 2004, p. 15-29.

Robson M. (2002). *Problem-Solving in Groups*. Gower Publishing Limited, Gower House, 2002, (185 pp.).

Sanz R. and Zalewski J. (2003). *Pattern-Based Control Systems Engineering*. IEEE Control Systems, vol. 23, No. 3, pp. 43-60, July 2003.

Senge P.M., (1990). *The Fifth Discipline. The Art and Practice of The Learning Organization*. Doubleday, 1990 (389 pp.).

Singpurwalla N.D. (2006). *Reliability and Risk – A Bayesian Perspective*, Wiley Series in Probability and Statistics, John Wiley & Sons, Ltd, 2006 (371 pp.)

Sorensen J.N. (2002). *Safety culture: a survey of the state-of-the-art.* Reliability Engineering and System Safety, 76 (2002), p. 189-204.

Speirs F. and Johnson C.W. (2002). *Safety Culture in the face of industrial change: a case study from the UK Rail Industry.* University of Glasgow, Scotland, May 29, 2002.

Weinstock Ch. B. and all, (2004). *Dependability Cases. May 2004*, Technical Note, CMU/SEI-2004-TN-016, (31 pp.).

Zalewski J. (2003). *Real-Time Software Architectures and Design Patterns: Fundamental Concepts and Their Consequences.* SCR 2003 (also: Annual Reviews in Control, vol. 25, No. 1, p. 133-146, July 2001).

Zalewski J. and all, (2003). *Safety of computer control systems: challenges and results in software development.* Annual Reviews in Control, vol. 27, No. 1, p. 23-37, 2003.

Safety Case Experiences from Harrier

Jeff Lucas
BAE Systems,
Farnborough, United Kingdom

Abstract

This paper details the experiences of the BAE Systems Harrier Safety Team in developing the Operational Safety Cases for the Harrier II GR Mk9/9A & T Mk12 including the Open Systems Mission Computer and its Operational Flight Program.

1 Introduction

The goal of this paper is to identify the challenges encountered over the last 7 years in developing and managing a whole aircraft safety case. The Harrier aircraft in question has a long history in service with the Royal Navy (RN) and Royal Air Force (RAF), see section 2. This service is considered tolerably safe given the current loss rate of aircraft through all causes. This is referred to as the 'legacy' claim and it sets the basis of all future safety arguments, the top goal being "at least as safe as the legacy aircraft".

This paper covers two specific safety cases; the aircraft level case and the case covering the Open Systems Mission Computer (OMSC) and its software. Both cases are produced by the BAE Systems safety team at Farnborough to cover the upgrade of the aircraft at the incremental Capability upgrades required by the RAF.

The development and continued management of the safety case during the upgrades have raised issues that the team have successfully overcome and a number of lessons have been learnt along the way.

The first of these, given the range of choice available in this day and age, is that it is important to select the correct toolset for safety case management. Alternative approaches are often required from those initially planned. The upgrade development process brought late changes which needed to be incorporated but could not be supported in the original safety case. The toolset, and those using it, need to be sufficiently flexible to cope with such uncertainty. The capability upgrade requirements, not surprisingly, developed over the years and the initial safety case structure became more complex. Continuous process improvement, in the form of generic modelling within the Goal Structured Notation, was used to handle this.

Additionally some of the arguments developed were not changing between one Capability release and the next. This created repetition and led to nugatory re-review of these arguments during the final stages of sign-off which is a time when it could be least tolerated. Using the 'legacy' claim detailed above was acceptable for the initial capability safety case, however subsequent arguments needed the previous capability to be put into context. As such there was a requirement to derive a clear definition and nomenclature for these past Capability standards.   Another opportunity for the safety team came when a weapon that had been in service around the world for decades was required to be covered in the safety case for the first time. Unforeseen, it presented a real challenge to the team's evidence gathering techniques. The arrival of new smart weapons caused some unexpected issues too. The questions raised challenged scope and responsibility boundaries previously considered to be well understood from long service experience.

At the OSMC level, the safety case was originally developed using a detailed and rigid process. Subsequently, this was found to have produced a case that was inflexible, over complex and prevented comprehensive and constructive reviews. In light of this, the entire case construction was overhauled to address each of these issues.

Finally the paper details the latest safety challenge, that of clearances with limited evidence using rapid technology insertion in support of operational requirements direct from the front line.

2 Harrier Aircraft Background

The Harrier I entered operational service with the RAF in 1969. The Harrier II aircraft is a development of the earlier versions of Harrier I, incorporating a number of aerodynamic, structural and systems improvements, which greatly enhance the operational performance of the aircraft.

Initially entering service with the RAF as the GR Mk5, all RAF Harrier II aircraft have been modified to the full 'Night Attack' standard the GR Mk7. The 'Night Attack' avionics are designed to allow Harrier missions to be performed equally well during the day or night. A two-seater training version of the aircraft was also introduced, the T Mk10. The GR7 aircraft are being upgraded to produce GR9 aircraft with a host of improvements in incremental stages.

GR7 Mission computing is performed using AYK code running on an ACCS 3500. GR9 aircraft Mission Computing is performed by the OSMC consisting of ACCS 3550 hardware utilising a LynxOS operating system with Application Support Package (ASP) and Operational Flight Programme (OFP) software. The OSMC is at the centre of the avionic system; controlling the avionic system mission databus, and performing weapon aiming calculations, data fusion from multiple sensor inputs and general control of avionics moding and switching.

The increased capability from the baseline is being introduced in 'Capability' stages, currently from Capability A to E. This staged approach introduces

Capability in an incremental development environment that includes major avionics upgrades and the introduction of new weapons and role equipment to address obsolescence and to enhance operational effectiveness. These include the introduction of Advanced Targeting Pod, Maverick, Brimstone, Paveway™ IV and CRV-7 Rockets (recovered from baseline GR7).

Concurrently the MoD embarked upon an engine upgrade programme with a view to increasing performance in high ambient temperatures and carrier operations. This programme produced a number of Harrier II (UK) aircraft fitted with the Rolls Royce Pegasus Mk107 engine; these aircraft are known as the Harrier GR Mk7A or GR9A. Unmodified, Pegasus Mk105 engine equipped, aircraft continue to be known as GR7 and GR9. All GR9 aircraft are capable of being fitted with the Mk 107 engine as a role modification should operations require it.

3 Capability Upgrade

This paper centres on the Harrier aircraft safety case and the supporting OSMC equipment safety case both of which are produced by BAE Systems. The safety case covered by this paper focuses on the changed elements for a particular Capability upgrade.

To date, three Capabilities have been released to the Customer and significant updates have taken place. During this life-cycle, the safety case construct, format and development processes have been subjected to constant challenge, refinement and improvement. To provide the necessary context, the architecture of one Capability is defined below in Figure 1. This represents the avionics upgrades only although delivered Capability demands physical changes to the airframe, wiring and external role equipment.

Given the number of diverse equipments being introduced or modified, the aircraft safety case builds relationships across a multitude of documents that represent individual components to be integrated into the main argument structure. Bringing such a level of complexity to the safety case requires careful handling to ensure the clarity of argument is not lost in the detail of the integration.

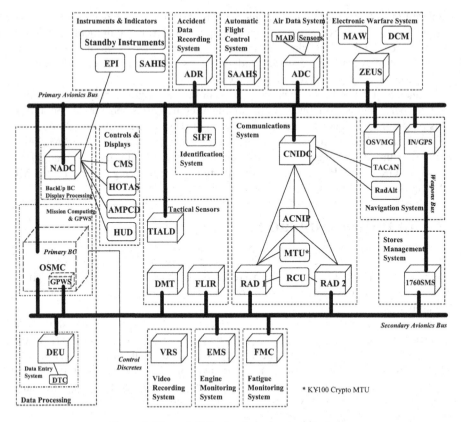

Figure 1 Upgraded Harrier Avionics Architecture.

3.1   Toolset

The safety toolsets utilised by the Harrier project to date consist of Microsoft Word safety cases, Excel hazard log and PowerPoint GSN that make for clunky and painful production. Utilising these tools with their known drawbacks have brought penalties in both safety case maintenance and time. The maintenance penalty directly impacting production time, this is becoming crucial as Capability changes are required to support Operational missions. There is, however, light at the end of the tunnel.

As Harrier transitions to Generic Aircraft Release Process (GARP), we are looking to migrate to the Adelard ASCE and HVR Cassandra toolsets. This aligns the Design Authority safety case detailed in this paper with the overall safety case at the platform level which is owned by the MoD.

This Platform safety case utilises the Design Authority safety case (BAE Systems safety case) plus all other operational elements not captured by the aircraft design

3.2   Flexibility

The primary purpose of the safety case is to support production standard certification at a specific Capability release. The production plan for the safety case follows a standard Preliminary, Interim and Operational level of maturity path with the Preliminary detailing the strategic approach, the Interim used as a maturity gate and the Operational safety case being the final version for certification release.

In early releases this plan worked as only the one set of requirements was being considered.   As the project matured, and new functions, equipment and requirements were added (and with increasing pace), this became untenable.   As such a new approach was required. To support the project effectively, the solution adopted was to cover these changes as addenda. These addenda directly augment the main safety case and argue the change to the final safety case, with non-interference having primacy.   This addenda safety case was given the term 'delta' and covers the process of producing a safety case specifically for the change but in the context of the final safety case and its claims.   For the project this proved successful. For the team it meant this became the standard, and subsequent releases planned for deltas to cater for ever later trial results driving ever later changes. Team pressure to produce safety cases to the same exacting standards at the end of the capability has increased.   In customer satisfaction terms the approach is an outright success giving a real opportunity to meet the operational needs and demonstrate the adequate level of safety required.

3.3   Models

As the aircraft level argument developed, a real problem with generating a structure which enabled a clear and concise argument became apparent. The solution to this came in the form of GSN models that could be utilised over and again. The issue for the team was deriving which model could adequately meet the variance of new and improved equipment, role equipment and weapons. This has been achieved, and is successfully demonstrated, as each new Capability required by the customer is now mapped to the model as part of the safety team's pre-contract assessment.

Figure 2 below details an example of this for role equipment. The structure has been used in several instances for the various role change pods that can be fitted. The detail is instantiated in each safety case for the evidence of the specific equipment. With the use of these generic models future Capability / Upgrades can be mapped and the argument structure and expected evidence can be assessed earlier to enable a higher level of confidence in the estimation when bidding for the contract.

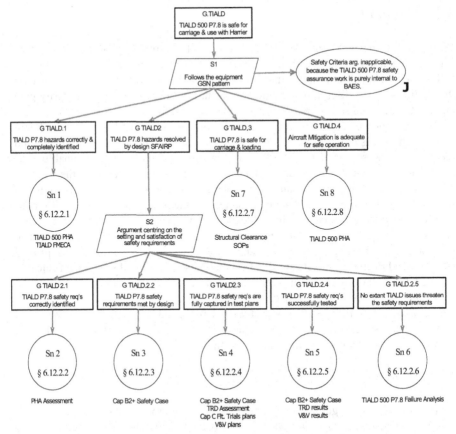

Figure 2 Generic GSN Model for Role Equipment

3.4   Generic arguments

With the increase of capability, the aircraft safety case became more focused on the standard three legged GSN pattern of Old, New and Non-interference (New to Old and Old to New). It became clear that the engineering approach to all the upgrades followed the same process (developed and improved through time and experience). As such, the front end of the safety case, which dealt with the safety engineering, development, build, configuration control etc., was becoming a safety case in its own right.

This was hived off into a separate document and turned into a generic process orientated safety case. Having produced that, all Harrier upgrades, from black box upgrades to new weapon introductions, are able to appeal to the generic aspects of an agreed process safety case. With each use it is assessed for validity and improvements to any of the processes drive an update. This has enabled the aircraft safety case to focus directly on the technical issues. The benefits of this are a much reduced document and not having to argue existing and agreed arguments time and again for each Capability release.

3.5 Legacy

Being an in-Service aircraft, the Harrier has accumulated significant and sufficient flying hours to support a legacy claim. The basis of the aircraft safety case is that the existing design is tolerably safe and that the upgraded aircraft is at least as safe as the existing system (GR7 or T10). This is considered a justified and pragmatic approach for such a mature aircraft.

As the capabilities have grown, the question of what constitutes 'Legacy' has become more pressing. This was resolved as the team approached the 3rd (Capability B2+) release. The 'Baseline' was defined as GR7, 'Legacy' as the previous capability/capabilities. As such the standard three-legged argument involving Old, New and Non-interference could be established for each of the incoming upgrades.

Another aspect of this has been the requirement to certify and underwrite a weapon of some maturity. Maverick has been operated since Vietnam and many aspects of the design can be traced back almost as far. The Harrier team was asked to liaise with Raytheon Missile Systems (RMS) to clear Maverick onto the aircraft. Interesting times were ahead! It soon became clear that evidence in support of the safety case arguments was going to be different and standard safety deliverables would either not be present or considered insufficient to meet today's standards. RMS personnel were undaunted and, after several visits to the desert oasis of Tucson, dusty files of design data were produced.

Traceability to the latest versions to meet the needs of picky British safety engineers soon became a sticking point. 'Grey Beards' were drafted in to throw some light on the subject matter of concern – these were gentlemen involved in the design back in the day whose memory and attention to detail would shame many today. In consultation with these enlightened beings, almost 625 system level hazards were derived, with design evidence items identified to mitigate nearly all. Standard Operating Procedures (SOP) were used appropriately for the remainder without loss of mission capability or increased pilot workload. These were then filtered down to 13 missile level hazards that covered all the aircraft level hazards identified by modern hazard analysis.

The lesson here was; never give up. Just because it hasn't been seen for some time doesn't mean that it's not there, that, once found, it's invalid or there is no quality underneath the dust once it's blown away.

3.6   Scope

The scope of the safety case was initially well understood and agreed. The aircraft design authority, BAE Systems, was responsible for the design of the aircraft and the integration of role equipment and weapons. These weapons were, by definition, 'legacy' and, as such, appeal was made to their safety on the existing aircraft. The interfaces were unchanged and weapon aiming was recovered from the AYK, assembler based, OFP functionality (GR7) and re-expressed using modern design methods (OOA/OOD) with the Ada 95 High Order Language for GR9.

Then the issue of scope was raised as new weapons and Mil Std 1760 smart interfaces were introduced. Harrier approached the governing bodies asking questions of the safety targets, boundaries of responsibility and which bodies were responsible for each of the various phases of a weapon release. No overt or definitive answers came. As such, the Harrier Weapons Project Safety Committee (PSC) derived a 'straw-man' to be offered to the interested parties. Over several iterations the weapon delivery phase diagram became the pan-platform agreed definition. This agreement was across all stakeholders involving the customer and external agencies alike.

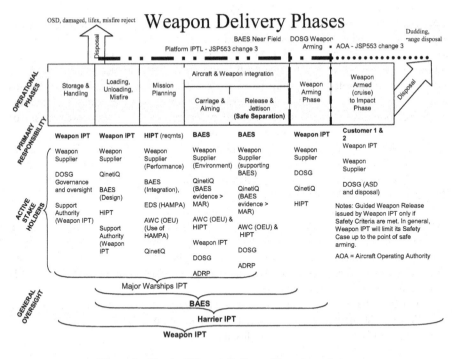

Figure 3 – Harrier Weapon Delivery Phase boundaries

Figure 3 identifies the phases, stakeholders and boundaries of responsibilities associate with the weapon delivery phases from storage, loading and eventual release / disposal.

4   OSMC Operational Safety Case

This section details some of the lessons learnt in the production of the Mission Computer safety case.

4.1   Construct

The Operational Equipment Safety case includes the complete set of safety arguments and all relevant evidence to demonstrate that the identified safety requirements have been met to the specified integrity level. The operational version of the safety case provides the arguments and evidence from code analyses through to the dynamic testing of the software in flight.

Historically, pre-operational OSMC safety cases were produced with the aspiration to support flight trials. This was difficult to achieve as the tempo of flight worthy code release challenged and, sometimes, outstripped the ability of the safety case to keep up. The plans created at the start of the programme, which presumed detailed analysis ahead of flight, were, in retrospect, considered unworkable. In mitigation, a strategy of limiting the flight envelope was derived. These limitations ensured that all safety related aspects of the mission computer were adequately handled. This resulted in an increased burden on the Aircraft safety case since it was required to provide these envelope defining arguments. However, one benefit of this approach was that these limitations could be employed time and time again. Given the fact that all that was required for re-use was a review for validity for the flight software updates, which were being produced at a rate of one every three months, this was a real benefit.

Early versions of the OSMC safety case were structured to specifically and rigidly meet the requirements of DEF STAN 00-55/2. In particular, the plan addressed all topics identified within Annex B.2 of Part 2 of that standard. The structure of the Safety Case is illustrated in figure 4 below:

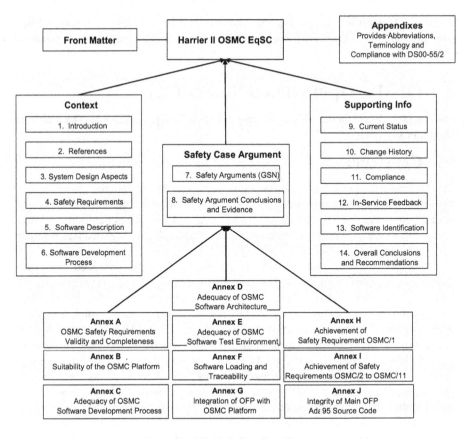

Figure 4– OSMC Safety Case Structure

The overall context and background information for the OSMC Safety Case is presented in Chapters 1 to 6. In particular, Chapter 4 describes the Safety Requirements for the OSMC and its OFP, and structures them into a number of functional areas. The Safety Case Argument is presented within Chapter 7, supplemented by its conclusions and a summary of evidence given within Chapter 8. Each set of conclusions and evidence summary relates to a detailed argument presented as a separate Annex to the OSMC Safety Case.

Annexes A to G and J provide arguments and evidence relating to the OSMC and its OFP as a whole, while Annexes H and I provide arguments and evidence for compliance with the Safety Requirements within one or more functional areas, as defined within Chapter 4. Appendices contain the usual abbreviations and definitions plus:

- Appendix C of the Safety Case provides a compliance matrix to demonstrate conformance of the Safety Case to Annex B.2 of Part 2 of DEF STAN 00-55/2.

- Appendix D demonstrates compliance between the Harrier Software Development Process, as used for the Harrier II OSMC OFP development, and the requirements of DEF STAN 00-55/2, interpreted for SIL S2 in accordance with clause 43 of that Standard.

In addition, a number of Annexes supplement the OSMC Safety Case. Each Annex has its own separate structure and pagination, although approvals are organised in conjunction with the Main Body of the OSMC Safety Case.

These Annexes present detailed Safety Case Argument Reports in support of one or more of the goals defined in Chapter 7. Material from these reports was used to generate the conclusions presented in Chapter 8.

This whole structure led to the issued safety case being a 1300 page tome and whilst comprehensive and informative its usability proved less than intuitive. This structure lasted two further iterations each of which burdened the review teams with its complexity. The cause of the excessive growth stemmed from not foreseeing the inevitable expansion of requirements and doggedly following standards.   It was time to step back and re-think the approach and, in support of the 4th Capability (Capability C) release, the OSMC Safety Case has been revamped.

The structure is similar in coverage but significantly lighter on duplication of data. Compression of the main body now realises a concise assessment of the entire safety argument with informative overviews directly linked into the detailed argument and supporting evidence. Figure 5 details the structure and, whilst similar, it has demonstrated a real improvement in clarity and usability.

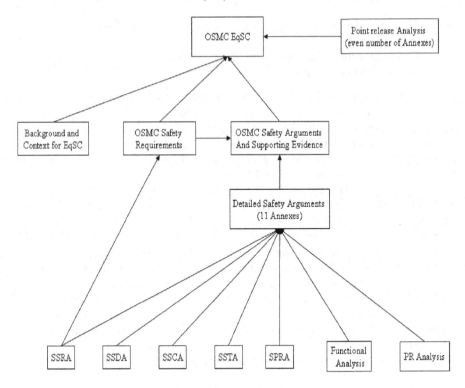

Figure 5 Revised OSMC Safety Case Structure

The net result of this format and construction change is; significantly more productive reviews, the finished product is easier to use, refinement of dissemination to executive population and better understanding of the overall risk retained against the requirements.

4.2   Deltas

The delta approach, detailed above at the aircraft level, has been used with particular success with the OSMC equipment safety case.   It has been seen that OSMC software changes introduced through the delta process have been used to overcome problems in some of the more rigid or less responsive equipments. As the software validation and formal testing approaches the end of its life cycle, the Harrier project has involved operational pilots which has enabled an operational sortie profile to be undertaken with the development software.

This may seem like an obvious thing to do but the early involvement has actually required a change in test philosophy. At one stage the Company would be unwilling to release a development aircraft to the operational pilot (RN/RAF) before significant flight testing had been completed. Now they are involved at a much earlier stage and it makes for a better, more mature, product at formal release. Fix cycles are now addressing not only essential (Cat 1) corrections from a functional or safety point of view, but those seen as operationally limiting as well. This brings the front line requirements directly into the project where rapid design and operational needs merge to resolve the issue.

From a safety perspective these rapid changes to the 'final' product have invoked some emotive arguments amongst the Harrier safety community. What is the level of change that is acceptable for a Delta? How much regression testing is required before a full qualification test run is required? How many lines of code are acceptable before a point release is no longer an appropriate solution and a full incremental release is required? Each of these questions is now raised to the core of the OSMC Safety Project Safety Committee for consideration and acceptance.

A baseline has been set for the maximum acceptable number of lines of code. Each of the proposed Deltas are inspected for the 'fixes' verses new functionality, and a community wide agreement is sought. Regression testing is argued through the delta safety case for the individual delta changes and why only that set of test parameters are considered necessary. Again communication at an early stage with the involved stakeholders and safety sponsors is sought. Communication at the earliest stage possible is considered the watch word of the Harrier safety team.

At one Capability alone more than 5 delta changes have been required in order to meet the functional and safety needs of an ever demanding operational customer. The demands are being driven by the circumstances in which he finds himself and the aircraft needing to provide the facility to complete the tasking in an efficient manner and without compromising safety.

5   Here and now

The Capability upgrades are the cornerstone of the Harrier aircraft success in recent times. However, that method of upgrade is proving overly long and is now being challenged. This stems from changes being identified quicker, with the setting of the requirements now taking weeks not months or years.

Rapid Technology Insertion (RTI) is the new approach. The aim is to get required functionality onto the aircraft, into theatre and supporting operations as quickly, safely and cost effectively as possible. It may enter service initially with some rough edges but the basic functionality and operational advantages are made available in a safety minded approach. Harrier RTI successes can be captured easily by looking at the Sniper Advanced Targeting Pod (ATP) as a use case.

The Lockheed Martin (LM) Sniper ATP has been integrated onto Harrier GR Mk.9 in response to an Urgent Operational Requirement (UOR). In order to minimise the time of the integration programme the decision was made to exclude any changes to the Harrier OFP and effectively tailor the Sniper pod software so that it works with the aircraft and its operating systems

This was the first real RTI and stemmed from a need for an enhanced targeting system. This was met after the requirement for a targeting device was identified to BAE Systems (this was prior to UOR status being declared). The requirement was to provide better targeting capability than the current TIALD pod in use with the RAF on Harrier, Tornado and lately Jaguar. BAE Systems approached the Sniper ATP vendor, Lockheed Martin, to discuss the feasibility of a Harrier aircraft integration programme. Initial funding was made available to Harrier project through BAE SYSTEMS private venture funding. Lockheed Martin took the same approach and provided significant product support, also through private venture funding. This internal funding was agreed by BAE Systems senior management on the grounds that the prospect of a rapid insertion being taken up by the RAF was considered high. The ATP pod came with in-service experience on non Harrier US aircraft, so from a safety perspective it was not going to be an undefined starting point.

After a series of discussions direct with LM engineers it was understood that an initial safety clearance could be given based on some basic understanding. The pod utilises 3 different laser modes one of which is advertised as 'eye safe' and the main tactical laser being much more hazardous than TIALD.

As such the Military Laser Safety Committee (MLSC) needed to understand the pod and the proposed Harrier integration. The approach was to open discussions direct with the MLSC and invite them to get directly involved on site in order for them to identify their requirements for a Laser fire clearance. The approach worked and after 3 way discussions between the MLSC, BAE Systems and LM, the basic understanding of what documentation would be required was identified. The basis of the hazards to be controlled stemmed from the TIALD work carried out during earlier Capability clearances where laser safety was the predominant concern. LM then undertook to provide a series of safety and certification documents. After several iterations this was achieved and safety scrutiny of the systems started. BAE Systems wrote a safety case to provide support to the flight trials and it was this that was utilised by MLSC to better understand the Harrier safety arguments and integration.

In a compressed programme of software development, rig testing and certification, the combined team conducted the first flight just two months after the first RTI integration meeting. Safety was assured through the aircraft systems controls but the touch time between standard safety engineering practices was significantly reduced. With the integrity of the overall aircraft safety assured this led the way for increased evaluation flights. The safety case covering the RTI made strong operational procedures mandatory and these are being rigidly adhered to by the operating forces today.

The lesson being learnt from this experience is that fluid safety engineering practices can live along side rapid technology insertion and has a place to assure that operational requirements do not outstrip the need for a safe operating platform. Both industry and customer have played their part in assuring that safety has been placed at the front of the requirements when considering these projects.

6   Conclusion

The Harrier project has taken the approach of supporting an essential element of the military projection wherever needed and without compromising the safety of the aircrew, personnel and third parties / non-combatants it involves in doing its duty.

Safety engineering has been embraced within the Harrier project as well as involving all external stakeholders along the way. There is a real understanding with the project that safety has a role to play in generating a product that endures and meets the customers' requirements.

Furthermore in the last 6 years of development the Harrier project has never failed to meet a key milestone objective and has delivered on-time, on-budget and to, or exceeding, the required military capability. It has done so within an increasingly safety conscious environment and without compromising safety. This has not been an easy task as long-established processes have been challenged. Behind the Harrier aircraft is a robust safety engineering practice that involves a safety community aligned to ensure safety is considered and adequately met through the development to delivery phase and beyond into service.

The key to this success is undoubtedly communication. This applies both internally, within the project, and, as importantly, to the customer and other stakeholders. Without this, the Safety Case for the Harrier aircraft clearances could not adequately support the changing environment in which the aircraft is required to operate.

Safety Culture

Investigation to Establish Whether Cultural Analysis can be used to Improve the Interactions Between Design, Safety and Operations Departments

Tim Smith
T F Smith Ltd
Bristol, England

1.0   Introduction

Background

This paper presents a study that was carried out to investigate the interactions between the design, safety and operations departments within an organisation. The study was carried out by the author in support of obtaining an MSc in Safety Engineering at Lancaster University. The author has over twenty-five years experience working in the nuclear and oil industries and has been involved in many projects during this time. While the majority of projects are successful there are always one or two that experience problems.

The MSc course in Safety Engineering reviewed a number of notable high-profile accidents in recent history. It is interesting that while there are technical causal factors to each accident, there are also cultural issues that contribute to many of them. A particular example is the Columbia space shuttle accident. The space shuttle was damaged during take off and exploded on re-entry to the Earth's environment. The technical cause of the accident was attributed to foam causing damage to the leading edge of the wing during take off which, on re-entry, caused the wing to overheat and the shuttle to explode. While there was a technical cause to the accident, there were also management issues and a notable cultural shift from an assumption of "you must prove it's safe" to "now you must prove it's unsafe or I won't take any management action" (Gehman, 2003).

The MSc course undertaken by the author had introduced the concepts of human factors, culture and behaviour based safety which inspired the author to investigate whether these concepts could be used to examine why some projects are successful and some fail. In particular it was thought that success or failure of a project can, at times, be dependant on whether the various departments that contribute to the overall project interact effectively. Thus, the aim of the study was to investigate whether cultural analysis could form the basis of a tool for assessing and streamlining the interactions between departments that contribute to the successful fruition of projects. The study was focused on the nuclear industry and investigated interactions between a design department, safety department and operations department.

There is a dual purpose to this paper firstly to present the methodology that was used in the study and secondly to present the results of the study. While the nuclear industry was the focus for the case study, the issues investigated are by no means limited to the nuclear industry and are common to industry and commerce as a whole. Thus, with some adaptation, the methodology described by this paper could be applied to interactions between other groups of people.

Structure of this Paper

This paper is split into eight sections. Section 1 and 2 introduce the paper. The paper is aimed at an audience with an engineering bias and Section 2 provides an introduction to some of the concepts of culture by answering some basic questions on it. The purpose of Section 2, as well as providing an introduction to culture, is to demonstrate that culture is abstract and conceptual, and therefore does not have absolute truths regarding interpretation nor application. This may be obvious to an audience from a social science background but can be overlooked by an audience with an engineering bias.

Section 3 reviews a number of cultural models to highlight that there are many ways in which culture can be modelled, and to explain Schein's model of culture (Schein, 2004) which was selected for the basis of the study.

Section 4 describes how Schein's model of culture was adapted to add structure. The purpose of this was to align the cultural model with the topic of this paper; as initial trials using Schein's model demonstrated that a pure academic application did not produce the desired results.

Section 5 presents a working trial using the adapted methodology and discusses the results.

Section 6 discusses a methodology for modifying culture. No attempt was made to modify culture within the organisation used for the trial as this was outside the scope of the study. Cultural modification (Schein, 2004) is expected to take at least two years to implement, which was in excess of the time available for preparation of the study. Section 7 presents a summary of this paper.

The Interaction between Design, Safety and Operations

In the nuclear industry projects often require complex bespoke designs for plant and equipment, that must be supported by robust safety cases to demonstrate safety through the full project life cycle. As well as meeting stringent safety requirements, projects must also be technically appropriate and be cost-effective to the industry. These complexities increase the potential for projects to fail. Contributing to the success of projects in the nuclear industry is the need for design requirements, operation needs and the safety objectives to be combined in a balanced manner so that the most effective solutions are obtained to meet the challenging industry standards. This balance requires the interaction of the three separate disciplines of design, safety and operations. Sometimes this interaction works well, but at other times the interaction falters or becomes skewed leading to over-safe or over-complex designs, cost or programme overruns, or specifications that can-not be achieved. The interaction between the design, safety and operational departments is shown diagrammatically in Figure 1. If the three departments interact effectively a project is likely to be a success. In a simplistic form, this is shown as the successful project area in Figure 1.

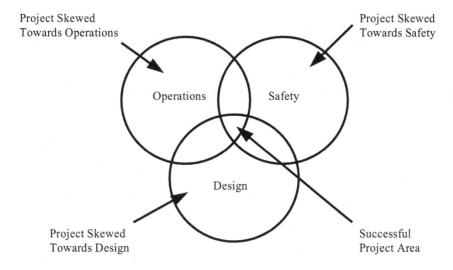

Figure 1 – Design, Safety and Operations Interaction

Before reviewing culture it is worth briefly explaining the function of the design, safety and operations departments in the context of how they are used in this paper, as the terminology in not common for every organisation. The broad function of the design department is to provide a technical solution to meet a known set of customer or stakeholder requirements. Depending on the specific application there will be statutory and legislative requirements that also need to be satisfied. The responsibility of the safety department (in the nuclear industry) is one of nuclear safety and the requirement to provide a robust safety case. The safety case is produced to justify safety during the full nuclear plant life cycle from design and operation through to eventual decommissioning. The study carried out by the author was undertaken in an end-user organisation and in the context of this paper the operations department combines both end user representation and the project management function. This is not true of every organisation and quite often they are considered as two separate functions. The operations department has a significant responsibility throughout a project life cycle and has a number of responsibilities that include such things as risk control, resource allocation, change control, planning, procurement and contractual matters. The operations department is responsible for the project management function and in a contractor organisation this is often termed the project department.

2.0   Organisational Culture

The first step in understanding the essence of organisational culture is to appreciate that it is a concept rather than an object (Ott, 1996). This distinction is crucial. An object can be discovered and truths established about it, for example, through empirical research. Unlike an object, however, a concept is created in peoples' minds and must be conjured up, defined and refined. Thus there are no ultimate truths about organisational culture that can be found nor discovered. Why is this important? Because when someone claims to have identified an organisational culture, that discovery represents nothing more than the results obtained from applying that person's concepts of organisational culture (via a concept-driven deciphering process) in a given organisation (Ott, 1996) at a given time.

Some insight to the concept of organisational culture can be gained from an analogy with the individual; that is the personality of an individual is akin to the culture of an organisation. In an organisational sense the term "culture" refers to "shared values and beliefs" that have been learnt or established over a period of time which are seen to characterise organisations. Thus the culture of an organisation can be considered as the attitudes, values, norms and customs of an organisation. In simple terms, culture in an organisation can be considered as "the way we do things around here" (Deal and Kennedy, 1988).

There are many definitions of culture and writers and researchers do not agree on a common definition. Kroeber and Kluckhohn (Kroeber and Kluckhohn, 1963) identified over one hundred definitions of culture and classified them under six headings. The classifications are given in Table 1.

Classification	Description of Definition
Descriptive	Comprise definitions that attempt to enumerate the content of culture, the items are taken to be similar in the lives of members of a given group.
Historical	Comprise definitions that emphasize an aggregate's joint social heritage or tradition.
Normative	Characterise culture by definitions that identify rules and ways of behaving.
Genetic	Characterise culture in terms of products, ideas or symbols.
Structural	Comprised of definitions that emphasize statistical regularities.
Psychological	Attach culture to the outcome of how children are raised, and refer to processes such as "adjustment", "learning" and "development".

Table 1 – Culture Definition Classification (Kroeber and Kluckhohn, 1963)

Subcultures

"Subculture" is the term used to describe different groups of cultures that may exist within an organisation. When researchers discuss organisational culture they are generally considering the values and practices that are shared across an organisation, however organisational culture does comprise of multiple cultures which can be associated with different geographic locations, different occupational groups or different departments (Black, 2004). Louis (Louis, 1986) and Martin and Siehl (Martin and Siehl, 1983) are three researchers who have made this point clearly. Kotter and Hesketh (Kotter and Hesketh, 1992) discuss organisations with multiple cultures and acknowledge that even in relatively small subunits there can be multiple and conflicting cultures.

The safety culture is also a sub-set of the overall culture of an organisation and is greatly influenced by the overall culture of the organisation. The term safety culture was first introduced by the International Nuclear Safety Advisory Group following the Chernobyl accident (IET, 2006). The safety culture might be described as the shared values and beliefs which characterise safety in organisations.

Why is Culture Important?

At a corporate level an appropriate culture can be the success of an organisation or if it is inappropriate can lead to low performance. Almost all books on organisational culture state or imply a relationship with long-term economic performance and provide numerous examples of successful organisations managing an appropriate culture. Hofstede (Hofstede, 1984), Schein (Schein, 2004) Deal and Kennedy (Deal and Kennedy, 1988) and Handy (Handy, 1993) are just a few of the writers who have made this distinction and it is probably fair to say that this is one point on which researchers and writers agree.

Safety Culture is important as although the immediate causes of accidents are often identified as human error or technical failure, the investigation and analysis of the circumstances surrounding major accidents such as Three Mile Island, Chernobyl, Kings Cross, the Herald of Free Enterprise and Clapham have revealed issues beyond the immediate causes. These issues relate to the wider considerations of the organisation's culture as a whole. Two quotations (IET, 2006) from different enquiry reports illustrate the point:

"...their belief in safety was a mirage, their systems inadequate, and operator errors commonplace..."

".....From the top to the bottom, the body corporate was infected with the disease of sloppiness."

It has become widely accepted from a number of accident investigations that basic faults in organisation structure, climate and procedures may predispose an organisation to an accident. The development of an appropriate safety culture within an organisation seeks to address this shortfall and create an environment where improvements in safety performance can be made.

The importance of subculture has been examined by Black (Black, 2004), who has shown that differences in organisational culture between departments can strongly influence business value and success. The research by Black (Black, 2004) has shown how organisational culture can provide a valuable framework for improving the working practices and "soft-skills" in corporate teams in general. Thus the subcultures in different departments within an organisation can influence how well they work together.

Is there a Right or Wrong Culture?

Kotter and Heskett (Kotter and Hesketh, 1992) identify three categories of culture performance perspectives. The first category is the association of a "strong" culture with excellent performance, or "weak" culture with poor performance. The second category is one of a strategically appropriate culture which states that, the direction of cultures must align with business strategy and motivate employees if they are to enhance company performance. Unfortunately there is no such thing as a generically good cultural content or "winning" culture that works well anywhere. Instead a culture is good only if it "fits" its context. That is the better the fit, the better the performance or the poorer the fit, the poorer the performance (Kotter and Hesketh, 1992). Black (Black, 2004) notes that organisations create more value when they align their culture with business strategy. The third category is of adaptive cultures; that only cultures that can help organisations anticipate and adapt to environmental change will be associated with superior performance over long periods of time (Kotter and Hesketh, 1992). These are three further areas on which researchers and writers on culture agree.

3.0   Selection of a Model Of Culture

Dimensions of Culture

Researchers use "dimensions" to compare different cultures (Black, 2004). Dimensions simply measure aspects of culture relative to other cultures. Standard types of culture may be identified by analysing dimensional scores from cultural identification models and surveys. Researchers and consultancies disagree both on the number of "standard" dimensions and on the nature of those dimensions (Black, 2004). There are many cultural models published. Each of the models defines a "standard" set of dimensions and a matching "standard" identification methodology. Some researchers openly publish their models while others hold their models as proprietary. An outline of some of the popular culture dimension models is provided in Table 2.

Selection of a Cultural Model

A number of cultural models were investigated to establish whether they could be used to analyse the interaction between the design, safety and operations departments. All of the proprietary models were discounted due to cost; these models could not be reviewed as it would have been necessary to procure each system to review the model. The remaining models, with the exception of Schein's cultural model, were also discounted as they are models which are based on categorising aspects of culture into a small number of discrete dimensions. There are two concerns with this approach. Firstly, this appears to oversimplify a complex interaction, culture is complex and describing it by simple classifications e.g. power culture or role culture (Handy, 1993) may not identify levels of cultural detail that would be necessary to identify differences between subcultures. Secondly, a concern arose with categorising aspects of culture into discrete dimensions as this does not allow direct conclusions to be drawn that can be applied to improve culture; but leads to a conundrum of what aspects are then desirable in preference to others i.e. there is a need for a subjective comparison. The objective of the study was not to categorise a culture but to investigate whether the interaction between departments could be improved, hence discrete categorisation models were viewed with some apprehension and rejected.

Researcher	Model	Cultural Type	Dimensions
Hofstede (Hofstede, 1984)	5D Model	National	Power-Distance, Individualist-Collectivist, Masculinity, Uncertainty Avoidance, Long-term Orientation.
Trompenaars (Trompenaars and Hampden-Turner, 1998)	6D Model	Organisational	Universalism-Particularism, Individualism-Communitarianism, Specificity-Diffusion, Achievement-Ascription, Sequential-Synchronic, Internal-External Control.
McShane (McShane and Von Glinow, 2000)	4 Types	Organisational	Control, Performance, Relationship, Responsive.
Deal and Kennedy (Deal and Kennedy, 1988)	4 Types	Organisational	Tough Guy Macho, Work Hard/Play Hard, Bet your Company, Process.
Handy (Handy, 1993)	4 Types	Organisational	Power, Role, Task, Person.
Schein (Schein, 2004)	Structural Concept	Organisational	Structural concepts of Artefact, Espoused Beliefs and Values, Underlying Assumptions.

Table 2 – Different Culture Dimension Models

Schein's cultural model was interesting for two reasons. Firstly because it utilises three successively deeper layers of culture which are visible on the surface and less visible with each deeper layer. This was considered desirable because it was thought that visibility of the layers might be related to the visibility or accuracy of the results obtained. The second reason for Schein's model being of interest, and probably more important, was that it is structurally conceptual. Structure is a desirable characteristic in an engineering environment and processes tend to migrate towards structure; for instance, option studies make use of multi-attribute analysis and HAZOP studies are structured via the use of a series of nodes and guide words. It is also interesting to quote a comment from one of the participants in the working trial who commented "I expect structure in everything [in the context of work] and have no respect for anything that is not structured." Schein's model being relatively structured in comparison to other models makes it more tangible when applied in an engineering environment. In engineering jargon it can be described as "a bottom up" process and the apparent structure of the model sets it apart from some of the other less structured cultural models. It should be noted, however, that some of the other cultural models rejected do share many of the ideas considered by Schein, but do so in a less structured or more abstract way. For instance Deal and Kennedy (Deal and Kennedy, 1988) consider values which are analogous to Schein's second level of culture but are applied in a much more abstract manner. Schein's model was selected as the preferred cultural model to investigate the interaction between the design, safety and operations departments.

Schein's Model of Culture

Schein

Schein (Schein, 2004) provides a formal definition of culture within a group as "a pattern of shared basic assumptions that was learned by a group as it solved its problems of external adaptation and internal integration, that has worked well enough to be considered valid and, therefore, to be taught to new members as the correct way to perceive, think and feel in relation to those problems".

Levels of Culture

Schein (Schein, 2004) proposes that culture can be analysed at several different levels. The term level meaning the degree to which the cultural phenomenon is visible to the observer. These levels range from the easily observable rituals to the very deep embedded values or beliefs that can be considered the essence of culture. The levels identified by Schein (Schein, 2004) are:

- Artefacts
- Espoused Beliefs and Values
- Basic Underlying Assumptions

Artefacts

At the surface of culture are the artefacts. These are the visible entities or phenomena that are seen, heard or felt when a group with an unfamiliar culture is encountered for the first time. Artefacts include the visible products of the group, such as the architecture of its physical environment, its language, technology and products, its published list of values, its rituals, dress code and so on. An important point of this level of culture is that it is easy to observe but difficult to understand.

For instance Schein (Schein, 2004) provides an analogy that the Egyptians and the Mayans both built pyramids but the meaning in each culture was very different; tombs in one, and temples as well as tombs in the other. The meaning of the artefacts within the culture becomes clear over a long period of time but to form an immediate understanding it is necessary to look at the next level of culture; the espoused beliefs and values.

Espoused Beliefs and Values.

All group learning ultimately reflects someone's original beliefs and values, their sense of what ought to be, which may be distinct from what is occurring in the real situation. Through reinforcement over a period of time these beliefs are transformed into the espoused values and beliefs of the group. These are the values that the group say they have and adopt; their judgement of what is good or bad. The espoused beliefs and values are not clearly visible but are only observable through representation in artefacts and behaviours. A company's mission statement is an example of an artefact that represents an espoused value (Schein, 2004).

Beliefs and values will predict much of the behaviour at the artefact level, but if not based on a learning reinforcement cycle may only reflect aspirations of the group. For instance a company may say that it values its employees but in practice may have total disregard for them. Often the belief and values based on aspirations can be abstract or contradictory in nature. For instance a company may claim that it has the highest quality product at the lowest price.

Basic Underlying Assumptions

The basic underlying assumptions represent the deepest level of culture. These are the non-negotiable ideas or beliefs that are so ingrained in the culture that they are not questioned nor directly communicated. They are essentially invisible to an observer and are taken for granted by the group. However, once uncovered, their meaning becomes very clear and they illuminate previously discovered values and artefacts. The basic assumptions tend to be extremely difficult to change as they are in essence the basis of the culture described by Schein (Schein, 2004).

4.0   Adapting Schein's Method

Adding Structure

An initial trial carried out by the author demonstrated that Schein's process could be used to decipher culture in an organisation but lacked direction in deriving aspects of culture that were relevant to the objective of the study. A natural progression by the author was therefore to introduce additional structure to Schein's methodology, with the objective of directing dialogue in cultural assessment meetings in a direction that aligned with the objective of this study. The idea was to apply a series of "cultural nodes" in a similar fashion to the approach utilised in a HAZOP meeting. A discussion could then focus around each cultural node to identify aspects of culture that were relevant to each node. It was thought that this might produce findings from the cultural assessment meetings that were less abstract and more aligned with the objective of this study.

Cultural nodes were selected by considering factors or aspects of a project that were perceived as important. These factors were considered to relate to a project life cycle and could be described by three main categories which broadly related to factors that; considered the key drivers of a project; considered the interaction between departments and considered the successful completion of a project. Research areas for safety culture were also considered. Each of these are reviewed below.

Key Drivers

Key drivers for the design, safety and operations departments were derived for the study and established six primary key drivers of a project. These are:

- User Requirements
- Cost
- Programme
- Quality
- Safety
- Technical

Interactions

"A Guide to the Project Management Body of Knowledge (Project Management Institute Standards Committee, 1996) presents nine project management processes that describe how project management elements interrelate. The management processes or project management knowledge areas are:

- Project Integration Management
- Project Scope Management
- Project Time Management
- Project Cost Management
- Project Quality Management
- Project Human Resource Management
- Project Communications Management
- Project Risk Management
- Project Procurement Management

Success Factors

It is very easy to make simplistic assumptions about project success criteria. That is, if a project completion time exceeds its due date, or expenses overrun the budget, or the outcome does not satisfy a company's pre-determined performance criteria, then the project is deemed a failure. However, determining whether a project is a success or a failure is much more complex and there are two main reasons for this. Firstly, as discussed in a paper by Pinto and Slevin (Pinto and Slevin, 1989), each stakeholder will have a different perspective of success. For instance, a project that meets budget and programme may be perceived as a success by a project manager or senior management, but could be technically inappropriate or may be perceived as a failure by the client. Secondly, that there are no universally accepted success or failure factors for a project, as the studies that have been carried out tend to tabulate individual factors for each project, rather than grouping them according to criteria. The study carried out by Belassi and Tukel (Belassi and Tukel, 1996) identifies a framework for determining success and failure factors in projects. The paper suggests that factors can be grouped into four main areas:

- Factors related to the project.
- Factors related to the project manager and the team member.
- Factors related to the organisation.
- Factors related to the external environment.

The key factors which lead to the success or failure of a project are summarised in Table 3.

Factors Related to the Project	Factors related to the Project Manager	Factors related to the Organisation	Factors related to the External Environment
• Size and Value • Uniqueness of project activities. • Density of project • Life cycle • Urgency	• Ability to delegate authority • Ability to trade-off • Ability to coordinate • Perception of his role and responsibilities • Competence • Commitment **Project Team Members** • Technical Background • Communication skills • Trouble shooting • Commitment	• Top Management support • Project organisational structure. • Functional managers support • Project champion	• Political environment • Economical environment • Social environment • Technological environment • Nature • Client • Competitors • Sub-contractors

Table 3 – Key factors that Influence the Success/Failure of a Project.

An explanation of the factors is beyond the scope of this study but is given in the paper by Belassi and Tukel (Belassi and Tukel, 1996). For the purposes of this study it is sufficient to note that success factors are diverse and extend beyond a simplistic measurement of the key project drivers identified above.

Research Areas

A lecture from the MSc course in safety engineering identified "key theme" research areas which were considered relevant to this work. The key research themes are:

- Communication
- Teamworking
- Personal Behaviours and Competence
- Leadership
- Learning

Cultural Nodes

The project drivers, project management knowledge areas, project success criteria and research themes were combined into seventeen cultural nodes. The derivation and origin of each cultural node is shown in Table 4. There was some overlap between the nodes in each group which can be observed by reading across rows in Table 4. The seventeen cultural nodes, Table 4, were "simple" descriptors which were considered to capture or envelope any aspect of a project. It was thought that any facet of a project could be described by one or more of the cultural nodes.

5.0   The Working Trial

The 10 Step Process

A second trial was carried out. The trial was similar to the first trial in that a presentation on culture was provided; this was followed by a group exercise to identify artefacts, espoused values and underlying assumptions. In the second trial, cultural nodes were used to steer the group discussions in a direction that aligned with the aim of the study. This demonstrated the methodology worked and following the second trial, a full working trial was carried out which is described below. The structure of the section follows the ten step process proposed by Schein (Schein, 2004), on which the adapted methodology is based, so that a comparison can be made with Schein's suggested methodology.

Step 1: Obtaining Leadership Commitment.

Schein (Schein, 2004) stresses that the requirement to analyse culture needs to be driven by a motivation to correct a problem or issue. This needs to be supported by the leaders of the organisation such that management "buy in" is obtained. The purpose of the study was to establish whether cultural analysis could be used as a tool to improve the interface between design, safety and operations. Hence in the context of this study management "buy in" was not necessary, particularly because there was no intention to change the culture as a result of the findings obtained from the investigation.

Project Drivers	Project Management Knowledge Area	Project Success Criteria	Research Themes	Cultural Node
	Project Integration			Integration
User Requirements	Project Scope			User Requirements
Cost	Project Cost			Cost
Programme	Project Time			Programme
Quality	Project Quality			Quality
Safety				Safety
Technical				Technical
	Project Communications Management		Communication	Communication
	Project Risk			Risk
	Project Procurement			Procurement
			Team working	Team working
	Project Human Resource		Personal Behaviours and Competence	Personal Behaviours and Competence
			Learning	Learning
		Project Manager and Team Members		Leadership
		Project Factors		Project Factors
		Organisation		Organisation
		Environment		Environment

Table 4 – Derivation of Cultural Nodes

Step 2: Selecting Groups for Interviews

A group size of three was selected and separate groups were interviewed representing the design, safety and operations departments. The rank level of members within each group was intentionally similar to avoid senior people inhibiting the discussions within each group. The three disciplines were segregated into homogenous groups to accentuate the difference in the perception of any subculture within each group. It was also considered that three groups would provide some triangulation (Guion, 2002) of data, which would not be possible if a single large group was considered.

Step 3: Selecting an Appropriate Setting for Group Interviews

A standard conference room was selected for each meeting. The meetings were held in June and July 2006.

Step 4: Explaining the Purpose of the Group Meetings.

The group meetings were introduced by the author of this study who explained the purpose of each meeting.

Step 5: A Short Lecture on How to Think About Culture

A ten to fifteen minute presentation was given to each group to explain Schein's (Schein, 2004) model of culture. The presentation proposed that culture was a learned set of assumptions based on the group's shared history and identified the three levels of culture proposed by Schein. The presentation was purposely short, to provide the minimum necessary knowledge for the participants to understand the concept of culture but still use it to decipher culture within the group.

Step 6: Eliciting Descriptions of the Artefacts

Schein's suggested approach is abstract in that artefacts are selected from general questioning of participants. The adapted approach was used to elicit descriptions of artefacts by the use of cultural nodes. The nodes used for the working trial were:

- User Requirements
- Cost
- Programme
- Quality
- Safety
- Technical

Each cultural node was selected in turn and each group was asked to identify artefacts against each cultural node. It was only necessary to identify two or three artefacts against each node to ensure a successful meeting; as early trials had tended to identify too many artefacts at the expense of detailed discussion at the deeper levels of culture. Points highlighting the discussion were recorded on a flipchart. Different coloured pens were used to distinguish between the cultural nodes, artefacts and deeper levels of culture. As pages were completed they were torn off and hung on the wall so that they remained visible throughout each meeting.

Step 7: Identifying Espoused Values

The question that elicits artefacts is "What is going on here?" (Schein, 2004). By contrast the question that elicits espoused values is "Why are you doing what you are doing?" (Schein, 2004). Artefacts were selected from each cultural node, in turn, and a general discussion was held to identify espoused values. The espoused values were added to the flipchart sheets against the corresponding artefact being considered. To aid discussion "guide word" prompts and "questions" were used in the meeting which comprised:

- Norms – e.g. what is considered acceptable behaviour?
- Values – e.g. what is considered to be important?
- Working Atmosphere – e.g. the social environment of the workplace.
- Management Style – e.g. the accessibility of managers.
- Structure and Systems – e.g. reporting systems.
- External Perceptions – what competitors think?

The guide words and questions were selected from a behaviour safety toolkit (Loughborough University, 2007) but only used if conversation dried up, and then tended only to be used on an individual basis; that is the most relevant guideword or question was selected to stimulate debate.

Step 8: Identifying Shared Tacit Assumptions

The objective of Schein's methodology is to explore and identify the deepest level of culture; the shared tacit assumptions of the organisation. For reasons discussed below the goal or value of the cultural analysis in the context of this study lies in identifying and understanding the lower levels of culture. Thus, there was more emphasis on establishing the espoused values of the group than driving the analysis to establish shared tacit assumptions. Nevertheless, some insight was gained into assumptions of the organisation but these were established via unprompted inspiration of each group as opposed to a stage of structured review. The assumptions established tended to "drop out" of the discussion, in that, during debate a sudden awareness occurred of some deeper aspect of culture. Following some discussion within each group these deeper assumptions could be identified and were annotated as a "mark up" on the flip chart.

Step 9: Identifying Cultural Aids and Hindrances

Cultural aids and hindrances were established through dialogue in the discussion groups by questioning whether artefacts, espoused values or shared tacit assumptions had a beneficial or detrimental effect on the project or interaction between the design, safety and operations departments. Where applicable, annotations were added to the flipchart sheets.

Step 10: Reporting Assumptions and Joint Analysis

Schein identifies the purpose of this step is to reach a consensus on what the important shared assumptions are; and their implications for what the organisation wants to do. The methodology adopted by this study took a different approach, and requested each group to review the cultural aids and hindrances with a view to describing what actions could be taken with respect to improvement. Again where applicable, annotations were added to the flipchart sheets.

Discussion of Results

For the working trial, three meetings were held to investigate culture within an organisation; one meeting was held for each group from the design, safety and operations departments. The meetings followed the format described above. It is somewhat unfair to provide a detailed discussion of the results of the analysis in the public domain, as this infringes on an organisation's privacy. Evidence does need to be provided to demonstrate that the process works, and some general statements can be made that illustrate the type of findings that were obtained from the investigations.

The results from each of the three meetings were consistent with each other and each group easily derived artefacts against each of the cultural nodes. The artefacts derived by each group were not the same as the artefacts derived by the other groups but this proved to be somewhat irrelevant when each group debated the espoused beliefs behind each artefact. During the discussions of espoused beliefs it was very notable that the dialogue migrated to common themes consistent between each of the groups. That is re-occurring issues were identified, in simple terms the groups were discussing and identifying the common beliefs of the organisation with respect to the node. In some respects the artefact served as a catalyst to open up a discussion that migrated to the organisation's espoused beliefs. From the discussions of the cultural nodes of user requirements, cost, programme, quality, safety and technical it was relatively easy to establish which were strong or weak aspects of culture and where problem areas occurred with the interactions or interfaces between the groups.

It was also noticeable that there were instances where one or more of the groups had an opposing belief to another group and therefore did not consider the view of the other group to be realistic or acceptable. These differences were again easily identifiable from the discussions and could have a negative effect on the interactions between the groups. It was interesting to note that these differences were generally passive in nature, in that a group with an opposing belief was not necessarily aware of the other group's differing belief, i.e. they were non-confrontational to the opposing group but acted so that everything would appear acceptable at a surface or artefact level.

It was also noticeable that cultural shifts in the organisation could be identified. This occurred where the culture had changed over a period of time due to external market forces or senior management realigning the direction of the organisation. The positive and negative effects from the cultural changes were debated by the groups.

Seventeen cultural nodes were originally derived but only six nodes were used in the working trial. From the trials carried out it was considered that selection of the around six nodes would provide meaningful results within a meeting scheduled for approximately two hours. Although not explicitly stated, it was intended to develop a continuous process technique that could be used within an organisation to examine cultural differences between departments. It was thought that this could be used periodically and to be effective it was considered that meeting durations would need to be restricted to approximately two hours. As the assessment is considered a process of continuous development, different groups of nodes can be selected from the set of seventeen with a view to investigating other aspects of the culture; or even a separate set of nodes established altogether. If different nodes are selected, there should be some recognition of the need to triangulate data to ensure that results are consistent.

6.0   Transforming the Culture

Schein

It is progressively more difficult to create change in each deeper level of culture (Schein, 2004). At the artefact level, change can be implemented with relative ease by adding or removing artefacts. At the second level behaviour changes are required to transform beliefs and values. At the third level of culture change must alter or refocus basic assumptions which is complex and difficult (Schein, 2004). Schein suggests a methodology for creating cultural change which is aimed at creating global change in an organisation and refocusing its basic assumptions. In this case, it is a simpler issue, the goal is to improve inter departmental working, which can be accomplished, in the main, by changes to the first two cultural levels. That is not to say that basic assumptions will not influence interdepartmental working, which is far from the truth. The point is that if basic assumptions are a concern these are better investigated and managed in a perspective of the organisation as a whole, and not as a focus in relation to specific departments within the organisation. An analogy is of the "cultural tail wagging the cultural dog" or in another sense if there are significant issues relating to basic assumptions of culture, these should be addressed as global business strategy issues and not as departmental issues.

This obviously leads to the question as to whether the first two levels of culture can be considered in isolation to the underlying assumptions. This can be answered by reference to work by Deal and Kennedy (Deal and Kennedy, 1988) who consider the importance of values (espoused beliefs) as an individual aspect of culture without reference to deeper assumptions. Martin and Siehl (Martin and Siehl, 1983) also adopt this approach in analysing counter culture.

Hofstede

Black (Black, 2004) suggests that Hofstede's (Hofstede, 1984) continuous cultural improvement model can form the basis of a cultural management technique, Figure 2. The process can be applied to cultural change at an inter-departmental level.

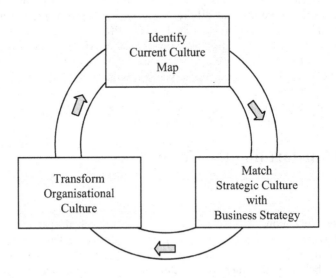

Figure 2 – Cultural Management Process

Cultural Map

The adapted Schein methodology proposed by this paper can be used to map aspects of culture within an organisation and suggest improvements that can be made to methods of working between departments. This will represent changes to the first two levels of culture i.e. artefact and espoused belief level. Changes to basic assumptions may also be desirable but these should be considered in the context of overall business strategy. This process can be considered as the "current culture map."

Matching Strategic Culture with Business Strategy

Section 4 provides a partial introduction to factors which are important in deriving key drivers and success factors for projects. The referenced material provides a basis for developing a business strategy for project management. The correct strategy will be specific to an organisation and should be aligned with the objectives of the organisation. Further discussion is beyond the scope of this paper other than noting that the results from a "cultural map" should be aligned or matched with an overall project management strategy.

Transforming Organisational Culture

The third step is the transformation of culture. This process is seen as a continuous improvement process. The readiness of an organisation to use and implement the findings from a continuous improvement programme will be dependant on the organisation reaching a level of maturity which is striving for improvement. Maturity models have been developed for safety culture (Health and Safety Executive, 2001) and the culture of project management (Kerzner, 2005), (Kwak and Ibbs, 2002). Both models propose five levels of maturity with the highest level of maturity corresponding to a willingness to adopt a continuous improvement programme. The lower levels correspond to the organisation implementing appropriate procedures and methods of working before reaching a state where it can adopt a process of continuous improvement. In effect: a prerequisite is that the company systems, procedures and methods of working should be streamlined to a high degree of effectiveness before embarking on a continuous improvement programme. This is not to say that the process could not be used at a lower level of maturity but at the lower levels it makes more sense to focus effort on more tangible aspects of the organisation such as optimising business systems and procedures.

When considering cultural change at departmental level, a sensible approach is to adopt a simplified change process such as that recommended by safety climate measurement (Loughborough University, 2007). This method is applicable as, although it relates to safety culture, it is aimed at changing or modifying subcultures within the organisation. The methodology (Loughborough University, 2007) makes use of action plans, feedback, follow-up and focus groups.

An action plan should be developed, with appropriate milestones, which should be linked to the organisation's business plan, vision or mission. The milestones should be realistic and understandable. The first stage in the planning process is to review the cultural map to identify issues where improvements can be made. These may relate to cultural misalignment between departments, where department culture does not align with business strategy or where it is considered there is general scope for improvement. Involving employees in implementing an action plan is recommended (Loughborough University, 2007) as it does ensure some form of "ownership" of the initiative. Individuals can be involved in project teams, focus groups, or through direct interviewing to gain their views. Involving them in focus discussion groups may be an expedient way of maximising the number of participants. A survey of potential cultural improvement strategies (Loughborough University, 2007) found that communication, consultation and involvement of as many employees as possible, ensured success in cultural change initiatives.

Focus groups are a form of group interview in which a moderator facilitates discussion among about five to ten group members (Loughborough University, 2007), ensuring that the group focuses on the topic of interest. The technique is characterised by the use of group interaction to produce insights that would be less accessible without the interaction found in the group. In the focus group, the moderator directs the discussion to the extent considered necessary, and thus exerts some control over the outcome. The use of focus groups as a follow-up from the cultural profiling will allow more detailed discussion on specific issues raised, actions to be formulated and, in some cases, for problems to be resolved.

7.0   Summary

To summarise, this paper has presented the following:

- A basic introduction to some of the concepts of culture. This has demonstrated that there are neither singular definitions nor absolute truths that can be established regarding its interpretation or application. Nevertheless culture is important and three desirable characteristics are to establish a strong culture, which is strategically aligned with objectives, whether they relate to safety, business strategy or department strategy, and to ensure that the culture is adaptive to a changing environment.

- Presented a step by step methodology that can be used to examine the interactions and interfaces between departments or groups of people within an organisation that work together to contribute to a common goal. The study investigated the interactions between a design, safety and operations department in the nuclear industry but the methodology described is equally applicable to the interaction between other departments in other industries; providing that the cultural nodes are changed from those used in this study to a group that are aligned with function of the organisation.

- Provided an overview of the results obtained from a working trial to provide credibility to the methodology described. The trial provided meaningful results and identified aspects of culture and issues that could hinder or aid the interactions between a design, safety and operations departments. These effects can influence whether a project is successful or fails.

- Suggested a methodology that can be used to create cultural change within an organisation. This is seen as a continuous improvement process that may take a number of years to complete (Schein, 2004).

8.0   References

Belassi W and Tukel O, A new framework for determining critical success/failure factors in projects, International Journal of Project Management Vol. 1996; 14, 3, 141-151.

Black R J, Organisational Culture: Creating the Influence Needed for Strategic Success, 2004, ISBN 158112211X.

Deal T and Kennedy A, Corporate Cultures, The Rites and Rituals of Corporate Life, Penguin Books, 1988, ISBN 0140091386.

Gehman H W, Chairman, Columbia Accident Investigation Board, The Columbia Shuttle Accident: Study in Safety Culture, 2003 INPO CEO Conference.

Guion L A, Triangulation: Establishing the Validity of Qualitative Studies, University of Florida, 2002. http://edis.ifas.ufl.edu/pdffiles/FY/FY39400.pdf

Handy C, Understanding Organisations, Penguin Books, 1993, ISBN 0140156038.

Health & Safety Executive, Safety Culture Maturity Model, Offshore Technology Report 2000/049, 2001, ISBN 0717619192.

Hofstede G, Culture's Consequences: International Differences in Work-related Values (Cross-Cultural Research & Methodology Series), Sage Publications, 1984, ISBN 0803913060.

IET- Health and Safety Briefing 07, December 2006 – Safety Culture, http://www.theiet.org/factfiles/health/index.cfm

Kerzner H, Using the Project Management Maturity Model: Strategic Planning for Project Management, 2nd Edition, John Wiley and Sons, 2005, ISBN 0471691615.

Kotter J P and Heskett J L, Corporate Culture and Performance, The Free Press, 1992, ISBN 0029184673.

Kroeber A L and Kluckhohn C, Culture: A Critical Review of Concepts and Definitions, Alfred A. Knopf and Random House, 1963.

Kwak Y H and Ibbs W, Project Management Process Maturity (PM)2 Model, Journal of Management in Engineering Jul/Aug 2002; 18, 3, 150-155.

Loughborough University Safety Climate Assessment Toolkit, 2007. www.lboro.ac.uk/departments/bs/safety/

Louis M, Sourcing Workplace Cultures: Why, When and How in Kilmann, Saxton and Serpa, eds, Gaining Control of the Corporate Culture, Jossey-Bass, 1986; 126-136.

Martin J and Siehl C, Organisational Culture and Counterculture: An Uneasy Symbiosis, Organisational Dynamics [0090-2616] Joanne yr: 1983; 12, 2, 52-64.

McShane S L and Von Glinow M A, Organizational Behaviour, McGraw-Hill Education, 2000, ISBN 0071163344.

Ott J S, The Organizational Culture Perspective, Harcourt Publishers, 1996, ISBN 0534109187.

Pinto J K and Slevin D P, Critical Success Factors in R&D Projects, Research-Technology Management Jan-Feb, 1989; 32, 1, 31-35.

Project Management Institute Standards Committee, A Guide to the Project Management Body of Knowledge, 1996 Edition, ISBN 1880410125.

Schein E H, Organisational Culture and Leadership, 3rd Edition, Jossey-Bass, 2004, ISBN 0787975974.

Trompenaars F and Hampden-Turner C, Riding the Waves of Culture: Understanding the Waves of Culture, McGraw-Hill Education, 1998, ISBN 0786311258.

Human Performance Improvement-
Reducing Significant Events in Nuclear Power

Don Goble

British Energy

Barnwood, Gloucester, England

Abstract

Over the past decade a great many improvements have been made in the nuclear power industry relative to technology and equipment. System improvements have added redundancy to safety systems, electronics have improved and become more reliable, and better equipment continues to enter the workplace.

These technological improvements have gone a long way in improving the reliability of nuclear power facilities. In order to obtain even further improvements, the industry has recognised the need for improving Human Performance.

Whilst a great deal of focus has been placed on human performance over the past decade, there continues to be many opportunities to improve in this arena. Unplanned reactor trips continue to occur, nuclear reportable events have not been eliminated, and industrial safety accidents remain in need of attention.

This paper explains the importance of human performance to British Energy (BE) and provides the drivers for continued improvement in human performance.

The paper outlines the elements of the British Energy human performance enhancement programme, in line with the World Association of Nuclear Operators (WANO) and the Institute of Nuclear Power Operators (INPO) Principles in an effort to reduce significant events caused by human error.

1   Introduction

Mark Twain once stated, "What gets us into trouble is not what we don't know, but what we know for sure that just ain't so". This saying is very much at the foundation of human error. Personnel regularly interact with the plant and perform their daily tasks assuming they are equipped knowing exactly what they need to do to be successful. The challenge is to help them understand that they "don't know what they don't know" and to assist them in recognising what good looks like.

Proper human performance programmes will have in place processes and tools to ensure that workers are set to work with the right level of knowledge to properly complete the task. This was the goal in mind as British Energy and the nuclear industry developed a strategic approach. However, attempting to change culture after decades of performing work in a manner different than what is expected from a rigorous human performance programme poses significant challenges. These culture changes exist not only with the workers, but also for the organisation.

Added to that is an aging workforce that in the whole of the nuclear industry continues to increase. An aging workforce does not mean that old dogs can't learn new tricks, but it poses challenges in that these same workers have experienced a variety of different improvement programmes come and go over the years. This makes it difficult to reassure workers that there is a reason to sign on to human performance. Age isn't as much of an issue as is the fact that workers in the nuclear industry have experience in excess of 20 and 30 years in many cases. New employees entering the industry have the benefit of human performance practices being core values and everyday expectations, making it much easier to embed.

---

2   Human Performance in the Nuclear Industry

The Institute of Nuclear Power Operators (INPO) in the United States recognised that in order to gain increased confidence in nuclear power operations from the public, additional focus needed to be paid to human behaviours. At the time, unplanned automatic reactor trips were prevalent at most power stations due to a number of issues including human error. Rework remained high, refuelling outages extended, adherence to work schedules was lower than expected, and equipment reliability was becoming a factor in capability of reactor output.

In late 1993, INPO established a Special Review Committee on Human Performance comprised of experts in human performance and senior utility representatives. This committee, along with several working groups, was asked to identify actions to bring about continued improvement in human performance within the commercial nuclear power industry. The working groups included utility operators, craft personnel, supervisors and managers as well as personnel from other industries. In November 1994, after a series of meetings with these working groups, the Special Review Committee recommended that "consideration should be given to developing and publishing a set of key elements, principles, or guidelines for human performance improvement."

Acting on this recommendation in April, 1995, INPO put together a Special Utility Committee on Human Performance to discuss a broad spectrum of issues affecting excellence in human performance. Drawing on the work of the Special Review Committee, the utility committee identified a number of individual and leader behaviours and organisational factors that promote excellence in human performance. These behaviours embody a number of professionalism principles and were presented to assist utilities in achieving excellent human performance (WANO Principles for Excellence in Human Performance, WANO-GL 2002-02).

The INPO document "Excellence in Human Performance" was subsequently issued in 1997. This document was adopted and reviewed to suit the WANO members' needs in 2002 with input from all WANO regional centres. The strategy developed is based on the following underlying principles:

1. People are fallible and even the best make mistakes.
2. Error-likely situations are predictable, manageable and preventable.
3. Individual behaviour is influenced by organisational processes and values.
4. People achieve high levels of performance based largely on the encouragement and reinforcement from leaders, peers and subordinates.
5. Events can be avoided by understanding the reasons why mistakes occur and applying lessons learned from past events.

In 2003, a WANO peer review visit outlined a number of areas for improvement relative to human performance within British Energy. The review stated that Human Performance tools and error prevention practices were not effectively implemented on a company-wide basis. This was evidenced by management personnel not consistently reinforcing expectations and coaching in the work area was (often) not evident. It was also found that there was an over dependence on "human performance" to compensate for poor or inadequate processes, procedures or programmes. Furthermore it stated that station personnel do not understand the need or the mechanics of the human performance error prevention techniques.

British Energy maintains and operates eight nuclear plants and corporate offices housing personnel who directly support these plants. Within British Energy, safety impact, fiscal value, operational reliability values, and the value of creating long term changes in people's attitudes and behaviours was not always recognised. British Energy also did not always get to the root cause of events. Many times the root cause ended at the point of the individual without reviewing organizational weaknesses. At the same time there was recognition that the world class nuclear plants operated better, in part, because of their embedded Human Performance programmes.

With that in mind, BE set out to establish a performance improvement programme. The programme incorporated several aspects including continuous improvement, corrective actions, operating experience, simulations and HU training, improved labeling, reward and recognition programmes, leadership workstreams, and introduction of human performance error prevention tools.

3   WANO Performance Objectives and Criteria

WANO has established performance objectives and criteria (PO&Cs) intended for use in its peer review visits to operating and near-term operating license nuclear power plants. Nuclear utilities are also encouraged to use these objectives in self-evaluations of their own performance.

For operating nuclear power plants, WANO review teams apply the performance objectives and criteria based on observed performance, with emphasis on safety and reliability.

The performance objectives are broad in scope. Each objective generally covers a single, well-defined management area. The supporting criteria are more narrow in scope and typically describe a specific activity that contributes to the achievement of a performance objective. Several criteria are listed under each performance objective.

The performance objectives are grouped into two basic areas. The first is a group of 10 functional areas that generally coincide with the management, operation, maintenance, and support activities needed to safely and reliably operate a nuclear powered electrical generating plant. These areas generally correspond to nuclear station organisational departments or groups that are organised to complete the function described. These functional areas are basic to an organisation and are as follows:

- Organisational Effectiveness Functions
- Operations Functions
- Maintenance Functions
- Engineering Support Functions
- Radiological Protection Functions
- Operating Experience Functions
- Chemistry Functions
- Training and Qualification Functions
- Fire Protection Functions
- Emergency Preparedness Functions

The second group of performance objectives generally correspond to those characteristics of an organisation that cross organisational boundaries because they apply to the entire workforce, and represent additional prevailing standards, attitudes, behaviours, and work processes and controls. This group is defined as "cross-functional" and includes the following:

- Safety Culture
- Human Performance
- Self-Evaluation (Learning Organisation)
- Industrial Safety
- Plant Status and Configuration Control
- Work Management
- Equipment Performance and Condition

The extent of the use of these performance objectives and criteria, both functional and cross-functional, by WANO peer review teams is determined by the director of each regional centre in accordance with WANO policies and guidelines and as appropriate to the needs of the station being reviewed.

The criteria listed may not address every activity associated with the performance objective. Therefore, meeting all the criteria does not ensure that the performance objective is fully met. Conversely, it is recognised that a nuclear station may effectively achieve the performance objective without meeting each specific criterion. For these reasons, WANO emphasises achievement of the performance objectives rather than focusing solely on the supporting criteria.

The criteria in this document are results-oriented. The methods for achieving the desired results are generally not stated. Thus, considerable judgement is required in applying the criteria. Consequently, these objectives and criteria provide a broad framework for reviewing performance in operational nuclear power stations, and in Near-Term Operating License plants. For purposes of this paper, we will only focus and discuss the human performance-performance objective.

3.1   Human Performance – Performance Objective

The behaviours of all personnel result in safe and reliable station operation. Behaviours that contribute to excellence in human performance are reinforced to continuously strive for event-free station operations.

CRITERIA
A. Individuals take responsibility for their actions and are committed to improve plant performance. They exhibit behaviours that support safe and reliable plant operation, such as the following:

1. Communicate frequently and precisely, and maintain expected standards for communication.
2. Make conservative decisions with respect to the reactor core, especially when faced with uncertain or degrading conditions. Verify assumptions before taking action.
3. Anticipate problems and take precautions or countermeasures before and during activities they perform or supervise. Inform management and coworkers of problems and potential problems and recommended solutions.
4. Search for and eliminate conditions that lead to human error. Reinforce the use of defences that mitigate the consequences of errors.
5. Focus attention on the task at hand to reduce the likelihood of error, including use of self-checking, checking by others (peers), and coaching and by encouraging personal accountability and responsibility.
6. Follow procedures or correct procedure deficiencies before continuing the task.
7. Practice team skills when working in a group. These skills include the following:
    a. Obtain necessary information by making appropriate inquiry.

　　　　b. Advocate their positions when potential problems arise.

　　　　c. Take initiative to confirm that necessary actions occur.

　　　　d. Resolve conflict to achieve the best solution.

　　　　e. Critique team performance to reinforce desired team skills.

　　　　f. Identify and promptly resolve obstacles to teamwork.

B. Leader behaviours promote excellence in human performance as exhibited by activities such as the following:

1. Reinforce open communication and a questioning attitude toward work activities.

2. Communicate and reinforce roles, responsibilities, expected behaviours, and high standards of performance for communication, teamwork, and performance improvement.

3. Establish conditions that reinforce desired job-site behaviours to reduce the potential for human error. Focus the attention of assigned personnel on nuclear safety-critical tasks such as changes in core reactivity and engineering-related activities.

4. Verify that individuals involved with a task accurately perceive the potential consequences of error and take precautions to avoid complacency.

5. Insist on uniform adherence to high standards of performance. Continually search for and eliminate organisational weaknesses that create the conditions for human error.

C. Managers establish conditions that support event-free performance as exhibited by activities such as the following:

1. Develop strategies, policies, processes, and practices that support excellent human performance. Identify and exemplify desired individual and leader behaviours.

2. Establish defences that prevent or mitigate the consequences of human error. Recognise communication as one of the most effective defences against events.

3. Identify and mitigate conditions that lead to human error.

4. Balance supervision, procedures, and individual knowledge and skill to support expected job-site behaviours. To maintain this balance, changes in conditions and resources are anticipated and corrective actions implemented.

5. Train personnel on conditions that lead to human error, on risk-important actions, on operating experience involving human performance, and on methods to enhance performance.

6. Evaluate human performance problems to determine and resolve causes attributable to the organisation, leadership, and the individual.

7. Create a work environment that promotes a high level of human performance. Accomplish this by optimising factors such as the following:

　　　　a. knowledge, proficiency, attitude, fitness, and limitations of individuals with respect to the tasks being performed

　　　　b. availability and quality of work documents, procedures, resources, and tools

c. working conditions, such as lighting, physical constraints, sources of distraction, schedule pressure, human-machine interface, and workarounds

d. effective use of operating experience and risk analysis insights

e. accuracy and quality of information transfer during prejob briefings and turnover of tasks or responsibilities (WANO Performance Objectives and Criteria 2005).

4   Performance Improvement Plan

The basis for most human performance programmes within the nuclear industry typically have evolved from a variety of documents and training programmes first introduced by INPO in the 1990's. British Energy was no exception. However, part of determining and developing the BE performance improvement plan (PIP), included benchmarking of several major utilities in the United States. These included South Texas Utilities, Exelon Corporation, and Entergy to name a few. The HU programmes at these companies had proven successful in reducing human performance errors and significant events over the previous several years.

British Energy recognised and accepted that human performance is probabilistic, meaning that people tend to focus on the probability of making an error rather than the consequences of their behaviours. As a result, it was vital to provide understanding to all levels of the organisation as to the value of a human performance programme as a core business practice.

When the PIP was first developed, it naturally was an add-on to the way that BE had conducted business in the past. Training programmes had to be unique in nature because of the new approach to the way staff would be asked to conduct work. A strategic approach was established to formalise the programme structure and create project plans. Overall, the PIP was designed to take three years to completely implement.

4.1   Strategy

The strategy was aimed at reducing errors, eliminating events and increasing operational reliability through Human Performance Improvement. Success would depend on effecting behavioural change at all levels of the organisation and the engagement of all staff and contractors in the application of error prevention tools and techniques, the elimination of organisational barriers, increased personal accountability and application of standards in the field.

The overall strategy was based on five levels of engagement and a location WANO assist visit.

Level 1 – Expectations and Individual Awareness

This was aimed at setting management Human Performance Expectations for leaders and all staff, raising staff and team awareness of human performance issues and steps that individuals may take to minimise human performance shortfalls within their sphere of influence.

Location Managers set Human Performance Expectations based on the INPO Principles for Excellence in Human Performance utilising the standard company tri-folds.

Each team was required to complete awareness workshops based upon the company Level 1 Human Performance Awareness course.   Teams were encouraged to explore and understand the basic error prevention tools and techniques and how these may be applied in the workplace to reduce the risk of error. Organisational barriers to Human performance Improvement were also discussed and identified. The workshops concluded with a team action plan that was presented to the relevant Department Manager detailing how the team intended to improve performance. The action plans adopted a common format, and contained actions to be included in the Team business plan and progressed via the normal line accountability process.

Following the initial awareness raising and team workshop, each Line Manager conducted a face to face meeting with the Location Director and Departmental Manager to align expectations and agreed "sign-on" to the Human Performance improvement programme the location was embarking on.

Level 2 – Organisational Barriers to Human Performance

This was aimed at addressing key organisational barriers to improving Human Performance identified during the Level 1 workshops, location WANO peer reviews and INPO Gap Analysis surveys.

Each problem area was analysed by a small team comprising Line Managers and subject matter experts culminating in a decision paper for Location Management consideration and approval.   Subject to approval, the team then spearheaded implementation through the Group Business Plans via the normal accountability mechanisms.

Level 3 – Positive Reinforcement and Personal Accountability

This was aimed at the positive reinforcement of the error prevention tools and techniques initiated during the level one awareness workshops and increasing personal accountability with the objective of effecting long term behavioural change in the field.

To effect this change, Line Managers were required to have a greater presence in the field applying observational and coaching techniques to reinforce good performance and challenge poor performance. This was achieved in two phases. The initial "high impact" phase aimed at equipping the Line Managers with the necessary observation and coaching skills to reinforce the Human Performance behaviours, tools and techniques. The second longer term "embedding" phase was aimed at establishing a continual Line Manager presence in the field reinforcing the ongoing application of Human Performance tools and techniques and revisiting each team to review progress with their Level one action plans.

In addition, individuals involved in human performance events were required to present and discuss the key aspects of the event with their team with an emphasis on steps that the individual proposes to take to minimise the re-occurrence. Line Managers were required to facilitate this discussion to identify areas for improvement.

Level 4 – Communications

Aimed at ongoing communications, a campaign was developed based on Operational Experience (lessons learned), Task Observations, and reinforcing the error prevention tools and techniques.

Level 5 – Human Performance Leadership – Monthly Line Managers Meeting

This was aimed at establishing a consistent ongoing application and reinforcement of appropriate behaviours, challenging inappropriate behaviours and maintaining a "focus" within the wider Management Team on Human Performance. Achievements were experienced through monthly Line Manager meetings focused on Human Performance to share experience, discuss events and messages to be disseminated, progress with team action plans and positive reinforcement in the field. In addition, Line Managers were encouraged to present results of team discussions undertaken as a result of an event (Level 3).

5   HU Implementation

$$R_e \ + \ M_d \ \rightarrow \ \varnothing E$$

| *Reducing* *Error* | and | *Managing* *Defences* | leads to | *ZERO* *Events* |

A model standard to the industry is displayed in the equation above. By reducing errors and managing defences, sites should eventually realise zero events. Zero events as referenced here is a vision. As long as humans continue to be fallible, there will always be errors that have the potential to lead to events. The basis behind proactive human performance programmes is aimed at addressing both.

5.1   Error Rate

When we begin to pay attention to human performance, error rate tends to decrease. But what are we actually paying attention to? We tend to pay attention to those things that are controllable or systemic. For example, procedures, training and organisational issues.

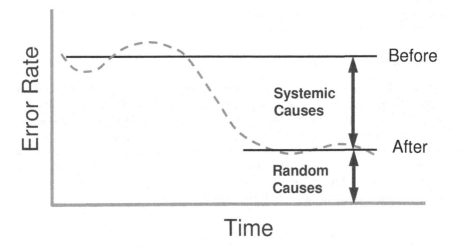

However there is an element of error rate that is uncontrollable due to random causes related to human nature. Because humans are fallible, there will always be the need to defend against these errors. The design of a HU strategy must tackle systemic causes and defend against random errors.

5.2   Types of Errors

There are two types of errors that are focused upon; active and latent. Active errors result in an immediate adverse consequence, whilst latent errors create a latent condition that may sit dormant for long periods of time until something triggers them.

One historical example of a latent error is the Apollo 13 disaster. In April 1970, an explosion originated in a tank of liquid oxygen when the crew activated a set of rotating paddles [trigger] to stir the liquid oxygen. The paddles had been bench-tested prior to the mission, but they had been connected to the wrong power supply [latent error]. The power supply caused the insulating material to be burned off of the electrical supply to the paddles [latent condition]. Once the paddles were switched on [trigger], a spark ignited the liquid oxygen causing an explosion that blew out the side of the oxygen tank.

The problem with latent errors is that personnel do not know when they have made an error. In order to minimise the significance and number of errors, the proper defences must be in place. One such defence is error prevention tools.

5.3   Human Performance error prevention tools

The most relied upon method for reducing active errors is the use of error prevention tools. Within the nuclear industry, there are a large number of error prevention tools that have been established. Following a review of the tools that were being utilised at other utilities, BE decided upon the following ten tools that would become the standard for the company:

- Self-check (STAR)
- Pre-Job Brief
- Questioning Attitude
- Peer Check
- Independent Verification
- Operating Experience
- Procedure Use & Adherence
- Clear Communication Techniques
- Observation & Coaching
- Post-job debrief

Each of these tools have been proven to help reduce significant events at nuclear plants in the United States. Whilst there have been several HU tools developed and used over the years within the industry, the key is to determine those tools that will work best for each specific company or facility. This is best determined by understanding what assets require protecting.

For example; all too often companies blend industrial safety programmes with human performance programmes. Whilst there certainly are overlaps, and human performance tools can improve work practices that will lead to improved safety behaviours, the primary purpose of a human performance programme is to protect the plant from people's actions. Industrial safety and radiological safety programmes should be designed to protect people from the plant. Why is this important to differentiate? Because if we don't understand the asset to be protected (i.e. plant equipment, environment, information, etc.) then it is impossible to identify the proper HU tools to implement. Furthermore, it is impossible to train workers on when and how to specifically use each of the tools.

5.4   HU Training Programme

Within British Energy a number of training courses were developed beginning with a HU foundation course. The foundation course provides an entry level of education surrounding human performance. This course introduced the Generic Error Model System (GEMS) highlighting skill, rule and knowledge based performance.

> Skill based performance – Highly practiced tasks that people are good at most of the time.
> Skill based error – Typically related to inattention to detail. Error rate approximately 1:10,000
>
> Rule based performance – Application of memorised or written rules (such as procedures) by matching the signs and symptoms of the problem to some stored knowledge structure.
> Rule based error – Typically related to a misinterpretation or misapplication of a rule. Error rate approximately 1:1000
>
> Knowledge based performance – Used only when staff have repeatedly failed to find some pre-existing solution either from experience, rules or training.
> Knowledge based error – Typically related to an inaccurate mental model of the task presented to them. Error rate approximately 1:2 (Reason 1997)

The primary learning objective is for staff to recognise when they have entered into knowledge based space. Because of the significant likelihood of error and the inability in nuclear power for trial and error, personnel must recognise when they have entered into a situation where they have no rules or training to guide them on a successful path. Quite often however, individuals will talk themselves into a method of completing the task thinking that it will end with a successful outcome. Many times staff will find some way of comparing the task at hand to something that they are familiar with, and reassure themselves that they know what they are doing. Inevitably the results are unfavourable nearly half of the time.

   Implementing error prevention tools and educating personnel will only go so far without reinforcement. British Energy developed a task observation and coaching programme to provide leaders with the skills necessary to encourage and reinforce standards and expectations that would lead to improved behaviours. Expanding on this, BE developed a Human Performance Leader Authorisation (HULA) programme.

The HULA began with authorising executive managers and working down through the rest of the organisation. This provided managers the opportunity to lead by example and to drive standards from the top down. The HULA programme consists of leaders being trained in the foundation course, task observation and coaching, HU tools and techniques and concluding with a task performance evaluation in the field. The evaluation (or authorisation) consists of a leader being observed in a task observation setting and evaluating his/her observation and feedback skills. This was initially performed by a HU expert within BE or a human performance coach. Several human performance experts were brought in from America to assist in training development and coaching of leaders. Their experience abroad provided additional expertise for BE to an area relatively new in the United Kingdom.

Now that the programme and the organisation have matured, the authorisation process is being transferred to the senior leadership team at each respective site. This serves to provide several organisational benefits including ownership and the ability for senior managers to be in the field more frequently and to continue to reinforce expectations. It has also helped to streamline the process.

A quality human performance programme will take knowledge based and latent errors into account and incorporate a series of defences [defence in depth] in order to minimise the significance of these errors. Effectiveness relies upon engineering controls, formal controls, management assurance & oversight controls and cultural controls. Examples include:

- Plant labelling
- Configuration control
- Role clarity
- Management oversight
- Individual Accountability
- Open reporting and communication

5.5   Station and Department HU Clocks

One key tool for a learning organisation is to learn from significant and lower level events in order to avoid having repeat events. Human performance clocks are one tool that is used throughout the U.S. Nuclear industry and was selected to be used at British Energy also.

The purpose of the clock is to be used in two efforts; a performance indicator to measure the average number of days between events, and as a communication tool to communicate events, the barriers that failed, precursors that existed and corrective actions taken to avoid similar events.

More specific information on the content of this as an indicator is contained in the Key Performance Indicator section below.

5.6   Key Performance Indicators

Early in 2005, a working group was formed at the request of INPO to develop a key performance indicator basis document. The Human Performance Key Performance Indicators (KPIs) are a method to determine site human performance program effectiveness in the prevention of events using common measures. They allow top executives to present human error performance information throughout the industry, whereby all sites are using the same measures and criteria for site events.

The program below outlines Site Event Free Day Criteria and Department Event Free Day Criteria established for and currently in use within INPO industry plants.

British Energy uses very similar criteria to that developed by INPO, however because of cultural, equipment and reactor technology differences, the terminology is subtly different. British Energy also incorporates other performance indicators in addition to Site and Department Event clocks, as do the U.S. plants. The combination of these indicators are intended to measure the health of human performance at both a site and fleet wide level.

5.6.1   Definitions

Error - An action that unintentionally departs from an expected behaviour.

Event - An unwanted, undesirable change in the state of plant structures, systems, or components or human/organizational conditions (health, behaviour, administrative controls, environment, and so on) that exceeds established significance criteria.

Site Human Performance Event Free Day (EFD) Reset – When an error (Re) committed by personnel during the execution of an activity (work package, procedure, etc.)

or

When an activity is executed as planned (Md - work package, procedure, etc.) and results in one of the following, it is considered a site event.

5.6.2   *Site Event Free Criteria*

Description
Nuclear Safety / Operational Event a. Event that requires emergency plan activation b. A reactor trip or turbine trip c. Unplanned mode change d. Unexpected / Unplanned reactivity change   3% power e. Unplanned entry into a technical specification action statement $\leq$ 72 hours f. Fuel handling errors that result in a damaged fuel bundle, or misplaced bundle ungrappled. g. Switching/tagging/wrong component error that results in work being released to the field and clearance verified by the performing department, or work performed that results in inadequate equipment or personnel protection. h. Unplanned increase to the on-line or shutdown risk threshold colour / number i. Mis-operation, mis-position, or improper configuration that creates significant transient or challenge to nuclear safety. j. Property damage to the facility in excess of $50,000
Radiological Safety a. Radiological event that would generate a Licensee Event Report (LER) b. Unplanned exposure that exceeds 100 mrem over the estimate for an individual's exposure c. Loss of radiological control: Loss of radioactive material which creates a measurable exposure rate at 30 centimetres outside the protected area, any technical specification high radiation area occurrence, or any technical specification very high radiation area occurrence d. Mis-operation, mis-position, or improper configuration that creates significant transient or challenge to radiological safety.
Industrial Safety a. Any event that results in a fatality or lost-time accident b. Mis-operation, mis-position, or improper configuration that creates significant transient or challenge to personnel safety.
Regulatory Event a. NPDES or OSHA violation or Hazmat emergency b. Security report per 10 CFR 73.71 (excluding loggables) c. Licensee Event Report (LER) per 10 CFR 50.72 or 10 CFR 50.73

5.6.3   *Department Event Free Criteria*

Department clocks are reset for any event that resets the site event free day clock. In addition to that, the following criteria is suggested as minimum generic criteria that will be used by all station departments. Criteria more specific to individual departments is also incorporated into their reset documents.

Description
Nuclear Safety / Operational Event
a. Inadvertent increase of on-line or shutdown risk level
b. Unplanned Tech Spec LCO Action Statement Entries
c. Event classified as a Reactivity Management Precursor
d. Unplanned power change
e. Property damage > $10,000
f. Component miss-positioning
g. Foreign Material Exclusion program violation or intrusion
Radiological Safety
a. Violation of Radiological Work Permit (RWP) or Radiological Controls
b. Uncontrolled Radioactive Material found outside the RCA
c. Unplanned contamination of space that is not normally contaminated
d. Personnel contamination event
e. Unplanned release of radioactive material
Industrial Safety
a. OSHA Recordable Injury
b. A preventable motor vehicle accident involving company vehicle
c. Chemical Control Program Violation
d. Industrial Safety Program Violations (OSHA) (i.e. lifting/rigging, confined space, fall protection, etc.)
Regulatory Action
a. Security Loggable event as per Regulatory Guide 5.26
b. Missed Tech Spec / TRM / ODCM surveillance
c. NRC green finding or Non-Cited Violation (NCV)

6   Embed Phase

There are many aspects involved with embedding human performance into the organisation and the culture. This is where many organisations fail and lose worker confidence. Most organisations are good at rolling out new initiatives including training and kick-offs, etc. The true challenge lies in embedding the values and benefits that come from such programmes. For example, scientists and/or engineers have difficulty in understanding why you need to prevent an event that hasn't happened yet because they can't prove that it will happen.

British Energy has either begun or completed embedding human performance into the organisation through the following initiatives.

6.1   Continuing training

Following the stand alone foundation training mentioned earlier, the next phase in the process was to incorporate human performance into continuing training. How was this done? At British Energy there are a number or technical and accredited training programmes that previously would have focused primarily on a specific type of equipment, system, etc. and not taken error prevention tools into account. For example, maintenance technicians would have conducted training on various aspects of a pump, learning for example about seals, impellers, gaskets, packing, lubrication, etc.

But now, human performance fundamentals are incorporated into the training. Prior to beginning training, workers will now conduct a pre-job brief discussing roles and responsibilities, expectations, protective equipment and so on. They would then be expected to properly use the error prevention tools including procedure use and adherence and various other tools. At the end of the task, a post job debrief will be conducted to identify lessons learned. This will include what went well and what can be improved the next time that the task is performed. The logic behind this is to "train as you work, and work as you train."

6.2   Paired Observations

Within the past year paired observations have become a mechanism to embed not only human performance, but also reinforce standards and expectations. Paired observations are conducted by various levels of leaders where one leader (generally a manager or coach) conducts a task observation side by side with another leader. This provides the manager to reinforce his / her expectations both with the other leader and the workers that they observe. Following feedback to the workers, the two leaders will compare notes and provide coaching to each other. At the conclusion, one observation is entered into an observation database to capture the results of the observation.

6.3   Reinforcement

One of the most significant methods of embedding any behaviour is through reinforcement. Reinforcement can take the form of both positive and negative. It can also take the form of conscious and unconscious reinforcement. Positive, negative and conscious forms are rather straightforward and self explanatory, but let's take a moment to explore unconscious reinforcement. By leaders turning a blind eye when workers are exhibiting poor behaviours, they are in essence approving of the behaviour.

At the same time, when leaders are only focused on the outcome and not with the method that it was accomplished, this can also be reinforcing negative behaviours. Within British Energy our focus has been to positively reinforce appropriate behaviours, and to address inappropriate behaviours through coaching in the field.

6.4   Accountability

In addition to reinforcement it is necessary to ensure that all levels of the organisation are accountable for their actions. Only when leaders and staff become accountable can they hold each other accountable. The theory of being your "brothers keeper" is one which is currently being implemented not just with British Energy employees, but with our major contractor staff as well. This is expected to further embed the standards deeper in the organisation.

6.5   Self-assessment

Now that the programme has had time to be incorporated into the mainstream of the organisation, the method for determining how well it is embedded is through the use of self-assessments. Assessments are conducted both from the corporate level and by station departments.

Corporate led assessments assess the effectiveness of implementation and use of the error prevention tools using the WANO PO&C's. Station departments often perform assessments that focus on specific aspects of human performance within their functional areas.

7   Conclusion

Human performance programmes around the world have resulted in improved performance, reduced errors, lower industrial safety accidents, etc. Within BE the benefits have been tremendous. In just three years since the inception of the HU programme at British Energy, the number of unplanned reactor trips and nuclear reportable events have each decreased by more than 70%.

There remain challenges that must be addressed as with any organisation engaged on a continuous improvement journey. Primarily;

- continuing to investigate and determine the root cause of events and identify effective corrective actions
- identify and strengthen defences through engineered and formal controls
- further embed the HU error prevention tools into existing processes
- engage suppliers and long term contractors.

British Energy's future relies upon continued safe and reliable operation of our nuclear reactors. This requires diligence and continuous improvement. The next step on this journey is the inception of a Nuclear Professional programme. The Nuclear Professional programme will combine the efforts of Nuclear Safety Culture and Human Performance. The combining of these two programmes will provide the basis for embedding the expectations for a proud and professional workforce through all levels of the organisation.

References

Reason J (1997). Managing the Risks of Organizational Accidents. Ashgate.

World Association of Nuclear Operators (WANO) Performance Objectives and Criteria (2005)

WANO Guideline, Principles for Excellence in Human Performance, WANO-GL 2002-02

Human Factors

A Human Factors Perspective on Safety Management Systems

Christopher Lowe
Human Factors Consultant
Bristol, United Kingdom

Abstract

The purpose of this paper is to discuss a method of framing some of the Human Factors issues associated with the Safety Management Systems approach, and to investigate some of the barriers and opportunities in using Human Factors Methods to enhance the functioning of a Safety Management System within safety-related industries.

1 Introduction

Over the past twenty years the role of the Human Factors engineering discipline in Safety Assessment has been defined in a number of different industries and some degree of best practice has been established (for example NUREG-1792, 'Good Practices for Implementing Human Reliability Analysis' (US NRC, 2005)). However, a trend in some industries has been to augment the traditional safety assessment approach with a more holistic 'Safety Management Systems' focus (recorded in documents such as the UK Railways and Other Guided Transport Systems (Safety) Regulations (ROGS, 2006) for example). While the guidance exists for Safety Specialists on Human Factors within Safety Assessment, the increasing focus on Safety Management Systems introduces a new set of Human Factors issues, and requirements for standardisation and best practice.

The purpose of this paper is to discuss a method of framing some of the Human Factors issues associated with the Safety Management Systems approach, and to propose a general approach to using Human Factors Methods to enhance the functioning of a Safety Management System within safety-related industries.

To deal with this topic, this paper first discusses different high-level models of Safety Management Systems that have been proposed by researchers and organisations in this area (for example, the UK Health and Safety Executive).

A 'Human Factors View' of these SMS models is then presented and discussed. This view describes, in Human Factors terms, safety management activities and the overlap between these practices and Human Factors methods and concepts (as represented by models of Human Factors Integration, for instance).

The implications of this view on Safety Management Systems is then used to derive and discuss some of the barriers and opportunities associated with the use of Human Factors methods within Safety Management processes (such as incident investigation and safety reporting systems, for example).

This paper concludes with a summary of the overlap between Human Factors and Safety Management Systems, highlights the best practice advice that can be given to Safety Management Specialists at this time, and outlines some topics for further research and development.

2 Human Factors and System Safety

The value of Human Factors considerations in the analysis of system safety is obvious and often stated: humans are associated with the procurement, design, operation, management, maintenance and disposal of all systems in some form, and therefore the associated successes and failures of those systems (Turner and Pidgeon (1994)). In addition, most theoretical models of accident causation recognise the centrality of humans to system safety (e.g., Perrow (1984)), both as unwitting contributors to safety incidents, and as important barriers and sources of recovery from hazards.

System safety in this sense is being used to refer to a dynamic, emergent state of a system that may not cause harm or loss. Human Factors (or ergonomics) is taken to mean the scientific discipline concerned with the understanding of interactions among humans and other elements of a system (International Ergonomics Association (2000)).

2.1 Safety Assessments and Human Reliability Analysis

Given this background, there is a long tradition of the consideration of 'human factors' in system safety, and in avoiding the 'potentially harm-producing' system states such as incidents and accidents (see, for example, Doerner (1996) for some historical case studies). Since at least the 1980s there have been a number of methods proposed to formalise the consideration of Human Factors in assessments of safety.

One grouping of Human Factors methods used to support System Safety is 'Human Reliability Analysis' (HRA). Kirwan (1994) provides an overview of these early methods. HRA is not the only cluster of Human Factors methods to support System Safety, but it is the method most closely associated with aspects of risk assessment and mitigation (a key process in safety management).

HRA has been used to consider Human Factors in System Safety Assessment in a number of different industries such as the nuclear industry (Kirwan et al (1996)), the rail industry (Hickling et al (2005)), and defence (Kennedy et al (2007)).

To reflect the progress made, some degree of best practice has been established (for example NUREG-1792, 'Good Practices for Implementing Human Reliability Analysis'). This best practice involves consideration of factors such as:

- Using standard methods that are supported by studies demonstrating their validity.
- Relating the HRA approach used to some recognised theoretical basis of human cognition and performance.

- Basing the HRA on a sound understanding of the human actions and performance shaping factors within the system, as represented through (for example) forms of Task Analysis or Activity Analysis.
- Integrating the HRA into the wider Safety Assessment process (such as hazard identification) and models (such as fault and event trees).
- Developing sufficient, correct, and actionable mitigations or human-related safety requirements that are based on Human Factors design principles.

However some researchers in both the Human Factors and System Safety fields are critical of some elements of this approach to the consideration of Human Factors within System Safety (Dougherty (1990), Hollnagel (2005)). These criticisms can be quite technical but one important noted disadvantage is that pervasive or distal performance shaping factors such as culture, work organisation, management and other social considerations are not sufficiently understood and represented within the current popular approaches.

2.2 A Safety Management Perspective

While the debate concerning HRA methods has been ongoing within the Human Factors community, other trends in the wider Safety Management community have also lead to an increasing emphasis on a Safety Management Systems (SMS) approach.

Broadly speaking, a SMS is an attempt to combine different safety functions (such as risk assessment, incident investigation, and safety monitoring) into a coherent whole (Dijkstra (2006)).

Three themes can be seen that have raised the profile of SMS:

- Theoretical concerns associated with classical Safety Risk Assessment approaches.
- The drive towards continuous safety improvement in high-reliability industries.
- The consideration of Safety Management as a business function that exists to control risks and therefore to control cost.

To some extent the criticisms of HRA approaches have also been applied to the wider classical Quantitative Safety Assessment approach (Hollnagel (2005)). In these criticisms there is a recognised need to account more for organisational and social factors in Systems Safety (Leveson (2004)). These criticisms also represent a move towards a more organisational consideration of safety incidents and accidents (Reason (1997)). This trend can be seen in the updates to the most recent version of the UK Railway Safety Management Guide (The Yellow Book – (RSSB (2007))).

In addition, high-reliability industries are often required to maintain or improve their safety records, even while the demands on the system increase. For example, this requirement is recognised by the Railway Strategic Safety Plan (2006) published by the Rail Safety and Standards Board of Great Britain. Within this plan, the UK Rail industry acknowledges the need to 'maintain safety in a period of change' as a safety objective.

Cases have also been made to demonstrate the cost effectiveness of SMS. For example, guidance material from the Civil Aviation Safety Authority of Australia (2006) stresses the fact that the economic impact of accidents can be greater, especially for smaller organisations.

To support all of these trends, a number of industries have recently (over the past decade) introduced or strengthened their 'Safety Management System' approaches.

The next section presents an overview of the definitions, philosophy, and generic processes associated with Safety Management Systems.

3 The Safety Management Systems Approach

The idea of the SMS has been established for some time and regulations and/or guidance exist in most safety-related industries for the application of safety management. For example, in the UK, regulations for SMS exist in the rail industry (the Railways and Other Guided Transport Systems (Safety) Regulations ('ROGS')) and in the provision of air transport (through documents produced by the UK Civil Aviation Authority, such as CAP 712).

A small number of these approaches will be discussed here, and the common features extracted.

3.1 Definitions of Safety Management Systems

The regulations and guidance within each industry defines the applicable scope and focus of the SMS for that domain. A few of these definitions are provided below:

- Nuclear industry: *"The safety management system comprises those arrangements made by the organisation for the management of safety in order to promote a strong safety culture and achieve good safety performance."* (International Nuclear Safety Advisory Group (1999)).
- Rail industry: *"The organisation and arrangements established by a transport operator to ensure the safe management of its operation."* (The Railways and Other Guided Transport Systems (Safety) Regulations (2006)).
- Air Traffic Management: *"Safety management is that function of service provision which ensures that all safety risks have been identified, assessed, and satisfactorily mitigated."* (Air Traffic Services Safety Requirements (CAP 670) 2003), or, *"A safety management system is an organized approach to managing safety, including the necessary organizational structures, accountabilities, policies and procedures"* (International Civil Aviation Organisation (2006)).

3.2 Common Factors in Safety Management Systems

Although these definitions are taken from different domains and different documents, key common elements of a SMS can be extracted from these definitions and the associated documentation. These common factors can be summarised in the following way:

- A SMS is a business function of the overall organisation.
- A SMS is a systematic and organised approach to solving safety problems.
- The purpose of a SMS is to achieve and maintain the necessary level of safety within an organisation.
- The implementation of a SMS involves management, organisation, responsibility, and competence ('human issues').

The SMS approach is responding to the requirement from regulators (often adopted into European or national law) and the general public for organisations to assess, manage, and demonstrate their overall safety to a declared tolerable level.

In addition, a SMS exists to assist an organisation to understand it's current level of safety, to communicate this level of safety to stakeholders, to prevent incidents and accidents, and to improve communication, morale, and productivity within the organisation.

3.3 Elements of a Safety Management System

The risk assessment approach discussed in Section 2 is part of the SMS approach but typically a SMS will have a wider remit and not just focus on safety assessment and mitigation (see for example CASA Australia (2006)). This is a slightly different approach to the traditional systems safety assessment. The SMS is more concerned with managing the safety of the organisation's activities throughout the lifetime of the operation of the system, rather than just the assessment and management of proposed changes.

For example, a typical SMS approach may include references to the following elements:

- **A safety policy.** This is a clear written statement of the organisation's view, attitudes, and objectives with respect to safety in relation to the other business processes.
- **Organisational arrangements to support safety.** This involves the organisation, supervision, recruitment, and training of staff to support the safety policy and processes.
- **A safety plan.** This involves elements of establishing standards and processes for safety, and conducting risk assessment and mitigation.
- **A means of measuring safety performance.** Processes and data are required in order to monitor the current and past safety performance.
- **A means of reviewing safety performance.** This element of the SMS exists to assess and understand safety performance against the safety objectives. This may involve processes such as incident investigation and safety surveys.
- **A feedback loop to improve safety performance.** This element of the SMS is associated with making sure that any lessons that are learnt, or any changes necessary for improvement, are properly accounted for by the organisation, and properly communicated to all relevant staff.

The generic HSE model of successful health and safety management contains these elements (HSE (1997), sometimes referred to as the POPIMAR model).

4 Safety Management Systems from a Human Factors Perspective

As Section 2 demonstrates, there is an established link between Human Factors and System Safety Assessment, through Human Reliability Assessment. Currently, in some industries, the extent of integration between Human Factors and Safety Management Systems is not at the same level of maturity (for example, EUROCONTROL (2005)). This may be due to the fact that SMS are a relatively new development when compared with Systems Safety Assessment.

4.1 The Value of a Human Factors Viewpoint

There are a number of reasons why it is necessary and valuable to look at SMS from a Human Factors perspective.

The SMS involves the people within the organisation. It is possible to make a distinction between the 'structural' and 'operational' aspects of a SMS (Cambon et al (2006)). The 'structural' aspects of a SMS refer to the formal policies, procedures, databases, and guidelines that the organisation may have in place to manage safety (in other words, whether the organisation has a SMS or not). The 'operational' aspects of an SMS are the activities and practices that occur 'in real life' (how the SMS may be actually implemented and integrated into the everyday working practices of the staff within the organisation).

The discipline of Human Factors stresses the importance of capturing and understanding the reality of operations. It is these activities, as they are performed in the operational context, which can have the influence on safety.

The structural and operational aspects of the SMS are linked and inter-dependent. The safety policy and procedures of the organisation must exist before the people within the organisation can implement them. The people within the organisation must be aware of the SMS, and be sufficiently trained, motivated, and knowledgeable to use it. Taken together, the 'structural' and 'operational' factors could influence the overall safety management performance of the organisation.

Therefore, the essential problem is that the existence of a SMS is not sufficient to provide assurance on a certain level of safety. If the SMS is not correctly implemented then the assurance on safety, and the system behaviours that the SMS is trying to control, may not be within the bounds and limits established by the organisation. This makes the study of Human Factors within SMS crucial.

4.2 Human Factors Models of Safety Management Systems

The first step towards improving or assuring the 'operational' aspects of the SMS is develop an understanding of SMS from a Human Factors point of view. An important aspect of this understanding is to characterise the SMS in terms that make it amenable to a Human Factors perspective, and then to construct or adopt a working model from this starting point.

From a Human Factors perspective, a SMS can be seen as a socio-technical system. A socio-technical system is a system that involves both social (interactions between individuals and groups) and technical (physical artefacts such as hardware and software) components and their interactions (Eason (1988)).

A SMS exhibits many facets that are common to socio-technical systems:

- A social dimension. This refers to the 'operational' aspects such as the interactions between the staff members (safety managers, incident investigators, front-line staff and maintenance technicians) to perform the activities that comprise the safety-related aspects of the organisation).
- A cultural dimension. This refers to the attitudes, values, beliefs, perceptions, and practices of individuals and groups within the organisation towards safety within the organisation.
- A technological dimension. In this sense, 'technology' refers to a broad description of the tools and artefacts that support safety management. This includes procedures, sources of information, databases, and other documentation.
- The fact that the overall performance of the SMS is dependent on the joint performance of all of the system components.

For example, a safety survey may rely on the interactions between the safety surveyor and the staff being surveyed, the attitudes of the people involved in the survey to the organisation's commitment to safety, and the tools and technologies available to support the process.

From this socio-technical viewpoint, many models have been produced to describe the activities involved in introducing and maintaining a SMS (for example, Hale et al (1997), Transport Canada (2002), McDonald et al (2000)). Essentially these models see safety management systems as involving the following activities:

- Creating or updating the safety policy.
- Writing or maintaining the company safety standards.
- Planning and organising the changes to support the safety management activities.
- Maintaining the safety management activities during normal operational practice. This includes critical sub-tasks of:
  - o Identifying hazards.
  - o Assessing the impact of hazards in relation to the tolerable level of safety.
  - o Introducing changes to eliminate or control the risk posed by the identified hazard.
- Monitoring and responding to the level of safety within the organisation. This includes:
  - o Surveying safety indicators during normal operations.
  - o Investigating and acting on safety occurrences.
- Providing feedback mechanisms for those involved in the SMS.
- Adjusting the SMS and changing to meet new challenges and requirements.

It can be seen that this model is based on the HSE model presented above, but takes more account of the Human Factors aspects of actually attempting to introduce or implement a SMS in everyday practice.

For the cultural dimension, recent studies have attempted to locate concepts from Safety Culture research within SMS frameworks (for example, Gordon 2006). A detailed discussion of safety culture is beyond the scope of this paper. However, these cultural aspects can influence the degree of commitment held by staff towards the SMS.

To summarise, from a Human Factors perspective a SMS can be seen as a socio-technical system that relies on the performance of people (the 'operational' aspect) and the sufficiency of the processes and procedures (the 'structural' aspect) in order to successfully function.

Given this viewpoint, it follows that there will be Human Factors challenges and barriers for those implementing the SMS. The next section presents some of these challenges and barriers.

5 Challenges for Human Factors from Safety Management Systems

Section 4 established that Human Factors models of SMS exist, and that they capture some of the socio-technical aspects of the SMS as a 'living' system, rather than as a collection of documents and procedures.

However, this viewpoint introduces special considerations if we are to focus on the success of the SMS. It is no longer sufficient to focus on the production of technically correct policies and procedures. The focus must be on the Human Factors of the SMS, and this falls into three areas:

- Consideration of the 'people issues' (the interactions and relationships) that determine the outcomes of the SMS processes as they are conducted (the 'operational' factors).
- Making use of best practice technical Human Factors methods in the SMS processes (the 'structural' factors).
- Methodological integration between Human Factors and SMS, because the SMS is concerned with integrating the different safety functions of an organisation into a coherent whole.

This following sections attempt to explain these points and to present some of the associated challenges that need to be addressed.

5.1 General Methodological Challenges

In addition to the practical and operational considerations associated with the use of Human Factors to support SMS processes, there are also broader methodological concerns to be addressed. Three general groups of methodological challenges can be distinguished:

- Theoretical foundations.
- Knowing what works and what doesn't in Safety Management.
- Integrating with the wider SMS.

These methodological concerns are related to some of the difficulties outlined in Section 2.2.

Of particular note are the barriers associated with integrating Human Factors methods (such as Task Analysis, Usability Testing, and Competence Assessment) into SMS in a consistent way.

Traditionally, an approach called 'Human Factors Integration' has been used to 'integrate' Human Factors methods with the broader design or procurement of systems (see, for example, UK MoD (2001)).

Human Factors Integration is a framework for planning and conducting Human Factors methods in such a way to support overall safety, efficiency, or user satisfaction requirements of a system. It is both a management framework and a set of methods.

Most approaches to Human Factors Integration focus on the engineering design of new or modified systems ((see, for example, Network Rail (2003)).

Human Factors Integration is an approach that reflects current best practice in Human Factors methods (Hamilton et al (2005)) and most safety-related industries have Human Factors Integration guidance available.

However, based on the publicly available guidance, current Human Factors Integration approaches are likely to be insufficient when considered against the scope and requirements of most SMS regulations. This is for the following reasons:

- Historically, Human Factors Integration has been associated with the design or assessment of physical products rather than the definition of services or managerial functions.
- Current approaches to Human Factors Integration stress the structured use of Human Factors methods, rather than the techniques for integrating Human Factors into the wider project (Lowe et al (2005)).

Perhaps a similar concept or framework is needed for the integration of Human Factors methods into SMS processes. This framework would address the specific concerns of SMS, and in particular stress the fact that SMS is an on-going management process, rather than an activity to 'design' or 'maintain' a suite of documentation.

This 'methodological' group of challenges is important but to some extent theoretical. There is much that can be done at the present time (without completely solving these challenges) to use Human Factors within SMS, as described in Section 6.

The next section discusses some of the 'operational' factors that may influence how a SMS is implemented.

5.2 Social and Cultural Challenges to Successful SMS Implementation

Some common barriers to successful safety management revolve around the 'people issues'. For example, the interviews reported in Brook-Carter and Leach (2006) support this view. Some of the social and cultural challenges in implementing and maintaining SMS may include:

- Lack of commitment from management or staff.
- The level of prioritisation given to safety by the organisation.
- Difficulties in finding suitably competent people to develop and implement the SMS.
- A culture that does not encourage open communication of safety threats
- Confusion regarding safety roles and responsibilities.
- Strain placed on personnel involved in SMS activities arising from projects, procedures and paperwork.
- Integrating safety management with other management systems (such as the Quality Management System).
- Problems in introducing or establishing change.
- Knowing where to start with safety management, or what to do next.

These challenges are related to the social and cultural dimensions of the SMS. As previously noted, the 'structural' and 'operational' aspects of the SMS need to work together in order for the SMS to be fully effective.

6 Human Factors Best Practice and SMS

Section 5 established the challenges faced by Human Factors in attempting to support the Safety Management Systems approach. Most notable amongst these challenges is the lack of any coherent methodological framework that could be used to combine Human Factors and SMS.

Therefore, at this point in time, the most cautious but useful Human Factors advice that could be given to Safety Managers regarding their SMS is likely to be in the form of 'Human Factors heuristics'. A heuristic in this sense is intended to mean a principle or rule of thumb that can be applied in a number of different situations in order to achieve a positive result.

This section presents some tentative Human Factors heuristics that can be used in SMS. The purpose of these heuristics is to present generic Human Factors guidance applicable to the whole SMS implementation process that would ensure safety awareness and acceptance by all in the organisation.

6.1 A 'human-centred' approach

This heuristic means that, when designing, implementing, or operating a system, those responsible should put the considerations of the people in the system ahead of procedural or technological considerations.

It is the people in the SMS that ultimately provide the safety function, rather than any technologies or procedures. Any safety procedure or technology will have been designed and tested by humans. Therefore, people already are at the centre of the SMS, and this should be recognised.

This means that the importance of human factors are recognised and applied to the design and implementation of the SMS.

Being human-centred with respect to the SMS has two further heuristics:

* Design to be compatible with people's activities and motivations.
* Involve people early in the development of the SMS.

Understanding activities and motivations recognises that human actions have a purpose. Those involved in the implementation of the SMS should ensure that they try and support the safety management goals and motivations of staff. This starts with trying to understand the activities and demands that people experience (through a method such as Task Analysis). This understanding can lead to safety management procedures that are easier for the target audience to perform, and therefore more likely to be followed.

Involving people early means that the SMS will be more effective if the people in the SMS have some say in how it is created, organised, and implemented. Ideally this should be done early in the lifecycle of the SMS.

This means that the managers, front-line staff, auditors, regulators, and others involved in the SMS should contribute to the development or update of the SMS and associated tools, methods and procedures.

While it is tempting to involve only experienced safety specialists in developing safety management activities, all concerned personnel have a valuable contribution to make to developing and maintaining an effective SMS. It should also be noted that it is never too late to involve staff in SMS; even if the SMS has been operational for a number of years, staff can be involved in updating the SMS.

6.2 Effective communication

Part of the effectiveness of the SMS depends on spoken and written communication. Communication related to the SMS can include safety process descriptions, safety briefings, training events, communications between team members or between different teams during operations or maintenance work, and emergency communications.

Communication should be timely (not occur too early or too late), relevant (relate to the correct topic), and clear (be unambiguous and use language understood by the audience).

For SMS, an important principle of the communication loop is feedback. Feedback in communication is essential for learning. Safety managers should pay special attention to the feedback (implied or explicit) that is being provided in safety management processes.

The communication principle also means that the organisation should have open channels of communication between and within functional levels. Colleagues should be encouraged to share successes, failures and lessons learnt in an atmosphere of non-judgemental cooperation. Managers should be open to feedback and criticism from subordinate staff, which should be offered in a non-confrontational manner.

The success of SMS also benefits from empowering staff with safety-related duties. Ways in which empowerment can be encouraged include:

- Using consensus decision making where appropriate.
- Taking care to adopt a transparent process using language that the target audience will be able to understand.
- Taking the time to fully explain management decisions and to clarify safety goals and values.
- Assisting employees with their safety activities and ensuring that feedback is always provided.

Employee empowerment strengthens participation, communication and personal responsibility. This allows safety improvement within the SMS to be continuous, innovative, and permanent and inspires other staff members to make their own contributions.

6.3 Appropriate rewards and sanctions

This heuristic is based on the psychology and sociology of incentives. An incentive is a response (such as a reward or sanction) by an organisation that is designed to encourage or discourage a particular behaviour.

Incentives should be appropriate, and also perceived to be appropriate by the members of the organisation.

There are important psychological factors involved in how rewards and sanctions are perceived by the individuals (for example, how an operator is treated after a safety incident report has been made). The application of Human Factors methods (such as observations and interviews) can be used to investigate these issues.

'Just Culture' is strongly related to incentives. Reason (1997) describes a Just Culture as an atmosphere of trust in which people are encouraged, even rewarded, for providing essential safety-related information, but in which they are also clear about where the line must be drawn between acceptable and unacceptable behaviour.

In order for a non-judgemental (or just) culture to emerge it is essential for senior managers to lead by example and promote the non-judgement ideal. It is vital for staff to trust that senior management truly believe in the concept.

From a safety management perspective, it is important to keep all of these facts in mind when thinking about 'human error'. Because of the innate variability of humans (and combined with the influence of the working environment), people are prone to slips or lapses at some point in time. This is unavoidable and it is important to design safety systems to take account of this by providing opportunities for the detection and recovery of errors.

It is recognised that safety managers face many challenges in introducing or maintaining a SMS (Kettunen et al 2007). A SMS can be a difficult system to 'keep alive', but an easy system to 'harm'. The SMS must adapt to changes in organisational personnel, structure, and priorities. At the same time, the safety processes must be adapted and maintained. This is a difficult undertaking but consideration of 'Human Factors' may be able to assist in this process.

The next section presents the areas for further research and the next steps.

7 Areas for Further Research and Next Steps

The previous sections have introduced the concept of a SMS, and presented a Human Factors viewpoint that can be used to understand SMS as a dynamic socio-technical system. This section will describe how this perspective can be taken forward.

7.1 Areas for Further Research

This paper has discussed some of the links between Human Factors and SMS. It has also highlighted a requirement for the following activities:

- More research into what exactly is successful (or not) in operational safety management systems.
- More research on the link between SMS and safety culture, in particular how the two concepts are interrelated and the mechanisms by which cultural factors become enablers for certain safety management processes.
- Initial research into an overall framework for Human Factors methods that is compatible with SMS processes.

7.2 Next Steps

Previous studies and practical experience have demonstrated the feasibility of considering Human Factors within Safety Assessment through Human Reliability Analysis methods (referring specifically to processes such as Hazard Identification and Human Error Quantification).

There is also some level of understanding in the Human Factors literature with regard to models of safety management systems.

What is needed at the present time is a systematic means of uniting these two perspectives into a coherent model for the integration and consideration of Human Factors within SMS.

In the meantime, some heuristics are offered in this paper to provide a way forward in the consideration of Human Factors within Safety Management Systems.

Acknowledgements
The author would like to acknowledge the contribution of the following to the ideas contained in this paper: Dominique Van Damme, Emmanuelle Jeannot, Joanne Stokes, Michael Nendick, W Ian Hamilton, Christopher Kelly, and Ian Patterson.

References
Brook-Carter, N., and Leach, P. (2006). Organisational Structures: The Influence of Internal & External Structures on Safety Management Performance. UK Maritime and Coastguard Agency.
Cambon, J., Guarnieri, F., and Groeneweg, J. (2005). Towards a new tool for measuring Safety Management Systems Performance. 2nd Symposium on Resilience Engineering, Antibes, France.

Civil Aviation Authority United Kingdom (2002). Safety Management Systems for Commercial Air Transport Operations. CAP 712.

Civil Aviation Safety Authority Australia (2006). Safety Management Systems: An Aviation Business Guide.

Dijkstra, A. (2006). Resilience Engineering and Safety Management Systems in Aviation. 2nd Symposium on Resilience Engineering, Antibes, France.

Doerner, D. (1996). The Logic of Failure: Why things go wrong and what we can do to make them right. Metropolitan Books (Henry Holt), New York.

Dougherty, E. M. Jr. (1990). Human reliability analysis - Where shouldst thou turn? Reliability Engineering and System Safety, 29(3), 283-299.

Eason, K. D. (1988). Information Technology and Organisational Change. Taylor & Francis.

EUROCONTROL (2005). Feasibility Study on Human Factors Integration in Safety Management Systems: Final Report. HFSMS/WP5.

Gordon, R., Kennedy, R., Mearns, K., Jensen, C. L., Kirwan, B. (2006). Understanding Safety Culture in Air Traffic Management. EUROCONTROL Experimental Centre, EEC Note No. 11/06.

Hale, A. and Glendon, A. (1987). Individual Behaviour in the Control of Danger. Elsevier, Amsterdam.

Hale, A.R. Heming, B.H.J., Carthey, J., Kirwan, B. (1997) Modelling of safety management systems. Safety Science Vol 26 No 1/2 pg 121-140.

Hamilton, W. I., Rowbotham, H., and David, R. (2005). Human Factors Integration in Support of Optimising Capabilities. ESAS 05, Bristol, 26th and 27th October 2005.

Health and Safety Executive (1997). Successful Health and Safety Management. HSE Books.

Hickling, N., Gaskell, L., and Clarke, T. (2005). Generic Human Reliability Assessment for Railways: Results. In: John R. Wilson, Beverly Norris, Theresa Clarke, and Ann Mills (eds.), People and Rail Systems: Human Factors at the Heart of the Railway. Ashgate.

Hollnagel, E. (2005). Human Reliability Assessment in Context. Nuclear Engineering and Technology, 37 (2), 159-166.

International Civil Aviation Organisation (2006). The ICAO Safety Management Manual. Doc 9859-AN/460.

International Nuclear Safety Advisory Group (1999). Management of Operational Safety in Nuclear Power Plants. International Atomic Energy Agency, INSAG-13.

Kennedy, G. A. L., Siemieniuch, C. E., Sinclair, M. A., Kirwan, B. A., Gibson, W. H (2007). Proposal for a sustainable framework process for the generation, validation, and application of human reliability assessment within the engineering design lifecycle. Reliability Engineering and System Safety, 92, 755-770.

Kettunen, J., Reiman, T., Wahlstrom, B. (2007). Safety management challenges and tensions in the European nuclear power industry. Scandinavian Journal of Management.

Kirwan, B. (1994) Practical Human Reliability Assessment, Taylor & Francis.

Kirwan B., Scannali S., Robinson L. (1996). A case study of a human reliability assessment for an existing nuclear power plant. Applied Ergonomics 27(5), 289-302.

Leveson, N. (2004). A New Accident Model for Engineering Safer Systems. Safety Science, 42(4), 237-270.

Lowe, C., Lock, D., Annan, B., Thompson, P., and Raistrick, P. (2005). In: John R. Wilson, Beverly Norris, Theresa Clarke, and Ann Mills (eds.), People and Rail Systems: Human Factors at the Heart of the Railway. Ashgate.

McDonald N, Corrigan S, Daly, C, Cromie, S (2000). Safety management systems and safety culture in aircraft maintenance organisations. Safety Science 34: 151-176.

Network Rail (2003). Company Specification: Incorporating Ergonomics within Engineering Design. RT/E/P/24020 Issue 1.

Perrow, C. (1984). Normal accident theory, living with high risk technology. Second edition. New York: Basic Books.

Rail Safety and Standards Board (2007). The Engineering Safety Management Handbook (Yellow Book), Issue 4. ISBN 978-0-9551435-2-6.

Reason, J. T. (1990). Human error. Cambridge, U.K.: Cambridge University Press.

Reason, J. T. (1997). Managing the Risk of Organisational Accidents. Ashgate.

The Stationery Office (2006). The Railways and Other Guided Transport Systems (Safety) Regulations 2006, ISBN 0110743075.

Transport Canada (2002). Safety Management Systems Regulations http://www.tc.gc.ca/CivilAviation/SMS/NPAs/menu.htm.

Turner, B. and Pidgeon, N. (1994). Man-Made Disasters, 2nd Edition, Butterworth-Heinemann, Oxford.

U.K. Ministry of Defence (2001). Human Factors Integration: Practical Guidance for IPTs. Issue 1, May 2001.

U.S. Nuclear Regulatory Commission (2005). Good Practices for Implementing Human Reliability Analysis. NUREG-1792.

Human Factors Safety Assurance for Changing ATM Systems

Stephen O. Clark, Steven T. Shorrock and Nic Turley
NATS Ltd.
Whiteley, UK

Abstract

The significant contribution of human error to overall system risk for air traffic management systems has been recognised for some time. It therefore follows that when changes are being made to an ATM system, an important part of the safety assurance for that system is the risk assessment and mitigation for the human element. NATS are in the process of making a number of significant changes to their ATM systems and have been applying formalised and structured techniques for the analysis of human error. One of these techniques, the human error reduction technique for evaluating systems (HERTES), is described with reference to its successful application on the recent implementation of a new control tower at Heathrow Airport. However, it is also recognised that whilst human error assessment is a necessary component of human factors assurance, in isolation it is not sufficient. A complete framework for human factors assurance has therefore been developed and is being applied across all NATS future ATM projects.

1 Introduction

NATS provides the air traffic management (ATM) service within the 'controlled' en-route airspace in the UK and at 15 of the UK's largest airports. NATS also provides the ATM service in the western oceanic region of the North Atlantic and some flight information services to pilots flying outside controlled airspace. In 2006 NATS handled nearly 2.4 million flights carrying around 220 million passengers.

These services are provided by around 1900 air traffic controllers. These controllers are supported in their task by an extensive technical infrastructure, which NATS is currently in the process of upgrading and enhancing through a £1 billion investment programme.

NATS has recently introduced into operational service a number of major new ATM systems, including:

- a new control system for the western oceanic region of the North Atlantic;
- a new control tower at Heathrow Airport; and
- electronic flight data systems at some of its airports.

NATS is also developing electronic controller tools and safety nets and is in the process of equipping a new area control centre at Prestwick in Scotland. Looking forward, NATS is currently working with various international partners to develop the next generation of operational concepts and technologies to support the 'Single European Sky'.

Before any changes are made to ATM systems, NATS undertakes risk assessment and provides assurance that the changes are acceptably safe. Traditionally, the risk assessment and mitigation processes have focussed heavily on the safety contribution of the technical systems. Robust and structured techniques to assess the contribution of the equipment to the risk have been in place and detailed safety requirements have been levied against the equipment.

However, the overall ATM system comprises both the technical equipment (surveillance, communications, flight data and support information), and people and the procedures. Moreover, history has taught us that around 97% of the most serious safety incidents occur when equipment is functioning normally.

NATS has therefore developed a human error analysis process to help assess the impact of new technical systems on the controller. This process is now at a sufficient level of maturity to allow us to apply it systematically to all our projects through our formal safety management system (SMS), and to set appropriate safety requirements to reduce the risks from 'controller error' (not just from equipment malfunction) to an acceptable level. One way of conducting this human error analysis is called HERTES – human error reduction technique for the evaluation of systems.

In this paper we describe the role of the controller in the ATM context. We then present the specific techniques that we have developed and are currently using to minimise human error in NATS operations. This is illustrated with an example of how these have been used to provide safety assurance and contribute to the success of the recent Heathrow Airport control tower project. We also describe how we are now developing more holistic human factors assurance (HFA) techniques.

2 The Role of The Human in Air Traffic Management

2.1 The ATM System

ATM systems are complex. They comprise integrated technical systems that are used by highly skilled and trained air traffic controllers to interface with highly skilled and trained pilots in accordance with structured rules and procedures. To understand the role of the controller, it is useful to reflect on the functional context in which they operate.

In general, commercial flights operate in controlled airspace. They file flight plans which indicate their proposed routings and timings from take-off at the departure airport to landing at the destination airport. The pilot will fly the aircraft in accordance with the flight plan, but must gain clearance from controllers to do so. The controllers provide the aircraft with clearances to fly in accordance with their flight plan wherever possible, but they may sometimes need to apply restrictions or alternatives in order to separate the flight from other air traffic in the airspace.

The airspace is subdivided into various regions and each region is controlled by a dedicated controller or team of controllers. They are responsible for the air traffic passing through their region of airspace and safety is assured by ensuring that prescribed minimum separation distances (laterally and vertically) between all aircraft in their airspace are maintained at all times.

In the course of a flight, an aircraft will typically cross multiple regions of airspace. The controllers must therefore also co-ordinate the transition of each aircraft between regions such that minimum required separations are also maintained at the interface, and to ensure that controllers in adjacent regions of airspace can safely accommodate the incoming flights into their own traffic flows without compromising their minimum separations.

The technical systems (comprising hardware and software) support the controllers in their task, but it is the controllers themselves who deliver the service. They formulate an overall traffic plan based on the demands of the individual flight plans of the aircraft within their region. They then deliver that plan by providing clearances to each aircraft as required.

The technical systems contain 'safety nets' but they are not 'safety interlocked' in a traditional engineering sense. A controller can issue an unsafe clearance, or a pilot can fail to follow a clearance leading to an unsafe situation, without the technical system intervening to prevent the error. Conversely, the controllers are able to compensate for errors and recover potentially unsafe situations before a safety incident occurs.

Some technical safety net systems provide automatically generated conflict alerts to the controller in the control centre, but these require the intervention of the controller to be effective. The ATM system also contains aircraft based safety nets, such as airborne collision avoidance systems, but these require successful intervention by the pilot to be effective.

Since the technical systems support the controllers in their tasks, a failure in the technical system results in these tasks becoming potentially more complex and difficult. Under such circumstances a safety incident may be more likely, but is not certain. An error by a controller may however directly result in an unsafe situation if swift recovery action is not taken.

2.2 Types of Controller Error

The types of error that controllers may make are currently grouped into four broad categories by NATS (Shorrock and Kirwan, 1999):

1. Perception.
2. Memory.
3. Decision.
4. Action.

Perception errors are where a controller fails to correctly detect, identify or recognise information which then results in their perception of a situation being at variance with the true situation (Shorrock, 2007). For example, a controller may mis-hear a faulty readback of an instruction from a pilot due to a strong expectation that it would be correct. Alternatviely, the controller may mis-identify an aircraft on the radar display due to a callsign that is similar to an aircraft nearby.

Memory errors are where a controller forgets or mis-recalls information or actions (either previous or intended) (Shorrock, 2005). For example, a controller may intend to monitor an aircraft, but forget to do so following a distraction. Alternatively a controller may believe that they have cleared an aircraft to flight level FL160, when in fact they have cleared it to FL180.

Decision errors are where the controller has access to the relevant information on which to base a decision, but misjudges the aircraft trajectory, makes a poor decision, or formulates a flawed plan. For example, a controller may clear an aircraft into conflict with another aircraft because they misjudge the required heading. Alternatively, a controller may ignore a short term conflict alert, assuming it is a false alert.

Action errors are where the controller is in possession of all the relevant information on which to base a decision, but they then simply make an error in the execution of the task. For example, an aircraft may be cleared into conflict with another aircraft because the controller inadvertently uses the wrong aircraft call-sign and issues a clearance to an unintended aircraft, which then responds to the instruction. Alternatively, a controller may intend to type "160" into an electronic flight strip but actually type "190".

An additional type of action is *non-conformance*. This is where the controller acts contrary to procedures and instructions. Non-conformances are a difficult area to consider in system development, but there are occasions where non-conformance can be predicted, e.g. where new systems require additional effort to achieve the same result.

3 Integrating Human Error Analysis into the SMS

Risk assessment and mitigation forms a key safety principle within the NATS SMS. All changes to the ATM system (people, procedures or technical systems) must be risk assessed and appropriate mitigation applied. This includes the contribution from human error.

3.1 NATS Project Lifecycle

NATS projects follow a typical project lifecycle comprising:

- Business analysis;
- Feasibility and options;
- Requirements specification;
- Design and build;

- Qualification and readiness; and
- Transition and operational use.

The opportunity for the consideration of human error to impact on the project exists throughout this lifecycle. The analysis process must therefore be aligned with the project lifecycle during safety planning.

In the early stages of a project the resources required to adequately address the impact of human error need to be considered as part of the *business* case. The earlier in the system development process any potential issues are identified the cheaper and more effective the resolutions to those issues are likely to be.

Ideally, the mitigations required against human error should be identified during the *feasibility and options* stage and articulated as part of the *requirements specification*. However, as human error is an emergent property of a system, it is often the case that the assessment of human error can only be done thoroughly at a relatively mature stage of system development.

For these reasons, it is therefore recommended that the human error analysis techniques are also applied iteratively throughout the project lifecycle. Human error identification should be revisited during the *design and build* stages of a project to ensure that previous assessments remain valid when considered against the emergent properties of the system within its context of use.

The outputs of the human error analysis process, in the form of safety requirements, must also be validated. Satisfaction must not only be proven during the *qualification and readiness* stage as part of the human factors assurance case, but also be monitored during *transition* and initial *operational use*.

3.2 Project Evaluation Criteria

The importance placed on the contribution of human error to system risk is now reflected by the requirement within NATS SMS for all projects that change the ATM system to be subject to some form of human error risk assessment. Each project must now be submitted for review by human factors specialists who will assess the changes being made for human error impact potential. Project managers are encouraged to submit their projects for review as early as possible in the development lifecycle, but all must be submitted no later than the start of the feasibility and options stage.

Initially, a project is reviewed against a set of criteria. These criteria are framed as questions covering the impact of the change on the three basic system elements (people, procedures and equipment).

People

- Will the proposed change result in a requirement for users to be trained in new skills?
- Will the proposed change result in changes to staffing levels?

Equipment

- Will the proposed change result in changes to or the introduction of new equipment (workstations, screens, input devices etc)?
- Will the proposed change result in changes to or the introduction of new HMI?

Procedures

- Will the proposed change result in changes to the design or implementation of procedures?
- Will the proposed change require the controller to do new or different tasks?

If the answer to *all* of these questions is *no* then the project is classified as having low human error impact potential and no further human error related risk assessment is carried out (unless the project scope is changed). In all other cases, the project will be assessed in more detail by appropriately qualified human factors specialists and a human error impact potential rating is assigned – either low, medium or high.

Low impact potential changes need not be assessed any further. High impact potential changes must apply the human error reduction techniques throughout the change lifecycle. In the case of medium impact projects the human factors specialists will work with the project safety manager to develop a safety plan which covers the areas of most concern for human error impact at appropriate points in the lifecycle, but the full human error techniques and involvement of human factors specialists is not mandated.

4 Minimising Controller Error due to Changes

New ATM systems may change the way in which the controllers perform their tasks. Electronic flight data systems require new data entry skills. They also change the ways in which the controllers scan, search for, store and recall information. New controller tools, enabled by the electronic data now available in the system, can change the ways in which the controller plans and manages the traffic pattern.

HERTES can be used to assess the risks from human error when changes are being made and ensure that appropriate mitigation is provided. The approach has been applied by NATS to various projects.

The method comprises a five step cyclical process that is applied throughout the lifecycle of a change to technical systems. The five steps are:

1. **understand** the change.
2. **identify** the hazards.
3. **mitigate** the risks.
4. **prove** the mitigations work.
5. **monitor** the system in service.

The most significant application of HERTES in NATS to date has focussed on the new air traffic control tower at Heathrow Airport. The new tower is required to support Terminal 5 operations and stands 87m high in a new location on the airfield. The technical systems in the tower were also upgraded and electronic flight progress strips (EFPS) were incorporated to replace the previous paper-based system. The tower went into operational service successfully on 21 April 2007.

A full safety case was produced in accordance with NATS' SMS. Consideration of human error and human factors safety issues formed a key element of the safety case and were central to the success of the project. A brief outline of the activities conducted to support the development and implementation of the tower is provided below following a description of each HERTES step.

4.1 Understand

The first step in the assessment process is to understand the nature of a change with respect to the potential for human error. The aim is to demonstrate that the changes to the system and context that may affect task performance have been examined and understood. This is a critical step because the risks affecting task performance can only be understood if the tasks, system changes, and context changes are understood.

System changes are identified via a variety of means, such as concept of operations, user requirements, existing safety cases, and individual and group consultation. The existing tasks (including mitigation and recovery mechanisms) performed by the controller are reviewed and changes to these tasks are assessed to determine how the revised system interactions might impact task performance. At this stage, it may be possible to consider task criticality, frequency, complexity, time available and time required for tasks, as these are fundamental task properties. This will generally involve some form of task analysis, but above all it is imperative that system users are consulted during this stage. Changes to the context of task performance are also identified. Such changes may involve the workstations, the user interface, procedures, task design, communications, etc. Step 1 recognises that even a seemingly minor change may significantly affect the user task when taken in context of the overall system performance.

In an airport control tower context, the controlling task involves co-ordinating aircraft ground movements and sequencing departing and arriving aircraft on the runways. At a busy airport this task is undertaken by a team of controllers. The controllers are based in a visual control room at the top of a control tower overlooking the airport. This is important as, when conditions allow, the controllers rely heavily on external visual information rather than radar displays. For the Heathrow project, two workshops were held to identify a list of changes and areas of potential impact to the users. The changes identified were as follows:

- External environment, e.g. change to location, change in height;
- Internal environment, e.g. significant changes to seating configurations for all controllers;

- Equipment changes, e.g. introduction of EFPS, new lighting panel;
- Method of operations, e.g. different methods of co-ordination between positions;
- Weather, e.g. tower may now sometimes be in cloud whilst there is good visibility on the airport surface;
- Operational roles, e.g. third ground movement controller when Heathrow Terminal 5 opens, assistants no longer involved in flight strip delivery;
- Training and experience, e.g. role of the on the job training instructors becomes more difficult due to the need to read from a screen rather than paper flight progress strips; and

Task analysis was used to describe the current controller and supervisor tasks, and to examine the safety significance of tasks and roles. This served as a basis for Step 2, identify.

4.2 Identify

Step 2 aims to identify and assess the potential human error risks associated with the changes, and set safety requirements to achieve an acceptable human error residual risk. Once the potential impacts of the system change on task performance has been assessed, the potential impact on system risk needs to be identified. This is done through hazard identification and risk assessment. In the context of human error, a human hazard is defined by NATS as 'any human action or omission that could cause, or aggravate the severity of, an incident or accident'.

The various standard hazard identification techniques used in risk assessment (e.g. HAZOP) can be adapted and employed for human error as they all fundamentally involve either a systematic consideration of error causes and effects, or a structured brainstorm of hazard scenarios. Many approaches are now available, including group approaches such as Human HAZOP, and single analyst approaches such as TRACEr - technique for the retrospective and predictive analysis of cognitive error (Shorrock and Kirwan, 2002; Shorrock, 2003). A typical human error analysis might analyse task step, error causes, context factors, barriers, frequency, severity, risk classification, possible mitigations and assumptions. One reference source during hazard identification is past performance of the system. Incident data can be reviewed to determine the types of human error previously experienced, and the frequency and severity of these errors.

The information derived is added to the project hazard log, and the process can be conducted more than once, for instance in the early, middle and late phases of a project.

Equally, significant potential benefits may also be identified at this stage, for instance human errors that are removed or reduced in risk. This can help to balance the risk assessment and provide information for use by decisions makers concerning risk tolerability.

As applied to the Heathrow project, this step involved workshops to assess first the high-level impact of each project change on each operational role, then to assess detailed impact of EFPS on each operational role.

A number of significant potential benefits were identified. These included the following examples:

- Controllers have improved views of runways and runway exit point, thus potentially reducing the risk of errors in detecting and identifying aircraft;
- The implementation of electronic and telephone co-ordination within the tower was expected to lead to more standardisation of co-ordination practices, thus potentially reducing the risk of co-ordination errors;
- The automatic update of information on slot times and stand numbers provides information earlier to controllers, thus reducing workload associated with these tasks; and
- The control room is quieter, thus reducing distractions.

Significant potential hazards included the following examples:

- The way in which departing aircraft are presented to the controller changed significantly such that delineation between aircraft 'lined up' and aircraft 'clear for take off' was less clear than was the case with paper strips. This could potentially lead to misperception of the runway status;
- New electronic systems typically increase 'head down' time, at least during earlier stages of use until greater expertise has developed. This could negatively impact situation awareness and lead to the failure to detect a conflict;
- The change in the position of controllers relative to the airfield could lead to errors in identifying aircraft; and
- EFPS afforded controllers the ability to discard an electronic strip with a single button press, which could lead to the accidental deletion of electronic strips.

While many potential hazards were raised during this step, most of these generally concerned workload, situational awareness, teamwork and communication, and specific new potential errors associated with flight data entry. Following the hazard identification workshops, the human factors team reviewed the findings and defined safety requirements for each potential human hazard identified.

4.3 Mitigate

The aim of step 3 is to specify, plan and (where appropriate) facilitate the activities to derive appropriate safety requirements. Where human hazards are identified, the attendant risks must be reduced to tolerable levels. This is achieved by ensuring that appropriate mitigations are determined as safety requirements. This poses two problems:

1. What is a tolerable level of risk?
2. What mitigations are appropriate?

The frequency and likely severity of the outcomes arising from human hazards are assessed and their tolerability determined from a risk classification matrix. Where a hazard has outcomes deemed to be intolerable then mitigations are required. The types of mitigation considered appropriate will depend on the level of risk to be mitigated and the relative contribution of the outcome severity. The types of mitigation that might be considered include:

- Equipment redesign to eliminate the hazard;
- Equipment redesign to reduce the frequency of the hazard;
- Equipment redesign to provide additional mitigation or recovery;
- Procedural changes to eliminate or mitigate the hazard; or
- Additional controller training to help reduce the frequency of, or mitigate, the hazard.

Each of these types of mitigation has different levels of effectiveness. Where the hazard has a high severity outcome or the degree of risk reduction required is relatively large, equipment design solutions are preferred over procedural or training solutions.

Eighteen human factors safety requirements were set for the Heathrow project, along with over fifty safety specifications. Specific mitigations involving design changes, procedure changes, inputs to the training programme, and performance requirements were agreed to meet the safety requirements and thus mitigate the hazards to a tolerable level.

Example mitigations are defined below for the hazards identified in the previous section.

- Changes to EFPS and training were made to ensure that air controllers were able to correctly ascertain the availability of the runway quickly and easily;
- Prior to entry into operational service ('O'date), significant training was required where controllers shadowed current operations from the new tower;
- This training also provided greater familiarisation with the new airfield position, thus reducing the potential for errors in identifying aircraft; and
- EFPS was redesigned to incorporate a 2-click process for hiding electronic flight strips from the runway bay, and to provide a dedicated retrieval button for strips dismissed in previous 5 minutes.

More generally, the hazard identification facilitated the development of realistic scenarios as a basis for simulation and training, such as unusual and high workload scenarios. The HERTES process had a significant input to the controller training programme. Controllers had to be trained in all aspects of the move to the new tower – equipment, orientation, procedures, and other transition arrangements – while simultaneously operating from the old tower. Training was achieved via a new £1.5 million 360 degree real-time simulator and a series of shadowing sessions conducted as whole or part watches, where controllers operated new equipment in the new tower while 'shadowing' the radio-telecommunications of towers working live from the old tower. Many of the hazards raised help to inform conditions and scenarios that controllers experienced in training. Similarly, much of the evidence gathered for the 'Prove' and 'Monitor' steps was gathered via training. In this way, the risk assessment process and the training programme went hand in hand.

4.4 Prove

Step 4 aims to gather evidence to provide assurance that the safety requirements have been met and that human error residual risks are acceptable. The evidence for step 4 needs to be gathered and documented to support the project safety case.

Activities undertaken during this stage will typically comprise simulation, testing or inspections with the objective of demonstrating that the human factors safety requirements have been satisfied and the specified mitigations are effective. If human factors safety requirements cannot be demonstrated to be satisfied then an assessment of the residual risk must be made in accordance with the tolerability criteria. Appropriate approvals are then required for acceptance of the residual risk.

For the Heathrow HERTES step 4, objective and subjective evidence was gathered from:

- Design changes;
- Procedure changes;
- Training inputs; and
- Outcomes from simulator training and shadowing, in terms of training team feedback and questionnaire feedback.

This activity aimed to assess the degree to which the safety specifications had been satisfied, the safety requirements had been met, and therefore the extent to which the hazards had been mitigated. Following the analysis and interpretation of the available evidence, the hazards initially raised were re-assessed in light of the mitigations, and residual risk levels were specified according to a traffic light system (red, amber or green).

4.5 Monitor

Step 5 aims to monitor task performance and context to ensure that the human error risks remain acceptable throughout a set transition period. This serves as further validation that the human factors safety requirements have been satisfied.

For Heathrow, during this stage, evidence was gathered via structured interviews and actual observations of performance via behavioral markers associated with workload, situation awareness and teamwork.

4.6 Limitations of Human Error Analysis

HERTES provides NATS with a tailored and structured process for identifying and mitigating sources of human error as change is applied to a system. HERTES delivers a clearly defined set of safety requirements against which detailed specifications can be written. These safety requirements form part of the overall requirements set for the system and can, therefore, be traced throughout the remainder of the system development process.

The safety requirements generated by HERTES provide an invaluable method for reducing sources of human error within ATM systems. It should be noted, however, that an analytical approach to the reduction of human error (e.g. through the application of HERTES and the consequent development of HF safety requirements) does not provide a sufficiently robust argument that all sources of human error have been identified and mitigated. This is because HERTES is typically only applied to parts of the system that are changing and because the hazard identification process relies upon experts to mentally construct what might go wrong. Moreover, it is not possible to prove that all sources of human error have been identified, let alone adequately mitigated.

Furthermore, a human error analysis (HEA) does not provide assurance that task performance will be acceptable. This is because HEA asks the questions:

- What errors will occur?
- How risky will they be?
- What should be done to mitigate them? and
- Have the mitigations worked?

None of these questions, either together or separately, asks "will task performance as a whole fulfil the aims of the project?" i.e. HEA focuses on the negative, on the exceptions.

A more comprehensive approach to human factors assurance (HFA) is now becoming favoured in which an analytical approach to the elimination of human error (e.g. HERTES) is *combined* with attention to a human factors framework based upon a set of established factors known to influence human performance within a system. The following section of the paper provides detail of the HFA framework that has been developed to guide human factors assurance on NATS system development projects.

5. HFA and Task Performance

The consideration of the potential for human error by users when designing new or changed ATM systems is important. However, through the application of these techniques, it has become increasingly apparent that the application of human error analysis techniques often tackles the symptoms rather than the disease. Intensive focus on human error analysis does not provide assurance that task performance will be effective (safe and efficient).

For instance, a system may be assessed as low risk from the point of view of human error, yet still suffer from poor usability and low user acceptance. Furthermore, spending the majority of human factors resource on HEA may, ironically, actually reduce the opportunity for error reduction in the design. This is because HEA generally requires a fairly developed task analysis, and such an analysis is often only available after the system (in a holistic sense) has been designed and is in a fairly developed state. At this stage, training and procedures often form the only error reduction and mitigation strategy that can be applied. This puts the burden on the controller and can remain a substantial element of through-life cost for the system's entire operational life.

For this reason, NATS is rebalancing attention to human error with more fundamental attention to task performance more generally, through design and validation. Human factors assurance techniques attempt to eliminate human errors at source. To use Reason's analogy (Reason 1997), instead of swatting mosquitoes, we are seeking more to drain the swamp.

Ensuring that the human component of the ATM system is able to perform to required standards (task performance) is the highest priority activity for human factors assurance during development of an ATM system. The objective of the NATS human factors assurance process is to provide a consistent and practical approach to ensuring that a system under development will be usable by the intended population of users, and that it will provide an appropriate level of safety and performance during operation.

The HFA approach recognises that there are two interrelated levels of assurance each underpinned by different system elements. These are:

- Task performance; supported by
- User-centred design.

These two levels together with their system elements are considered to form a triangle of assurance. This is illustrated in Figure 1 and described in this section.

5.1 User-Centred Design

A system's usability is directly influenced by its design characteristics. The principle of user-centred design is that the end solution incorporates an understanding of the needs of the people who will use it. This means that users are actively engaged throughout the project lifecycle.

However, user-centred design does not mean that the users get everything they ask for! The skill of good user-centred design is to understand the underlying user requirement, and then to incorporate this into design decisions and trade-offs which are communicated back, understood and accepted by the users.

If a user-centred design process is not followed, then there are two main risks. First, the system may be deficient in meeting the users' needs. Second, the users may reject the system. A good user-centred design process will make the entire design process more cost effective by early identification of requirements and through user buy-in.

User-centred design is underpinned by six key elements:

1. User interface.
2. Equipment design.
3. Workstation.
4. Physical environment.
5. Training.
6. Job and task design.

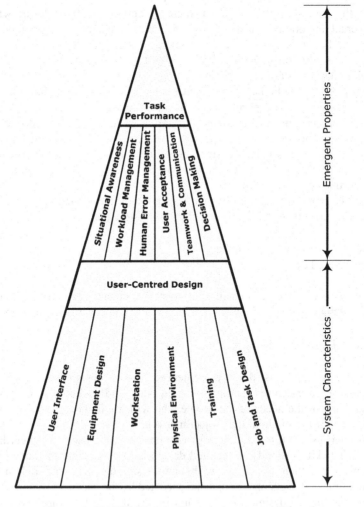

Figure 1: NATS' Human Factors Assurance Triangle

5.1.1 User Interface

The user interface incorporates everything that the user interacts with in order to use the system. For ATM this includes:

- Information on the radar display;
- Menu options;
- The layout of telephone panel buttons, and
- Flight strip design.

A poor user interface design is likely to lead to increased user errors and dissatisfaction. It can also distract the user's attention from the primary task towards error recovery tasks. Conversely, a good user interface allows the user to focus on their core tasks and does not cause unnecessary workload. A good user interface design will also be quicker to learn, thus reducing training time.

5.1.2 Equipment Design

Equipment design refers to the design of individual items of equipment such as a display or an input device. It includes, for example, the size and shape of the items, the viewing angle of a display and the visual and auditory specifications such as speaker volume.

Equipment design provides the elements through which humans can interface with the technical system. The design and selection of equipment needs to take into account the physical and mental performance constraints of the human.

5.1.3 Workstation

The workstation is the physical furniture at which the user works. It includes the working surfaces, the chairs, the desk (and any integrated items e.g. headset socket).

The workstation accommodates the equipment that the controller needs to use. If the workstation is inadequate, then use of that equipment is also likely to be sub-optimal.

5.1.4 Physical Environment

The physical environment includes all aspects of the physical environment within which the operation is located. This includes the thermal environment (e.g. temperature and humidity), the lighting environment (e.g. brightness) and the auditory environment (e.g. volume of noise).

5.1.5 Training

Training is the programme of tuition that is given to a user to enable users to perform their job. Appropriate training ensures that the requisite knowledge, skills and attitudes are available within the population of users to enable them to perform their tasks to the required level. Training is also often used as a means to ensure overall safe system performance so it is vital that the training provides users with all the skills they need to operate the system.

5.1.6 Job & Task Design

Job and task design has a significant impact upon the desire and capacity of individuals to perform. If this is inadequate it can lead to poor motivation, increased staff turnover and reduced job satisfaction. All of these factors can contribute to poor overall system performance and can increase through-life costs of a system.

5.2 Task Performance

Task performance is a function of the emergent properties of the system. These cannot be directly designed, but can be managed. Moreover, by tackling safety through task performance, this can also have the additional benefit of improving overall operational effectiveness.

We can set 'task objectives' at the beginning of the project to inform our design work. These task objectives can then be validated towards the end of the project.

Within the HFA framework, the task performance objective is underpinned by six key elements:

1. Situational awareness.
2. Workload management.
3. Human error management.
4. User acceptance.
5. Teamwork and communication.
6. Decision making.

5.2.1 Situational Awareness

Situational awareness is the integration of information to build a mental picture of the current traffic situation, and the use of that picture in perceiving events and making decisions. Within the controller community it is also sometimes referred to as 'the picture'. Situational awareness can be considered at both an individual and team level.

Loss of situation awareness is likely to lead to reduced task performance (unless that loss of situational awareness is compensated for). In particular, inadequate situational awareness can lead to controllers becoming reactive to events instead of planning ahead and they will be less able to deal with problems or unusual circumstances.

5.2.2 Workload Management

Controller workload is proportional not only to the volume of traffic but the complexity of that traffic and the extent of the controller's responsibilities. Workload is both cognitive (e.g. scanning for information) and physical (e.g. moving strips).

Workload is primarily a subjective measure and can be influenced by state of mind, experience and other factors. An important aspect is whether the user is able to perceive and respond to their own workload demands.

Both high workload and low workload can increase the likelihood of human error and can reduce situational awareness. An optimal balanced workload level is required for effective task performance.

5.2.3 Human Error Management

Human error can occur when there is a mismatch between the demands of a situation and:

- An individual's perception of the demands of the situation;
- An individual's intended response to the situation; or
- The actual response made by the individual.

Human error is in some ways necessary for task performance. Errors are unavoidable, and indeed necessary for learning, and so the system needs to be designed such that errors can be detected, interpreted and corrected or mitigated. Human error management is therefore one of the key elements of task performance.

5.2.4 User Acceptance

User acceptance is the extent to which the users accept that the system is fit for purpose. This is a complex area that is influenced by many factors (including some not under the remit of human factors). Some of the key factors that influence user acceptance are:

- The quality and quantity of user involvement during the development process;
- Peer pressure and cultural issues;
- Familiarity with the system; and
- System qualities.

User acceptance is also an indicator of the degree to which safety related issues have been appropriately addressed during the system development lifecycle.

5.2.5 Teamwork and Communication

Teamwork is a measure of how effectively a group of people work together. It is a product of many factors including the skills, knowledge and attitude of the individuals in the team, workload sharing, communication and cooperation. Ensuring the ATM system supports effective teamwork improves both the safety and effectiveness of the operation.

5.2.6 Decision Making

Decision making concerns the mental and social processes leading to the selection of a course of action among variations. The decision making process produces a final choice (e.g. an action or an opinion).

Consideration of factors influencing decision making in the design of a system can help ensure that relevant information is provided, highlighted, or emphasised to help the decision making process.

6 Conclusion

It is critical to manage the risks from human error while making changes to complex human centred systems such as ATM systems. Failure to control human error means that risks associated with the operation of the system can become intolerable.

The risks from human error must be managed throughout the lifecycle of change: human hazards need to be formally identified early in a project lifecycle; appropriate mitigations need to be specified as safety requirements and safety specifications; evidence of the safe operation of the system must be collected. This whole process contributes to the safety case for the system.

NATS commitment to managing and removing sources of human error is demonstrated by company policy that all projects that change the ATM system must be assessed for human error potential. This is a requirement of NATS safety management system. Formal and structured techniques have been developed to support this requirement, including the HERTES method which was recently used successfully on the new Heathrow Tower project.

However, NATS recognises that control and management of human error is only part of an overall approach to human factors assurance. A framework for human factors (which includes human error) has been developed and this is being applied across all NATS future ATM projects.

7 References

Reason J. (1997). Managing the Risk of Organisational Accidents. Aldershot, United Kingdom, Ashgate.

Shorrock S.T. (2003). The Retrospective and Predictive Analysis of Human Error in Air Traffic Control. PhD Thesis, Nottingham, UK: The University of Nottingham.

Shorrock S.T. (2005). Errors of memory in air traffic control. Safety Science, 43 (8), 571-588.

Shorrock S.T. (2007). Errors of perception in air traffic control. Safety Science, 45 (8), 890-904.

Shorrock S.T. and Kirwan B. (1999). TRACEr: A technique for the retrospective of cognitive errors in ATM. In D. Harris (Ed.) Engineering Psychology and Cognitive Ergonomics: Volume Three - Transportation Systems, Medical Ergonomics and Training. Aldershot, United Kingdom, Ashgate.

Shorrock S.T. and Kirwan B. (2002). Development and application of a human error identification tool for air traffic control. Applied Ergonomics, 33, 319-336.

8 Acknowledgements

The authors would like to acknowledge the immense contribution made to the development of the HERTES method over recent years by Lynn Springall of NATS, and to other members of the NATS Human Factors Group who have contributed to the human factors assurance process.

Achieving and Improving System Safety

Practical Ways of Improving Product Safety in Industry

Gabriele Schedl and Werner Winkelbauer
Frequentis AG
Vienna, Austria

Abstract

Looking at various industries it very soon becomes obvious that many safety aspects of a product usually are a result of customer or market requirements instead of an in-house based safety-oriented mindset. Producers usually behave *reactively* instead of *proactively*.

It is essential to understand, that safety needs to be incorporated into a product from the very beginning of the product design. Trying to force it onto a product as an afterthought, once the product design and development have already been completed is doomed to lead to mediocre results - at best.

There are a lot of pre-conditions increasing the difficulty to handle the safety of a product, e.g.:

- Various divisions within one company have to meet different safety standards
- One product is used in several domains
- Unequal safety and domain know-how of employees in different departments
- Last but not least, a poor safety culture. Safety has to be defined at the very top of a company and communicated to all employees.

This paper aims to discuss the role of safety in a company and how to handle increasing safety requirements from legislation and regulation and from different markets, e.g. different standards.

1 Introduction

FREQUENTIS is a producer of voice and data communication systems in many different areas, like air traffic control (ATC), public transport, maritime and public safety. Our customers are spread around the world. Most of our products are used for safety-related or critical tasks. Therefore our customers often demand or need a safety case, partly to be allowed by the authorities to "go live" with their system. This is a particular challenge for our safety work, as different standards in varying depth of compliance are to be fulfilled.

In our view, just fulfilling the required standards is not sufficient to achieve safety. At Frequentis, we are always striving to actually improve the safety of a target system, instead of merely following the standards word-by-word. The urge to develop a company-wide, safety-oriented product development strategy must emerge from within the company itself, and cannot only come out of external pressure.

2 What is Safety?

To find safety improvements we first have to answer the question: "What is safety in the true sense?"

To get a comprehensive picture, we have to split this into three sub-questions:

- What is system safety all about?
- Why is system safety necessary?
- What do we need for system safety?

2.1 What is System Safety all About?

The main objective of system safety is minimizing the risk of accidents, if possible, before they happen.

This should be done with reasonable costs by using a systematic approach. Testing safety into the system is not sufficient for achieving safety!

Beyond the most obvious and outstanding goal of saving human lives, the important benefit of real system safety also lays in saving huge amounts of money, as accidents or incidents are usually very expensive, with respect to both direct and indirect (loss of reputation, etc.) costs.

2.2 Why is System Safety Necessary?

In the past, we were faced with simple systems which included a small number of defined inputs and outputs, comprising only simple components. A single person could understand them completely and could predict failure conditions and consequences thereof.

Systems are not that simple any more. The system complexity is continuously increasing, pushing us to better understand how the system behaves. We face higher performance of single components due to increased levels of integration on chips, as well as ever higher interaction of "intelligent" systems (systems of systems). This can be seen in "simple" commodity devices (a modern mobile phone is as powerful as a supercomputer was 20 years ago) as well as in worldwide communication networks, such as the telephone system, the internet, or the various voice and data networks for Air Traffic Management, where subsystems are partly controlling each other.

Consequences of specific causal factors are often not easily predictable. Even seemingly "small" causes can result in considerable effects. This means that the system behaviour can no more be fully understood by a single person and therefore safety can no more be managed by individuals! Safety has to be performed by a systematically managed group of people in a methodical way, in order to ensure completeness and to avoid omissions.

In addition to the fact that systems become more complex, they also become more and more safety-related, as more and more processes in our daily lives are controlled by automated systems: e.g. fly and drive by wire systems, distance sensors in cars, medical devices such as pacemakers, etc. On the one hand, all these phenomena make our lives safer, as humans are replaced by machines, which tend to have a lower failure rate. On the other hand, however, the focus of safety shifts more and more from "safely operating human controlled systems" towards making the systems as such inherently "safer" by design, which is exactly the task of system safety!

2.3 What do we Need for System Safety?

Key points for system safety are:

- The commitment of the very top management of the company. This is usually expressed in a safety policy, which highlights the importance of safety, the safety culture and the responsibility of all employees.
- A structured organization-wide safety management system, comprising the safety organisation, its tasks, competences and responsibilities, trainings, a hazard tracking system, etc.
- Safety Engineering - the hands-on safety work in projects, following a defined safety process and comprising various analyses, calculations, documentation, etc.

In any safety-related role, competence takes a greater importance as systems are analysed, but there is no feedback until things fail with possibly serious consequences. This becomes even more critical as safety activities are "open loop activities", which can often not be finalised during the development of the system, while a trained safety engineering group is involved.

2.4 Requirements for Product Development

When improving the safety-oriented product development strategy of a company, the following aspects of the system in place must be considered:

2.4.1 Methodology

It is important to be in touch with the latest developments in the field. Sticking to possibly outdated safety analysis and implementation methods might reduce the quality of the output. The chosen methodology must be state-of-the-art to be in line with the technological developments of the analysed products. Regardless of how much thought one invests into choosing the methodology, the question of whether the methodology actually suits the technology can rarely be answered without any reasonable doubt.

2.4.2 Motivation of the employees

Without having highly motivated and well trained employees, even the best intentions are probably in vain.

2.4.3 Mind-set

It is important to develop and actively propagate the safety-oriented mind-set in the company, especially with respect to the question "how does one single step in a given process affect the safety of the resulting product"?

Implementing "System Safety" in a company demands a holistic approach. It is necessary for each of the employees involved in the design/production process both to possess the domain-specific know-how (i.e. "how do I build the product in accordance to the functional requirements in a way which makes sense for the user"), and to know how to do it from the safety point of view (i.e. each employee must also be well trained on the topic of "System Safety").

3 Problem Areas

3.1 One Product for Different Domains

When a product is used in different domains and/or different countries, various domain-specific requirements often have to be fulfilled, which usually generates additional effort. To make it worse, such requirements sometimes even contradict each other. Due to limited budgets caused by rather hard competition on the market, it is necessary to perform the work as effectively as possible.

3.1.1. Standards Quagmire

The choice of applicable safety standard is often one of the challenges when working in different domains. The difficulties in meeting industry standards are due to the large number of standards (refer to Figure 1) as they vary along both "dimensions": each country can have its own standard for each domain (ATC, rail, public safety ...). Thus there are so many safety standards available, some generic, and some domain-specific ones. Some of them have already been cancelled but are still demanded by customers.

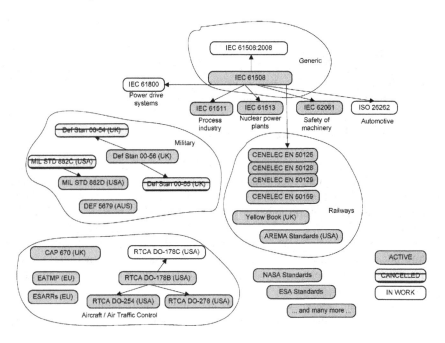

Figure 1. Standards Quagmire

3.2 Safety and Domain Know-how of Employees

It is well known that safety is a SYSTEM property. For that reason, safety always has to be considered in the context of the complete system, including not only the software, the hardware, the people and procedures, but also the environment. A system can be safe in one environment, but unsafe in another. Thus you cannot make single subsystems "safe", as most safety problems arise due to subsystem interaction (this is often referred to as "emergent system properties"). A typical example is "safe software" – a term which as such is meaningless, as software alone is always safe. It is very important to keep in mind, that the system consists of more than only hardware and software.

The system design has to be safe in the first place, but "safe" can be ambiguous for a specific system. Different usage of one system, e.g. used in different countries, domains or with different usage patterns, may have impact on the safety requirements. Therefore the employees must have extensive domain know-how to implement critical functions in a safe manner.

Some person-specific key issues threatening safety are:

- Insufficient education
- Ignorance
- Information overload

With higher education and experience people are more trained to see interrelations and are in the broad tendency more aware of consequences.

3.3 Safety Culture in the Company

There are two extremes of possible safety cultures: either the safety awareness of single persons is quite high, but organized safety is rather unknown or vice versa (as visible organised safety infrastructure sometimes causes people to completely hand over self responsibility to the organisations perceived as "being in charge").

Both extremes allow for one party (individual or organisation) to have "good" culture but are still missing the, in our opinion necessary, combination. Surely a more extremely bad position is when neither exists and a more extremely good position is when both are.

To increase the safety awareness, it is very important to define and commit to safety at the very top of the company and communicate this clearly and unmistakable to every employee!

It is essential to make people aware of the fact that

- Safety is everybody's responsibility (not only of a couple of safety specialists in a separated department, writing extensive safety documentation),
- Safety is definitely one of the core properties of a (safety-related) system, and
- Safety must be a basic requirement from the very beginning, not only a goal for the final system.

Considering safety in a company strategy can help a lot but safety is too often forgotten, as senior management do not address strategy in the context of safety.

3.4 Project Specific Problems

Projects can never be executed in the perfect environment and with the boundary conditions as inherently assumed in most of the standards and by many authorities. There are always areas of tension between the various stakeholders (customer, supplier, end-user, authorities, etc.) and gaps between theory and real life.

Some "Highlights" are:

- Tough Schedules: Many customers do not have the knowledge and experience of what tasks are possible in which time, sometimes not even within their own organisations. Due to various pressures, this often results in time schedules impossible to adhere to. To win the contract, a supplier still has to commit to such schedules, forcing him into a situation to decide where to make cutbacks. As functionality usually is the customer's main focus, these cutbacks unfortunately often affect quality and safety.

- Limited Resources: especially in the project business, where future orders are hardly predictable, companies always have to find compromises between building up sufficient resources and avoiding unnecessarily high personnel costs. In case of unexpected orders, this can lead, among many other influencing factors, to very limited resources. The effects of having limited personnel resources available for performing a required task are usually quite similar to the effects of tough schedules.

- Increasing Complexity: As detailed in the beginning, the complexity of systems is continually increasing. New technologies emerge with growing rates, the number of requirements as well as the amount of information to be processed by single persons, reaches unprecedented scales.

3.5 Lifecycle Problems

There are many different possible sources for problems with a product at any time during its lifecycle. Some of those are quite obvious, easy to understand and predict, whereas others might easily be overlooked during development, analysis, production and operation. It is often insufficient only to fulfil the requirements and to simply follow the relevant standards. Deeper understanding of the operational usage, the environment, as well as any other boundary conditions, is necessary to build a safe system.

Some typical "troublemakers" are:

- Shallow requirements analysis, leading to inadequate design concept
- Poor specification (design, components, processes, procedures, etc.)
- Improper processes (coding, manufacturing, etc.)
- Inadequate testing due to complexity
- Inadequate storage (corrosion, etc.)
- Inadequate shipping and handling, causing product damage before arrival at the customer
- Inadequate problem fixing, introducing new errors during the maintenance period

- Inadequate environment protection, as many chemicals and electrical signals can cause damage to the environment and to the long-term health of humans

These problem areas are always to be taken into account, independently of the domain or the required standards. Therefore, comprehensive safety activities are necessary.

4 Practical Ways to Improve Safety

Probably the most important questions to be answered prior to the systematic improvement of the company-wide safety culture and implementation of a respective strategy are:

- "Which safety aspects are of interest for the whole company?" and
- "How are we doing things *today*?"

We started with this internal assessment about ten years ago and defined an internal safety programme which has been continuously improved up to now.

4.1 Implementation of a Safety Management System

4.1.1 What is a Safety Management System?

What are the key issues of a safety management system?

- The approach is management led: systematic safety management starts at the top
- The scope is organisation wide: the safety manager is the focal point and driving force for the safety activities
- Everyone is responsible: this begins at the very top of the organisation and cascades down through the hierarchy
- The philosophy is prevention: safety management is not only a reactive but also a pro-active discipline aiming at minimising the risk of an accident as far as reasonably practicable
- And the theme is continuous improvement

Before implementing such a Management system we have to define the major parts:

- The reactive part, which deals with system correction after incidents and accidents (this is also called Organizational Learning) and
- The proactive part for hazard management and preventing accidents and incidents. If our systems pose risks, we must understand them; we must

assess them against tolerability criteria and reduce those risks which are not tolerable.

To be able to perform all necessary tasks within the company, a comprehensive safety management system was introduced. Its main components are briefly described in the following paragraphs.

4.1.2   Safety Policy

As it is essential that the importance of safety is understood both by the very top of the company and by all other employees, an internal safety policy, valid for every single person in the company, was written down, including a statement from the CEO about the importance of safety and his commitment to the implementation of safety.

Thus the safety department has his full support to drive changes and improvements in the whole company which are necessary for success.

It is indispensable for the management to understand that this is not only a written word on paper but represents the required safety culture and the implementation of the management responsibility!

4.2 Generic Safety Process

Having customers in various countries and domains results in many different standards which are to be followed. This can be managed with the definition of a generic safety process that comprises the basic principles of all those standards as most of them anyway differ more in wording than in intent.

The challenge is to define a solution which does the following:

- Helps to make the systems safer
- Is applicable to the respective domains and types of development
- Fulfils international standards
- Helps to demonstrate the safety of the systems, including the software, in a safety case

In the following the safety process phases, as shown and linked to the project phases in Figure 2, are briefly detailed.

4.2.1 Planning Phase

In the planning phase the customer requirements have to be assessed and the respective process and resources planning is performed and detailed in a System Safety Plan.

4.2.2   Preliminary Hazard Identification

The safety core-process itself starts with the Preliminary Hazard Identification (PHI), sometimes also called the Preliminary Hazard Assessment (PHA).

During that phase a preliminary hazard list with severities is created via brainstorming and the use of historical data and checklists. Outputs are the preliminary hazard list, including severities and hazard target rates, and initial development process integrity level allocations as detailed in various standards, e.g.: Safety Integrity Level (SIL) in IEC 61508 or CENELEC EN 50128.

4.2.3 Functional Hazard Assessment

The Functional Hazard Assessment (FHA) asks the question: "How safe does the system need to be?" considering the required functionality and the specific environmental context of the system.

A typically used technique in that phase is the Functional Failure Modes and Effects Analysis (Functional FMEA) to find all theoretically possible failure modes which then can be traced to hazards.

The preliminary hazard list is revised and safety requirements are derived.

4.2.4 Preliminary System Safety Assessment

The Preliminary System Safety Assessment (PSSA) asks the question: "Does the proposed design reach the safety objectives?"

The causes of hazards and functional failures are broken down, e.g. via Fault Tree Analysis (FTA). Other typical techniques are the Failure Modes, Effects and Criticality Analysis (FMECA) and the production of a Reliability Availability Maintainability Modelling and Prediction Report (RAM MPR), containing reliability block diagrams of the system.

This can lead to further requirements, e.g. that additional redundancy is necessary to meet the hazard target rates.

4.2.5 System Safety Assessment

The System Safety Assessment (SSA) asks the question: "Does the system as implemented achieve tolerable risk?"

All previously performed analyses are updated with the latest available data and all safety targets and safety requirements have to be verified to determine whether they are met.

4.2.6 Safety Case Report

Finally, a safety case report is produced, which is a living document which has to be kept up to date during the whole life-cycle of the system, especially when there are changes to the system or its environment.

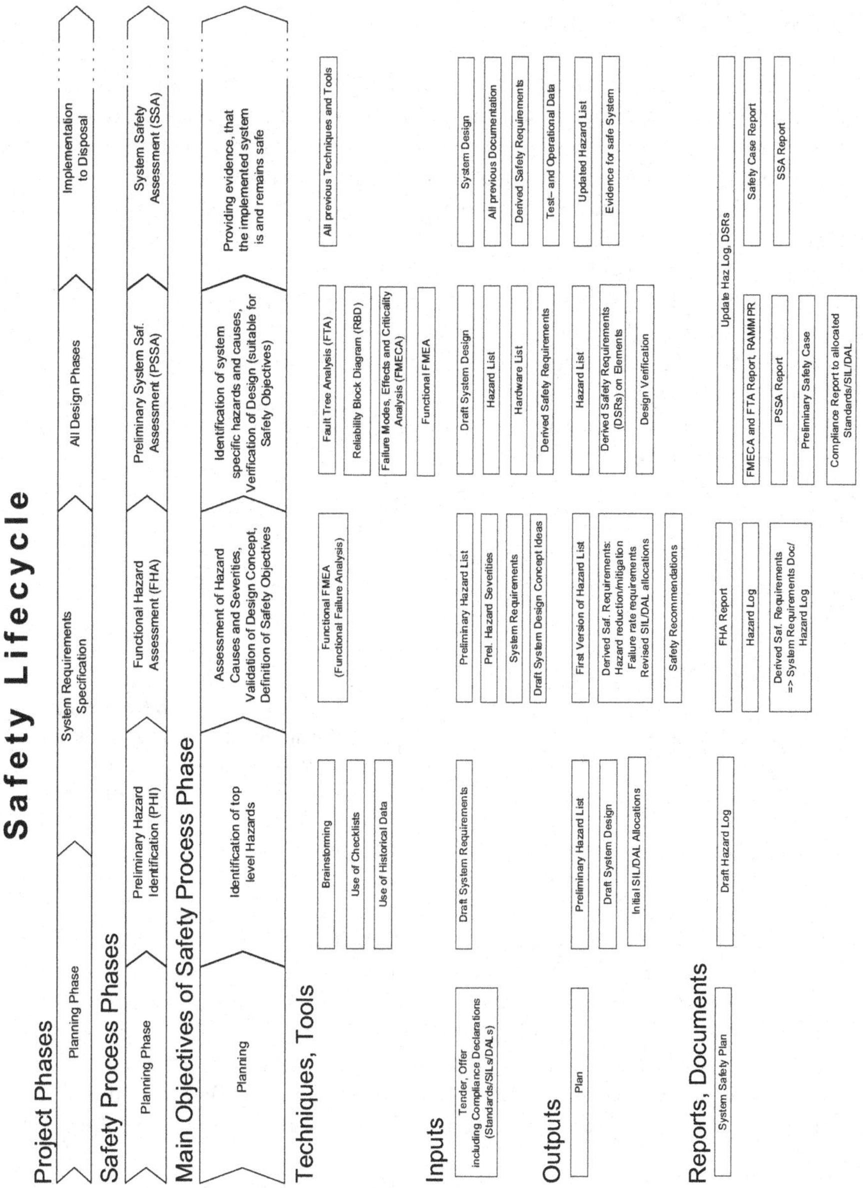

Safety Lifecycle

Project Phases

Planning Phase → System Requirements Specification → All Design Phases → Implementation to Disposal

Safety Process Phases

Planning Phase	Preliminary Hazard Identification (PHI)	Functional Hazard Assessment (FHA)	Preliminary System Saf. Assessment (PSSA)	System Safety Assessment (SSA)

Main Objectives of Safety Process Phase

Planning	Identification of top level Hazards	Assessment of Hazard Causes and Severities, Validation of Design Concept, Definition of Safety Objectives	Identification of system specific hazards and causes, Verification of Design (suitable for Safety Objectives)	Providing evidence, that the implemented system is and remains safe

Techniques, Tools

- (Planning)
- Brainstorming / Use of Checklists / Use of Historical Data
- Functional FMEA (Functional Failure Analysis)
- Fault Tree Analysis (FTA) / Reliability Block Diagram (RBD) / Failure Modes, Effects and Criticality Analysis (FMECA) / Functional FMEA
- All previous Techniques and Tools

Inputs

- Tender, Offer including Compliance Declarations (Standards/SIL s/DALs)
- Draft System Requirements
- Preliminary Hazard List / Prel. Hazard Severities / System Requirements / Draft System Design Concept Ideas
- Draft System Design / Hazard List / Hardware List / Derived Safety Requirements
- System Design / All previous Documentation / Derived Safety Requirements / Test– and Operational Data / Updated Hazard List / Evidence for safe System

Outputs

- Plan
- Preliminary Hazard List / Draft System Design / Initial SIL/DAL Allocations
- First Version of Hazard List / Derived Saf. Requirements: Hazard reduction/mitigation Failure rate requirements Revised SIL/DAL allocations / Safety Recommendations
- Hazard List / Derived Safety Requirements (DSRs) on Elements / Design Verification

Reports, Documents

- System Safety Plan
- Draft Hazard Log
- FHA Report / Hazard Log / Derived Saf. Requirements Doc/ => System Requirements Doc/ Hazard Log
- Update Haz Log, DSRs / FMECA and FTA Report, RAMM PR / PSSA Report / Preliminary Safety Case / Compliance Report to allocated Standards/SIL/DAL
- Safety Case Report / SSA Report

Figure 2. Safety Process

4.3 Software Safety Lifecycle

As more and more critical safety functions are realised with software, the software development process becomes a vital part of the safety assessment. The development standard has to provide respective evidences and comprise a rigorous System Safety Assessment (including software safety analysis) as well.

During the Functional Hazard Assessment the critical functions and system hazards are identified, which are broken down to system level and further either to hardware or software level. During the software safety analysis, potential software failures, contributing to these system hazards are identified, based on the software architecture. On the other hand, the results of the software safety analysis have to be considered at the system level as well. Therefore software safety analysis is an integral part of the system safety analysis.

Figure 3 shows the relationship of the software safety lifecycle to the safety process phases and the project phases.

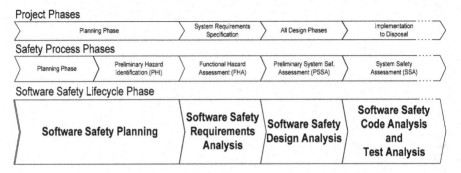

Figure 3. Software Safety Lifecycle

The development process has to be designed in such a way that sufficient evidence for the safety case is produced automatically if it is correctly followed. Analyses at system level are carried out prior to the related analysis of software, but software analysis should begin as soon as the essential input documents are available (for example a preliminary hazard list based on former experience).

The software safety requirement analysis evaluates software and interface requirements and identifies errors and deficiencies that would contribute to a hazard.

The software safety design analysis verifies that the safety-critical portion of the software design correctly implements the safety-critical requirements and introduces no new hazards into the system.

The software safety code analysis verifies that the safety-critical portions of the design are correctly implemented in the code. This is to be done during code reviews.

Finally software safety test analysis demonstrates that safety requirements have been correctly implemented and that the software functions safely within its specified environment.

4.4 Dealing with Different Domains

To make it possible to use one product base for different domains, it's important to improve domain know-how in the company.
One necessary step therefore is to determine the critical functions of a system according to the domain.

In the following an example for various uses of a Voice Communication System is given, which shows that the critical functions differ according to the application:

The product used in the maritime area has the following top level safety-critical functions:

Fct_1   Radio reception of voice
Fct_2   Reception of DSC Distress call
Fct_3   Radio transmission of voice
Fct_4   Radio Watchkeeping
Fct_5   Radio Cross Connect
Fct_6   Legacy Recording
Fct_7   Radio Remote Control
Fct_8   MOD Database connection
Fct_9   Alarm & Message Centre
Fct_10   Ship list

The product used in the civil air traffic management area has the following top-level safety-critical functions:

Fct_1   Set radio channel to "Rx"
Fct_2   Set radio channel to "Tx"
Fct_3   Radio transmission of voice
Fct_4   Radio reception of voice
Fct_5   Phone: Initiate Call
Fct_6   Incoming call indication
Fct_7   Accept call
Fct_8   Priority call
Fct_9   Terminate Call
Fct_10   TMCS - system configuration

Whereas the product used in the defence area has the following top-level safety-critical functions:

Fct_1   Radio Access : Assignment, RX/TX, PTT, SQU
Fct_2   Phone Communication, initiate, accept and terminate phone calls with call hold and call forward
Fct_3   Radio Remote Control
Fct_4   Stuck PTT handling
Fct_5   Network wide Radio access
Fct_6   Participate in Conferences, LOOP, Meetme, successive, line and preset conferences
Fct_7   Priority access to phone and radio communication resources
Fct_8   Secure non secure voice communication handling
Fct_9   Configuration and Monitoring by TMCS
Fct_10   Networkwide User/Role/Mission Management

These functions are the basis for the Functional Hazard Assessment, for the identification of possible hazards. In workshops with experts - to combine technical, domain and safety know-how - various techniques are applied. This includes brainstorming, use of historical data and functional failure modes and effects analysis to identify possible failure modes, their operational effects and the respective severity. Based on the safety-relevant failure modes, potential hazards are determined and respective risks are allocated according to the risk matrix.

Derived safety requirements are defined to reduce those risks which are not in the acceptable area of the matrix and to address safety issues emerging during discussions in the workshops. These safety requirements form a mandatory part of the system requirements and have to be fulfilled and verified accordingly.

Finally, sufficient analysis and documentation (preferably a safety case) are needed to demonstrate the fitness for purpose, i.e. that the system can be used safely in a domain under specified conditions.

Following these procedures gives us the possibility to develop products for use in the safety-critical area, even without a customer, as long as we have the necessary domain know-how.

In this way we are able to fulfil most of the safety standards, as the common requirements of the safety standards are:

- Identification of risk
- Assessment against tolerability criteria
- Definition of mitigating actions or features
- Assessment of residual risk and
- Demonstration of safety

The real objective of safety – maximise safety within the bounds of possibility – is herewith successfully addressed. Keeping in mind that safety is a system property and cannot be introduced into an existing system easily or cost-effectively; this is in our understanding the right way to achieve safety by addressing it from the very beginning of the system lifecycle on.

4.5 Company-wide Hazard Log

The main goal of the internal companywide hazard log is to act well in advance instead of reacting to problems, which is both a safety benefit and a commercial one, as we all know about the cost explosion of problem solving over lifecycle time.

The hazard log is a database containing all our systems at customer sites and all known hazards with respective data. After contract award, new projects are entered into this database. When a new hazard arises, information is gathered by the safety department and passed on to all departments which could possibly be influenced. Then the respective development department is instructed to solve the problem. Every hazard, once defined, stays in the hazard log, even if it is closed company-wide, and projects remain in it over their whole lifecycles.

Hazards are assigned to all projects or systems where they might possibly contribute to accidents. As soon as a new project is acquired, all known hazards of the corresponding product family are checked for applicability. All open hazards of the same product are automatically assigned. It is then the task of the project manager either to show that this hazard is not applicable or to implement the solution when available.

Out of the hazard log a checklist was created, asking for the root causes of these hazards. The questions are assigned to different roles in a project where development is performed. The respective employees get their questions on a sheet and have to answer these questions and return the filled-in and signed sheets before the system integration phase begins.

This serves as an aid to prevent repetition of the same hazardous errors by different people as the developers get the information and have to think about the specific problems.

It is under the responsibility of all employees to pass on all necessary information which could affect safety in any respect to their managers and to the safety department. Additionally information is controlled via the web tool ERRSYS, a company-wide error-tracking tool for all kinds of errors and incidents with an incorporated workflow for the management of these errors. This tool is mandatory to be used beginning, at the latest, with system integration.

The ERRSYS database is scanned for hazardous entries by safety personnel. All this information then serves as input to the hazard log.

4.6 Safety Working Group

The Safety Working Group regularly performs meetings with participants from different development teams, the quality management department, the manufacturing team and the safety department. Information is passed on to the management board, the project management department, the maintenance department and all heads of the various development teams.

The objectives are to enable company-wide hazard processing, to pass on and discuss information, to identify risks in development projects as early as possible, and to have an information board for results of monitoring activities and subcontractor evaluations.

One of the main goals, apart from hazard processing, is the establishment of an information network with decision making competence.

4.7 Safety Monitoring

The latest addition to the process is Safety Monitoring for development projects. The objective is to assure compliance to the agreed processes, traceability, and performance of safety reviews, achievement of project milestones in time and, in that way, to reduce the overall risk. All findings are reported to the head of the development department to give him a quick overview of all development projects in work.

Safety Monitoring is implemented mainly with the help of several meetings where the necessary development process level is determined, the implementation of the planned tasks is supervised and, finally, the lessons learned are discussed.

4.8 Safety Program for Product Releases

A comprehensive product release process ensures that products are very mature when released. Parallel to the comprehensive quality management process, the safety process starts with general safety requirements which are checked for applicability and allocated to the respective projects. It continues with several tasks, like performance of a Functional Hazard Assessment, production of a hardware RAM Modelling and Prediction Report and a Failure Modes, Effects and Criticality Analysis for a typical configuration, and the use of the previously mentioned hazard checklist. Finally all issues of the product release checklist are to be fulfilled in order to get the official release.

4.9 Safety Education

The implementation of the safety policy is supported by several internal trainings which can be accessed by every employee, comprising system safety, software quality management with focus on software safety, reliability engineering, and a special training programme called the Safety Certificate.

The Safety Certificate is an extensive training programme consisting of several mandatory and optional modules like "Foundation to System Safety", "Hazard Identification and Management", "Software Safety", "Safety Case", and an examination and an upgrade module to renew the validity of the certificate after two years.

It is intended that only those employees who hold a certificate are allowed to work on safety-critical projects.

To gain the necessary knowledge themselves, the safety specialists participate in external trainings (in the USA and Great Britain), attend safety conferences and are members of relevant societies (e.g. the International System Safety Society and the Safety-Critical Systems Club) as there are not yet many possibilities for a complete safety education in central Europe. An additional goal of these activities is the early recognition of new or revised legal requirements.

5 Conclusion

The intended goal is to maximise safety within the bounds of possibility and to determine the residual risks. Regulation and standards only may help to increase safety, but that alone is not sufficient.

It must be the supplier's own interest to make systems safe, not only on demand of regulators or customers. For that reason, an appropriate safety culture has to be developed in the company, emphasizing the responsibility of every single employee. If safety is a cultural element, it does not matter which standard or regulation has to be fulfilled for a specific project, as safety is automatically implemented as an inherent system property.

We have defined a comprehensive safety management system which helps us to make our systems safer, but we are also aware of the long way still laying in front of us. Being a growing company, with the responsibility to positively influence and develop the mind-sets of new inexperienced employees, one of the most important and challenging tasks for Frequentis is not only to make sure that the necessary domain know-how is accumulated, but also to ensure that the mind of every single member of the company is firmly set on safety as a part of the company-wide culture.

References

Winkelbauer W., Schedl G., Gerstinger A. (2006). Safety Case Practice – Meet the Challenge. In Redmill F and Anderson T (eds.): *Proceedings of the Fourteenth Safety-critical Systems Symposium, Southampton, UK*. Springer-Verlag, London, 2006

Prototyping versus Formal Development

Dr Mike Ainsworth MBCS CEng

Westinghouse Rail Systems Ltd,
PO Box 79, Pew Hill, Chippenham SN15 1JD
Tel: +44 1249 442351
Email: Michael.Ainsworth@wrsl.com

Abstract

Guidance on safety-critical development usually advocates very formal development methods, but heavyweight methods can be expensive, and on many projects informal development also plays a part. This paper looks at the advantages and disadvantages of various development styles, and discusses how they can be blended to create a methodology which is both safe and practical.

1 Introduction

Engineer: "There's a problem in our system design – the code fix is 2 hours work, but the re-certification will take four weeks."

Manager: "We can't afford to fix it – let's find a workaround instead"

This happens on projects, and it isn't making systems safer. Most long-term projects will experience some changes, either as a result of customer requirements evolving over time, or as a result of functionality being descoped due to timescale pressures. Change isn't always a sign of failure – sometimes the system is better as a result of new knowledge, but to deliver complex systems we need a safety management and development process which can cope with change.

2 Development Processes

Consider some typical development processes:

2.1 Formal V Lifecycle

Example process: Formal specification, proof of correctness, UML design with SPARK annotations, SPARK code with proof of conformance to specification, unit testing, system testing.

Advantages: High degree of confidence at each stage (zero defect methodology). Encourages each stage to be fully defined and correct before proceeding.

Disadvantages: Little visible progress early on. Long time before you get to hardware, so risk of integration issues. Desire to complete stages in order can result in 'analysis paralysis'. Requirement/design changes can create significant rework.

2.2 Prototyping

The term "prototyping" can be used to cover a wide range of different activities. In this paper the term refers to the development of software with simplified or partial functionality in order to de-risk projects (e.g. prototyping key algorithms and protocols), or "mock ups" for demonstrating proposed functionality in order to clarify requirements (especially for user interfaces).

Example process: Visual C++ (often with no documentation whatsoever)

Advantages: Rapidly build something to show to customer/management.

Able to try things out quickly. Lots of off-the-shelf code libraries to use as building blocks.

Disadvantages: May need to move to a completely different toolchain to create formal development. Difficulty of understanding the code and creating documentation after the fact.

2.3 Incremental/Agile Development

Example process: Build up functionality incrementally, using real toolchain and target hardware.

Advantages: Some functionality available early to show customer/management. Changes can be accommodated, although with a risk that re-factoring is needed.

Disdvantages: Either have lots of verification rework, or verification gets postponed until end of project. Risk that major re-design is needed part way through.

2.4 Model-based Development/Round-trip Engineering

Example process: Software specified in UML, automatic code generation, ability to reverse engineer any code changes back into the UML.

Advantages: Strong traceability between design and code. Automatic code generation reduces the likelihood of simple coding errors.

Disadvantages: If code generation includes functionality rather than just the structural skeleton the developers can end up debugging UML, and design tools are not usually designed for debugging.

Very close linkage between design and code can compromise the independence of testing and review, because the design ends up identical to the code.

2.5 A better process?

A perfect process which works for all projects is probably unachievable, and indeed it is often important to tailor the process to match the type of system being produced.

The need to de-risk complex areas and accommodate changes to requirements over time further complicates the development process, and experience is that changes and rework are often a major cost impact on projects.

All of the processes described above have their advantages and disadvantages. If we want a process which can cope with change without expensive rework, we need to look at two main factors:

- How do we design a development process which can cope with change? And

- Why is rework so expensive?

3   Where Does the Money Go?

Project Phase	Faults found (%)	Effort (%)
Specification	3.25%	5%
Z proof	16%	2.50%
High-level design	1.50%	2%
Detailed design, code & informal test	26.25%	17%
Unit test	15.75%	25%
Integration test	1.25%	1%
Code proof	5.25%	4.50%
System validation test	21.50%	9.50%
Acceptance test	1.25%	1.50%
Staff familiarisation		1%
Project management		20%
Safety management		7%
IV&V non-testing		4%

Table 1 Process Metrics for a SIL4 Development

The figures in Table 1 are taken from [1] and give a breakdown of the effort and faults found during the SHOLIS project (the pilot project for Def Stan 00-55). There are a couple of interesting features in these statistics:
1.   48% of the total effort was spent on verification activities.
2.   Designing, coding and informal testing (getting to a basic working system) was around 25%.
This suggests:
1.   When the development team claim that the system is mostly working, there's still a long way to go.
2.   Verification is a major cost driver (and therefore a good target for process optimisation).

4   Costs of Change

The figures from the SHOLIS project are based on a single pass through the lifecycle, where a well-defined system was implemented over short timescales with limited change.

If we look at the costs involved in reworking verification evidence, the costs involved can vary substantially:

Project Phase	Days per module (initial)	Rework
Specification	1.5	0.5
Z proof	0.7	5
High-level design	0.6	0.5
Detailed design, code & informal test	5.0	1
Unit test	7.4	5
Integration test	0.3	0.5
Code proof	1.3	5
System validation test	2.8	10
Acceptance test	0.4	5

Table 2 Rework Costs (estimated)

Table 2 is an estimate of the costs involved in the initial development activities and the costs of rework for a small change. The initial development cost is estimated per module by assuming 5 days to design and code a typical module and then scaling the other activities in line with the SHOLIS effort metrics. The rework costs are estimates based on experience with similar projects.

- Small changes to code can result in significant rework of verification materials – in particular unit test and proof are very fragile when things change.
- Integration and system tests may seem to require a disproportionate amount of effort, but the effort for reworking these activities tends to be fairly fixed regardless of the number of changes involved. Unless there are major changes to functionality, the system validation tests are usually a fixed amount of time dictated by the time taken to run the tests.

In Figure 1 below we extrapolate the rework costs for changing a number of modules.

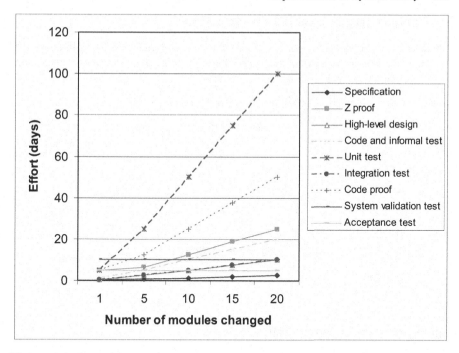

Figure 1 Estimated rework costs

Acceptance and validation testing tend to be a fixed amount of time regardless of the number of small changes. Unless changes are major the impact on these high-level tests is negligible.

Coding and unit testing activities are linear with the number of modules changed. Since code proof is partially automated it is assumed that only half the changes would affect the proof.

For specification and Z proof it has been assumed that 25% of code changes would affect these activities.

One factor which significantly changes the equation is the level of automation. Automated techniques such as static analysis and model checking may need a complete re-run when the system changes, but because the analysis is completely automated, the costs involved are negligible. Although automation can be very beneficial, there is a need to ensure that any verification activities are applying some form of independent checking, and not simply testing the code against itself. The advent of automatic code generation and round-trip engineering sometimes results in projects where the design and code are effectively identical, so code-level tests and reviews become largely meaningless.

Since change seems to be inevitable on most major projects, the question becomes "how do we make our verification cost-effective, and minimise the amount of rework?"

5   Architecture-based Development

Which parts of the system specification do we need to define first? Architecture and interfaces define the fundamental shape of the system, the technology, and often define the relationships between project teams.

Consider a (very simplified) train protection system:

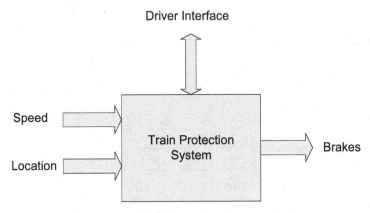

Figure 2 Simplifed Train Protection System

There are a number of difficult requirements areas that will need to be defined (e.g. under which circumstances the brakes are applied). A high-level view of the functionality seems simple:

"Apply the brakes if the speed is too high, or if the train will be unable to stop before a dangerous location."

In practice, the functional specification becomes more complex:

- Do you design the system to stop safely under worst-case braking conditions or average braking conditions?

- Do you allow for sensor inaccuracy?

- Is the driver allowed to override the system?

These issues need to be understood and agreed prior to final acceptance test, but can (and usually do) change during the course of the project without major impact. Many of these decisions involve complex trade-offs between safety, performance and usability which cannot easily be established at the start of a project. Very formal development methods sometimes lead you into defining these details at the start, in which case either the specification will be wrong, or it will take so long to produce that the project gets cancelled. (Or the critical factors are left as user configurable data, thus moving the problem on to the customer).

The basic system architecture (and many of the technology decisions) are often driven by safety and RAM considerations (and cost!) rather than detailed functionality:

- Do we need redundancy? (or diversity?)

- What SIL are the functions being implemented?

- How often do we need to sample inputs?

- What reaction time do we need?

- Do we need to read back outputs?

These basic architectural constraints are often independent of minor requirements tweaks. From a project management perspective, small changes in one area are manageable, changes which impact across other systems or projects can cause major problems. Boehm [6] estimates that 80% of rework comes from 20% of defects, and that the major rework tends to be caused by defects which affect the architecture. To control the impact of change across the system, we need to define:

- Interfaces (both external and internal) under normal and failure conditions, and

- Information flow through the system.

An architecture-based approach would therefore concentrate initially on how the interfaces worked (What is the valid range for speed? How often is it updated?), how information flows around the system (e.g. the braking function will be based on speed and location, and probably modified by some settings on the driver interface), and leave the precise details of the functionality to be defined as the development progresses.

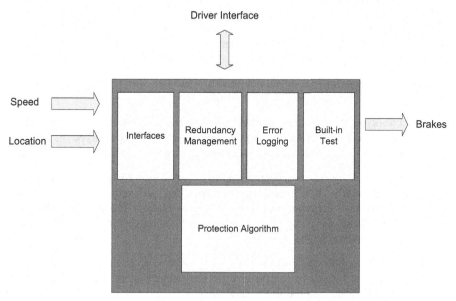

Figure 3 Architecture of a Train Protection System

If we get the architecture right, then we can make changes to the system functionality without having wide-ranging impact on the code. At the start of the project, the requirements need to be good enough to define the project scope and the basic nature of the system, but don't need to define every detail.

At lower integrity levels there is an increasing use of COTS components such as real-time operating systems and single-board computers which provide some pre-existing elements of an architecture. However COTS systems rarely provide all the features necessary for a safety-related system (or if the features are available they often require extensive tailoring).

For safety-critical systems where COTS components are not viable the architecture can have significant cost and complexity impact. For example, Johansson [4] looks at a number of different possible architectures for a train braking system and argues that a triple-modular redundant system is often overly expensive for mass production systems. Even if we try to reduce the hardware costs, we still have to meet onerous RAMS targets.

Having a clear understanding of the architecture provides an environment which is resilient when changes are made, but as an additional benefit, the architectural interfaces often define the boundaries between different teams within the project. Getting the architectural interfaces defined early on allows teams to work in reasonable isolation, so that changes in one area shouldn't impact other teams. The architecture provides the mental roadmap that everyone uses to navigate around the system.

It is also worth noting that architecture is one area where safety-critical systems tend to be different from mainstream software development, both in terms of gross factors such as redundancy and more subtle issues such as robust error handling and diagnostics. This can result in people underestimating the amount of work involved in getting a safety-related system working reliably and safely.

Prototyping and incremental development can work well with an architecture-based approach, provided that we follow some simple principles:

- Prototype with the real hardware if possible, otherwise you run a risk of major integration problems late in the project. If you prototype on a PC, at least make the software architecture realistic to reduce migration problems.

- Always design the *whole* architecture, even if you are going to implement incrementally. For example, error handling and redundancy should be present in the architecture from the start even if the precise behaviour hasn't been defined. Adding architectural features later on will require major changes to the system.

- The exception to all this is when prototyping is used to create non-functional mock-ups (e.g. user interfaces) where there is no possibility of the code being re-used in the final system.

6   Prototyping the Process

One of the risks with prototyping is that sometimes the only tool used is the compiler, leaving a large number of verification tools and methods to be implemented at the tail end of the project. This can result in poor quality software (i.e. works most of the time, but lacks resilience) and substantial pressure to only make minimal changes during formal verification, which can reduce the effectiveness of the verification techniques, and hence reduce the effectiveness of removing systematic errors.

A good way of dealing with this is to prototype the process, as well as the system. We can make sure that all the tools and techniques are working by applying them to samples of code during the prototype phases. Although tool vendors often claim that their tools work out of the box with minimal training required, in practice, new tools can need careful tailoring and some experimentation to find the best way to use them.

Although the full verification process will not be applied during prototyping (to avoid nugatory work), there are areas where it is sensible to apply some verification. High-impact design decisions should be reviewed – in particular, the architecture should be assessed to make sure that it is adequate to support the end system.

Techniques which are either highly automated (e.g. static analysis) or which require relatively little time (e.g. code reviews, system tests) can be applied as we go along because they are relatively lightweight to maintain. Assessments of verification techniques [2,5,6] have consistently found that code and design reviews are one of the most effective techniques for verification with Boehm giving a median level of 60% fault detection. Using a combination of directed reviewing against high level requirements using scenarios and checklists for common low-level mistakes can increase this to close to 90%. Increasing levels of automation, and mechanised formal methods techniques [3] can make more complex verification feasible to do as we go along, but care is need to ensure that the verification is of benefit in reducing systematic errors, and not simply proving the code against itself.

System tests will evolve as the system changes, but the maintenance overhead is usually reasonably small. Techniques which are heavily tied to the code and which require cumbersome manual analysis (e.g. unit testing) are better left until the code is stable. Although the traditional approach suggested in most safety standards is to use a bottom-up test strategy, experience on a number of projects is that unit testing is a substantial cost which tends to only find fairly minor problems (or finds a potential fault which could be hazardous under circumstances so unlikely that they may never occur). Integration and system testing on the other hand tend to find more serious faults which result in operational problems or serious hazards. One approach which has been used successfully on some WRSL projects is to measure code coverage during system-level tests. Well-written black-box tests typically give around 70% code coverage. Assessment of the uncovered code finds that it is usually either:

- An unusual but realistic path (in which case we can add more test cases at system level)

- Defensive code which can't be easily triggered at system level (in which case we leave it for unit testing)

- Complex algorithmic code where the full set of paths are too difficult to cover with system tests, or where there are complex interactions with data – in this case unit testing is probably the best approach for this area of the code.

- Unreachable code (left over from previous functionality, or provided to support future applications). This can be removed or justified as appropriate.

Verification techniques also need to be applied early enough in the development lifecycle to have an effect, even if only on a sample of the code. For example, if coding standards specify layout or style guidance, then it should be checked early on, at least for samples of code – at the end of the project the pressure to deliver will be so high that stylistic issues will stand no chance of being implemented, to the detriment of future maintenance and support.

If every tool and process has been applied at some point during the prototype development, then the eventual formal verification will be de-risked, and some realistic metrics will be available to allow verification activities to be planned.

7   Where does Safety Management fit in?

The safety management process for the project has to be adjusted slightly from that described in safety standards such as IEC61508 to reflect the fact that some important details will not be known at the start of the project, but will be defined as the project progresses. We need to distinguish between factors which have to be defined at the start of the project, and factors which need to be defined at some point, but which can be allowed to resolve themselves over time. A modified lifecycle is shown in Figure 4.

The initial system requirements need to be sufficient to give a clear scope for the project, but don't need to be detailed enough to be testable or to completely define the functionality.

Hazard analysis then has to be sufficient to confirm the basic nature of the safety issues involved and the SIL of the functions to be implemented. These factors will have a significant impact both on the architecture of the system, and on the processes to be followed. Even though many functional details may be unclear at this point, we can define the architectural safety requirements.

The development and verification processes may need to be tailored to fit the type of system being developed. The preliminary safety analysis needs to identify any specialist verification techniques that are required (e.g. do we need timing analysis of the software?) so that these techniques can be trialled during the early stages of the project.

Once the basic architecture has been designed, it can be reviewed to make sure that it is fit for purpose. As the basic architecture begins to take shape, early integration tests can be applied to verify that basic connectivity and performance is as expected.

In addition to defining the architecture, there are also a number of common tactical policies which will be used throughout the system and which need to be defined at this stage if the system development is to be consistent. The common tactical policies will cover issues such as memory management, error handling policy, locking of resources etc. in both normal operation and failure conditions.

An additional benefit of formalising the architecture early on is that it also formalises the interfaces between different project teams. Experience suggest that safety problems tend to occur at boundaries – not just system boundaries, but also boundaries between teams where potential misunderstandings can arise. Formalising the interface definitions early on hopefully minimises this, or at least provides a clear mechanism to manage problems.

The main functional development then proceeds incrementally on top of these foundations, gradually increasing the amount of functionality available and refining it in response to system testing.

During this main part of the development, the safety engineer has to keep track of the evolving functionality, and ensure that safety requirements are defined or updated as necessary. Having good traceability between the safety analysis and the requirements/design documentation is useful for this, although the level of formality for the traceability often starts off fairly basic and becomes more detailed as the system develops.

The system will be subject to code/design reviews and as much automated analysis as possible (e.g. static analysis). Testing will concentrate on system level tests with some more detailed testing for complex or high-risk areas. The safety engineer can look at the results of these activities to identify any general quality issues, and any significant points can be used to update the process. For example, early application of static analysis tools often identifies systematic nuisance errors which can be avoided by tightening up the coding standards.

Any remaining areas which require detailed module testing will then follow on once the code is complete and stable.

The final version of the code will then be subject to formal validation tests and any other final assessment required to produce the safety case (e.g. vertical slice analysis – checking the traceability of sample requirements through to implementation and verification).

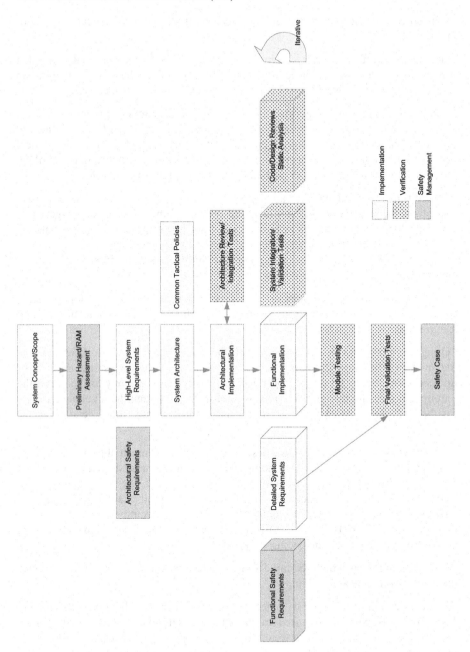

Figure 4 Architecture-based Lifecycle

8 Conclusions

Very formal, waterfall-style, development works well on short projects with very clear goals and familiar technology. It doesn't react well to changes, and can sometimes create 'analysis paralysis' as developers try to nail down every last detail.

At the other end of the spectrum, prototyping can be an important strategy on many projects, but completely uncontrolled prototyping can result in systems which are uncertifiable without major re-design.

Architecture-based development provides a framework which accommodates change and allows a system to be developed incrementally. Detailed design decisions can be deferred if they don't impact on the overall architecture, but safety and RAM requirements which have a major impact are factored in from the start (a major de-risking factor).

Prototyping and early development should include prototyping the process as well as building example systems. In the early stages, verification should concentrate on techniques which are cheap, effective and easily maintained – saving the difficult and expensive techniques until the code is stable enough to avoid substantial rework costs.

Requirements and detailed functionality have to be correct at the point when a system is delivered, but the architecture has to correct all the way through.

9 References

1. Steve King, Jonathan Hammond, Rod Chapman, Andy Pryor, *Is Proof More Cost-Effective Than Testing?*, IEEE Transactions on Software Engineering, Vol 26 No 8, August 2000.

2. Jorgy Rady de Almeida et al, *Best Practices in Code Inspection for Safety-Critical Software*, IEEE Software, May/June 2003.

3. Allan Wassyng, Mark Lawford, *Software tools for safety-critical software development,* International Journal on Software Tools for Technology, 8(4/5): 337-354, 2006.

4. R Johansson, *A fault-tolerant architecture for computer-based railway vehicle brake systems,* Proc. Instn. Mech. Engrs., Vol 218 Part F, 2004.

5. Robert L Glass, *Inspections - Some Suprising Findings*, Practical Programmer, Communications of the ACM, April 1999.

6. Barry Boehm and Victor R Basili, *Software Defect Reduction Top 10 List*, IEEE Computer, January 2001.

Systems Approach to Unmanned Air Vehicle Development and Certification

Richard Sleeman, Andrew Cox, Jenny Colledge
BAE SYSTEMS, Autonomous Systems and Future Capability(Air)
Warton, UK

Abstract

It is widely recognised that Unmanned Air Vehicle Systems are the next evolutionary step for aerospace usage, taking on roles that are too dull, dirty or dangerous for manned aircraft. Major strides have been made in recent years in developing these systems. However, whilst the military has been successfully using UAVs in combat environments, certification issues have so far prevented exploitation these systems, in any significant way, for commercial or state roles. Even in military roles, the need to fly over populated areas and in airspace alongside other airspace users is recognised.

This paper outlines the UAV developments of BAE Systems and, in particular, outlines the challenges, approaches and progress in flight certification of UAVs.

1. Introduction

It is widely believed that Uninhabited Air Vehicle Systems are the next evolutionary step for the Aviation Industry. There has been an explosion of effort on UAVs, with more than 30 nations currently developing and manufacturing in excess of 250 models, operating approximately 80 types of UAV, and covering a wide range of system performance factors including speed, altitude, mission duration and payload capability. Whilst the military has been successfully using UAVs operationally for some time in limited roles, it has not been possible to exploit these systems for commercial or state applications or even to fly military aircraft in transit flights through un-segregated airspace. This is mainly due to certification and qualification issues.

This paper discusses the challenges, approaches and progress in flight certification of UAVs and outlines some of the recent work undertaken by BAE Systems in this area. The details in this paper have been derived from BAE Systems Autonomous Systems and Future Capability (Air) business at Warton in conjunction with its partners BAE Systems Australia IAS (Integrated Autonomous Systems) and BAE Systems Insyte.

2. Background

There are a huge range of UAVs in development, from machines weighing a few grams to vehicles the size of a Boeing 737.

At the lower end of the scale, the differences between UAVs and model aircraft are hard to define. High technology is accessible and available to all and regulation is limited, at least, for small vehicles. With none of the constraints of having a human onboard, there are opportunities for new capabilities, configurations and lower risk deployment of new technologies. It should be of no surprise that universities have proven to be a hotbed for UAV development. Regulations for small UAVs very largely mirror those for radio controlled aircraft and are currently governed by national authorities. In the UK, operation of such vehicles is limited to flights below 400ft and within sight of the operator. However, as an example of what small UAVs are capable, Aerosonde have flown a 13kg UAV across the Atlantic[1].

At the top end of the range, Global Hawk, has a wing span of nearly 40m and an unrefuelled range of over 20000km[2]. In most respects, this class of UAVs is just like a manned aircraft.

Of course, the major difference between a conventional aircraft and all UAVs is the lack of a pilot on board. It is often remarked that large airliners "pretty much fly themselves" these days and it is true. So what does the pilot do? Consider the pilot's role in fault detection, where the pilot might

- Detect a fault (for instance, through aircraft handling)
- Locate the fault (maybe by looking through a window)
- Diagnose the cause of the fault
- Prognose whether the fault is likely to be critical soon, or if the mission can continue
- Decide on the course of action
- Communicate the problem and any action to Air Traffic Control, an airfield or other air users
- Take responsibility for the consequence, such as continuing a flight of an impaired aircraft

Some of these faults are fairly predictable, some are not. A bird strike is a classic case of an unpredictable event; a low flying military aircraft might encounter one or more birds at any time; the damage might be anywhere on the aircraft and might be negligible or potentially catastrophic. The pilot has to decide whether he is safe to carry on, to divert or, where possible, to eject. Replicating these processes on a UAV requires considerable effort. The adaptability of a pilot to make difficult decisions, often based on incomplete and diverse information sources, and then take responsibility for those actions is hard to replace.

---

[1] http://www.aerosonde.com/drawarticle/4
[2] http://www.northropgrumman.com/unmanned/globalhawk/techspecs.html

A number of studies over the years have considered what would be needed to enable UAVs to operate routinely in a similar manner to manned aircraft. These have identified a range of technology, regulatory, procedural and social/political barriers.

Technical challenges include:

- Sense & Avoid other air traffic
- Safe separation from other air traffic
- Dependable and secure communications for command and control
- Provision of suitable radio bandwidth for command and control and mission systems
- Providing the ability to dependably monitor, comply and respond to Air Traffic Control instructions & rules (including avoidance of prohibited airspace)
- Dependable Emergency Recovery (including forced landings)
- Management of faults to a similar level afforded by pilots of manned vehicles
- Automatic take-off and landing systems
- Weather detection / protection
- Auto Taxi
- Interoperability with other UAVs
- Autonomous behaviour/ decision making
- Man-machine interface
- Obstacle/ terrain avoidance (if low level flights required)

Regulatory developments - since current regulations often assume solutions with a human onboard - developments include:

- Design and Production Approvals
- Tailoring of existing manned regulations for UAVs

Procedures/ Training aspects include

- ATC / Aerodrome requirements
- Licensing of UAVS operators, pilots, commanders and ground crew
- Security of ground station, communication links, etc to prevent disruption of UAVS operator (eg hijacking), whilst controlling flight

Social/Political issues include;

- Product Liability
- Public Acceptance
- Export legislation

A number of projects are underway to address these issues. BAE Systems has been active in a number of the working groups, including the JAA[3] UAV Taskforce, the UK ASTRAEA programme and the ASD[4] UAV Certification and Qualification Working Group. ASTRAEA[5] is a UK national programme that focuses on the technologies, systems, facilities and procedures that will allow autonomous vehicles to operate safely and routinely in the UK. Involving some of the largest defence companies in Europe, research associations, regional bodies and UK Government departments, the ASTRAEA programme is breaking new ground in areas such as Collision Avoidance, UAV Fault Management, Decision making and autonomous re-routing as well as tackling regulatory issues. EUROCAE[6] Working Group 73, involving European industry and regulators, is currently developing UAV regulatory proposals and standards.

3. BAE Systems' Demonstrators

BAE Systems has also been active in demonstrating UAV technologies, flying its Raven, Corax and Herti systems in the last few years.

Figure 1. Raven demonstrator

---

[3] Joint Aviation Administration
[4] AeroSpace and Defence Industries Association of Europe
[5] Autonomous Systems Technology Related Airborne Evaluation & Assessment
[6] European Organisation for Civil Aviation Equipment

Raven, shown in Figure 1, was first flown in 2003, and demonstrated

- Advanced flight control systems for novel air vehicle shapes to create highly survivable, strategic UAV systems
- Rapid engineering - 10 months from start of project to 1st flight
- Fully autonomous flight from take off to landing

Corax, Figure 2, an ISTAR[7] weapon system demonstrator, again was developed in a short timescale (10 months from start of project to first flight).

Figure 2. Corax demonstrator

It was flown in early 2005, and demonstrated;

- A long endurance configuration
- Highly advanced low cost composite technology
- Advanced FCS technology to control this 'next generation' jet powered vehicle

Both these UAVs were designed to fly on a test range. However, the third BAE Systems UAV, Herti is going further.

The initial version of Herti, Herti D, benefited from using common systems, power plants and ground stations with other BAE Systems UAV programmes. Recognising that the airframe requirements for a long endurance UAV were essentially the same as a glider, Herti D was developed using the structure from a commercial motor-glider and had its first flight took only 7 months after initiation of the concept.

---

[7] Intelligence, Surveillance, Target Acquisition, and Reconnaissance.

Figure 3. Herti demonstrator

A more developed prop-driven version of Herti flew one year later, this time in Macrihanish in Scotland, achieving the first fully autonomous mission of an unmanned aircraft in UK airspace.

Figure 4. Herti demonstrator

All of these vehicles were flown in airspace segregated from other air traffic and over unpopulated ground. In the terminology of the UK Civil Aviation Authority's CAP 722 document (Civil Aviation Authority 2004), this is referred to as Group 1. The other groups from CAP 722 are shown below

Group 1: Range
Those intended to be flown in permanent or temporarily segregated airspace (normally a Danger Area) over an unpopulated surface (normally the sea following 'clear range' procedure.

Group 2: Segregated Airspace
Those intended to be flown in permanent or temporarily segregated airspace (normally a Danger Area) over a surface that may be permanently or temporarily inhabited by humans.

Group 3: Uncontrolled Airspace
Those intended to be flown outside Controlled Airspace (Class F & G) in the United Kingdom Flight Information Region (UK FIR).

Group 4: Controlled Airspace
Those intended to be flown inside Controlled Airspace (Class A-E) in the United Kingdom Flight Information Region and United Kingdom Upper Information Region (UK FIR and UK UIR).

Group 5: All Airspace Classes
Those intended to be flown in all airspace classifications.

Figure 5. CAP 722 groups

3.1. Groups 1 & 2

Test range flying removes the safety burden from many aspects of the vehicle and its systems and allows many aspects of UAV systems and operations to be developed and demonstrated, for example:

- Operating procedures
- Autonomous operation
- Sensor and mission systems.

By creating the conditions to rapidly develop, test and refine the operating characteristics of the system through experience, BAE Systems has been able to bring Herti to a level of maturity within only a couple of years.

The basic principles of the safety case for Group 1 flying were;

- An assumption that the probability of loss of vehicle is 1
- The range is sterile, therefore the probability of loss of life is 0
- The vehicle must be prevented from leaving the range segregated airspace in order to maintain the probability of loss of life at 0.

Critical to the safety case for operating any vehicle on a range is the Flight Termination System (FTS). The FTS is designed to terminate the flight of the vehicle within the range on command from the ground, thus preventing the vehicle leaving segregated airspace. The FTS is designed as a separate system and is the principle focus of any safety argument, specifically, the loss of communication with the Ground Control Station, determining the termination boundary such that no vehicle debris can exit the range, and ensuring that there are no dormant failures in the FTS.

Over the last year or so Herti has been developing functionality and expanding its flight envelope. However, the next step in terms of flight clearance is to tackle Group 2, i.e. flight over populated areas.

For Group 2 operation a few issues are immediately clear:

- The prime tenets of the Group 1 safety case do not hold; even over a lightly populated area, there is a finite probability of loss of life, so the probability of loss of the vehicle must be much less than 1.
- Since Group 2 still requires sterilisation of the airspace, the vehicle must still be prevented from leaving the segregated airspace. However a simple "cut-down" termination system cannot be used due to the danger it poses to personnel on the ground.

The safety philosophy for the UAV, therefore, changes between Group 1 from Group 2.

In principal, the requirements for flight clearance of UAVs over populated areas should be no different to those for manned aircraft and certification authorities have declared equivalence to manned aircraft as their core tenet for UAV clearances. One of the major challenges for UAVs certification is how to translate this into hard requirements. Manned aircraft have firm, long established regulations, formed over the course of the last hundred years, learning often from flight incidents. Such regulations do not yet exist for UAVs, so the emerging industry is faced with defining standards and regulations at the same time as trying to meet them.

A number of technical issues have to be addressed in taking on a Group 2 clearance, including;

- Selection of an appropriate Certification basis
- Identification of acceptable failure metrics
- The level of autonomy, from remote pilot to fully autonomous system
- Availability of RF Bandwidth
- The complexity of the system

3.2. Certification Basis

Traditionally, UAVs have been developed and certified against military requirements. However, the utility of UAVs, such as Herti, makes them equally attractive to both state operators (such as the Police, Customs and Excise, Fisheries protection etc.) and civil operators. So, the choice between Military and Civil certification is partially influenced by the business need to be able to offer the system to a number of disparate customer groups. Although military certification is natural AS&FC[8] home ground, a military clearance is difficult to transfer to a civil customer base and potentially needs changing for each application. Civil certification is however readily transferable between civil and state customers and should be reasonably transferable into the military domain (i.e. Herti use as a civilian reconnaissance asset is not significantly different from any military role). Hence, the preferred approach within AS&FC for Herti is to follow a civil regulation approach.

At the present time, two regulators need to be considered in the UK, the Civil Aviation Authority (CAA) for state operated and experimental systems and the European Aviation Safety Agency (EASA) for general civil certification.

Since there is not yet a Certification Standard for UAVs, the nearest manned equivalent must be selected as the basis for certification. CS-23 (EASA 2003) has been selected as the "closest neighbour" for Herti, based on its size, kinetic energy, capability and intended use. However, just as for sophisticated manned aircraft, special conditions must be agreed for UAVs. These represent deviations from the baseline specification, which was written around a plane with control rods and a pilot. Analysis suggests that about just over half of the paragraphs in CS-23 are directly applicable to UAVs.

Deviations range from canopy regulations to survive bird strike through to requirements for cockpit displays. In the canopy case the requirement is redundant

---

[8] Autonomous Systems and Future Capability (Air), BAE Systems Warton

and AS&FC would propose to the regulator that compliance is not required. For the cockpit display however there is an argument that the requirement should be transferred from the air vehicle to be a regulation against the ground station.

Therefore AS&FC would expect to show compliance to the CS across the entire UAV system and not specifically against the vehicle. This is conventionally done by use of the Acceptable Means of Compliance (AMC) document (EASA 2003) published by the regulator, in this case EASA. AS&FC have assumed that the AMC can be directly translated to apply to the Ground Control System (GCS). For example AS&FC shall use the DO178B (RTCA/EUROCAE 1999) standard for critical software in the GCS, as would be used for software on board a manned aircraft.

4. Failure Metrics

Manned aircraft regulations ensure acceptable levels of fatalities and injuries for aircrew and passengers. However, what happens when you don't have occupant on-board? Current regulations for manned aircraft generally don't define requirements for injuries or fatalities of over flown third parties. The general assumption is that if we minimise the risk of catastrophic loss of the aircraft and the risk to people onboard, that the risk to people off-board must be acceptable. By and large we don't segregate catastrophic loss of vehicle from loss of life. For a UAV, this is clearly incorrect since it is quite conceivable that we might be willing to accept loss of the low cost vehicle in some circumstances. However, we cannot accept a consequent loss of life. Agreeing an acceptable risk to third parties and the criteria by which we judge it, remains the subject of debate.

5. Control and Autonomy

Intimately intertwined with the UAV system is the level of control. Expanding on the cockpit displays issue, if the vehicle is remotely piloted then the UAV operator will need all the information that a pilot would expect within a cockpit. This should be extended to include those cues that are not provided to the pilot via instrumentation, for example vibration and engine noise as these are invaluable aids in retaining situational awareness of the aircraft state.

Alternatively, a vehicle such as Herti without a manual pilot which operates autonomously requires a control interface that is not a direct read across from its manned pilot equivalent. In these cases the UAV operator has a different level of control and the instrumentation required on any display is therefore different. The strict requirements of CS-23 or any of the other CSs may need interpretation and agreement with the CAA to ensure that the compliance against the code does result in a safe system.

These new issues will, again, have a great deal of bearing on how the system is operated. If a manual pilot is removed then compliance is relatively straight forward but this creates a dependence on the communications link to be available 100% which is almost certainly not achievable. Also the advantages of using a UAV in this role rather than a traditional manned vehicle seem minor.

If, however, the UAV is to operate autonomously then the relationship between the UAV operator and the vehicle will need to be considered. What level of control should the operator have? How should the operator, vehicle and ATC communicate and how should any commands be implemented by the vehicle? These are the next hurdles to be tackled.

6. RF Bandwidth

The availability of suitable and adequate radio bandwidth presents the most often quoted limitations to the utilisation of UAVs. The World Radio Communication conferences (WRC) are held every four years. It is the job of WRC to review, and, if necessary, revise the Radio Regulations (ITU[9], 2004), the international treaty governing the use of the radio-frequency spectrum and the geostationary-satellite and non-geostationary-satellite orbits. The next WRC conference that could address the frequency allocations for UAVs is in 2011. Any change to spectrum allocation in favour of UAVs (if it is agreed) would have to be assumed to take several years to implement. This must be assumed to be a restriction on large scale civil UAV operations, unless palliatives (such as more extensive use and clearance of autonomous systems) can be provided.

7. Complexity

The final strand in this section of the paper is to look at system complexity. In the previous sections we looked at how aspects of the baseline CS-23 may be deleted, replaced by a code from a simpler CS or transferred to another part of the UAV system. With system complexity we have a different problem altogether that the manned codes are not really suitable for.

Taking the baseline CS-23 and looking at avionics system safety, the regulation provides a high level requirement but no guidance on how that should be fulfilled. This would appear to be on the assumption that a CS-23 vehicle will not include sophisticated critical avionics systems. In reality, there was an Federal Aviation Administration (FAA) advisory circular (FAA, 1999) published recently which discusses and provides guidance for reducing the DO178B DAL levels for CS-23 aircraft. The discussion is based on the proviso that overall safety is enhanced by providing the General Aviation (GA) pilot with situational information with a limited assurance level rather than pricing such systems out of the market by applying overly strict development standards. As a UAV, Herti requires as a minimum a fly by wire system which needs to be covered under the safety analysis. The only CS which deals with equipment in this category is CS-25 for large aircraft (EASA 2007). Liaison and discussion is therefore required with the CAA to determine which aspects of CS-25 or its Acceptable Means of Compliance should be the source of requirements for Herti.

---

[9] International Telecommunications Union

Figure 6. Herti demonstrator

8. Next Steps

Group 2 represents a major step over the experimental and "war-time only" clearance offered in Group 1 and opens the door to state and civil UAV operations as well as an expansion of military capability. However, in the longer term, the objective is for UAVs to operate routinely in the same manner as manned aircraft, which requires that they fly safely alongside other air traffic in un-segregated airspace.

Whilst it is tempting to consider Collision avoidance as the only real issue for flight in unsegregated airspace, this is too simplistic. If UAVs are to be accepted by the air traffic control, other air users and the public, then they need to behave like other air users. They need to taxi from the apron much like other aircraft, follow instructions much like other aircraft, they need to maintain a safe separation from other aircraft, they need to behave rationally after failures. UAV entry into the airspace is likely to be as much about fitting in, as it is about absolute safety. Fortunately, the march of technology is separately transforming the airspace to be more UAV friendly, and programmes such as the Single European Skies initiative (SESAR)[10] should make the process easier.

The ASD Certification and Qualification Working Group suggested a timescale for progressing through the clearance steps, shown below in Figure 7.

---

[10] http://www.eurocontrol.int/ses/public/standard_page/sk_ses.html

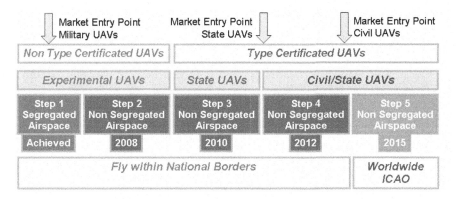

Figure 7. Clearance timescale

9. Conclusion

In summary, the growth of the UAV market presents several regulatory challenges. The CAA has defined a set of airspace criteria to allow for the gradual expansion of vehicles from range operation to a routine operation in civil airspace.

BAE Systems are currently developing the Herti system in both air and ground aspects to make the transition from Group 1 to Group 2. Expansion beyond this into Group 3 and 4 will bring further challenges.

To achieve Group 2 certification for a UAV system no single code of requirements is applicable. The UAV system provider needs to agree with the regulator the baseline certification standard to be used and what appropriate tailoring measures are to be taken, so that at the end, compliance can be shown to be achieved and that all parties believe the system is sufficiently safe.

10. References

Civil Aviation Authority 2004, *Unmanned Aerial Vehicle Operations in UK Airspace – Guidance*, CAP 722, 2nd Ed. Norwich:TSO

EASA 2003. CS-23: 2003, *Certification Specification for Normal, Utility, Aerobatic and Commuter Category Aeroplanes*. Brussels: EASA.

RTCA/EUROCAE 1999. DO-178B:1999, *Software Considerations in Airborne Systems and Equipment Certification*. Washington DC: RTCA, Inc.

ITU 2004. Radio Regulations. Geneva: ITU

FAA 1999, *Equipment, Systems and Installation in Part 23 Airplanes*, AC 23.1309-1C.

EASA 2007, CS-25:2007. *Certification Specification for Large Aeroplanes*. Brussels: EASA.

Safety and Risk Analysis

Safety Analysis: Thoughts on Methods and Experience

Michael Ellims
Pi-Shurlok,
Cambridge, United Kingdom

Abstract

If one opens a book on safety and reliability engineering, one is confronted by the number of available techniques that can be used to analyse the safety and/or the reliability of a system. However in the author's view, often not enough emphasis is placed on the role that experience plays in building a safe system. In this paper I examine some of the issues associated with using common methods and the role in which experience mitigates some of their weaknesses.

1 Introduction

The aim of this paper is to examine the relative importance of method and experience in systems safety analysis. Here method refers to the various techniques that can be used to analyse the system under consideration. These can range from methods to control and organise the whole analysis process such as that laid out in IEC 61508 (2002) which considers the complete lifecycle, to more targeted techniques aimed at a particular part of the problem. Methods or techniques that fall into this second category including HAZOP, FMEA (in its various guises e.g. DFMEA) and fault tree analysis (FTA). There are of course a mind boggling number of different techniques that have been proposed for performing safety and hazard analysis. The Federal Aviation Authority System Safety Handbook (FAA 2005) for example lists 131 "different" techniques for performing hazard and reliability analysis, some of which are complimentary and others provide essentially similar functionality.

It is the author's view that central to the use of these techniques is the experience of the practitioners performing the analysis activities. This central role is highlighted in guidance provided by organisations such as the Health and Safety Executive (2007) whose guidance document on managing competence for safety-related systems states "for a person to be competent, they need qualifications, *experience*, and qualities appropriate to their duties", the emphasis is mine.

Exactly what constitutes experience is somewhat ill defined, and although the related competency guidelines[1] provide some information on the matter, that information is framed in terms of assessment of practitioners. In this paper I shall examine a small number of aspects related to performing the hazard analysis process and try to show how experience is essential in both driving the process forwards and in gaining a satisfactory outcome.

The paper is divided into two parts. The first section lays out the stall on what I believe to be the major aspects of both experience and method. The second examines a small number or areas within the area of safety analysis and attempts to demonstrate how weaknesses in technique can be mitigated by experience.

2 Experience and Method

2.1 Experience

What is experience? The Oxford English Dictionary (OED) defines experience as "actual observation of or practical acquaintance with facts or events" and as "knowledge or skill resulting from this".

This definition is useful in several ways. For example it explicitly states that experience is not simply a matter of book learning, the reading of learned papers or even training. Indeed training in some cases can actually be counter productive in the short term giving an unwarranted confidence in ability McCammon (2000)[2]. Having said that, this type of information is not without its merits as it is impossible for the individual to observe all phenomena that may be relevant and learning from other peoples experience is one of the major achievements of civilisation.

This observation and the OED definitions suggest that when dealing with safety analysis we need to consider two separate but tightly interlinked factors which make up "experience". The first of these is domain knowledge, the explicit knowledge of particular situations, applications, devices etc. The second is understanding, that is the ability to take the domain knowledge and reapply it in the same or similar environments, to new situations, to derive general principles and rules, and to recognise when a similar but not necessarily identical situation occurs.

What we consider domain knowledge also needs to be further expanded on. There are two distinct forms of domain knowledge that are necessary for the execution of a hazard analysis, domain knowledge of the system being analysed and domain knowledge associated with conducting the hazard analysis itself.

---

[1] The author is possession of a copy of the draft document, Competency Guidelines for Safety-Related Systems Parishioners. The most recent version can be obtained from http://www.theiet.org/publishing/books/policy/comp-crit.cfm

[2] The author has actually got the avalanche thing very, very wrong, when much younger and much less experienced.

2.1.1 System Domain Knowledge

How does one obtain domain knowledge of a system? One slightly extreme view is given by Harrisberger's Fourth Law of the Lab which states that, "experience is directly proportional to the amount of equipment ruined" which is perhaps a little unfair. However another chief engineer at Pi-Shurlok has commented that "your not a real calibrator until you've broken your first engine". By this definition the author is not a real calibrator, but has come close on several occasions.

Engine calibration is an example of one method for obtaining experience and perhaps Harrisberger's law somewhat overstates the case. Experience can and will be obtained via success instead of failure, although probably at a slower rate. This is clearly illustrated by the fact that the author has been driving for many years and must have been acquiring experience in the process. However uneventful trips are not memorable. Perhaps luckily, as my employment is closely associated with the automotive industry I have a misplaced fondness for old vehicles that have low purchase costs, what is sometimes know as "bangernomics".

Vehicles such as this have provided a wealth of experience via failure, their root cause (age usually), their effects and how an average driver[3] copes with those failures. For example a naive hazard analysis of an engine that considered it seizing might assume that this would be a life threatening failure. However experience with seizures (two over a three year period) shows that the momentum of the vehicle and the fact that only one cylinder at a time is normally affected means that in reality this may not be much worse than running out of fuel (once). Of course that doesn't carry over to single cylinder motor cycle engines where instead you get dumped on the roadway and eventually wind up in hospital (again once).

These failures, and many others have provided a wealth of experience that I can apply di rectly in my employment. However, and more importantly, these experiences allow one to interpret data that can be accessed from other sources such as the vehicle recall bulletins issues by Vehicle and Operator Services Agency (VOSA 2007) which are published twice a year. Without experience the incidents are only information, useful in itself however the experience allows it to be applied more directly.

The same is true of interpreting information derived from other sources such as books and learned papers. In addition much written material provides something that is usually absent from domain knowledge obtained though experience. It provides the framework for organising other knowledge. Written material explicitly organises a body of knowledge in a way that is not done explicitly by most individuals.

2.1.2 Domain Knowledge of Hazard Analysis

Domain knowledge in the area of hazard analysis is acquired in much the same manner as that of systems, by doing (hopefully without the broken lab equipment).

---

[3] I assume I am somewhere around average as I don't think I'm the worst driver as I haven't caused any accidents on the road and I know I'm not the best.

Domain knowledge in this area is made up of a number of aspects. At its most basic level it comprises knowledge of the techniques and methods themselves. However this is by no means enough.

It also includes knowing at what level the analysis should be applied and what granularity of component should be considered. Just as with building a system from concept though to realisation it is a hierarchical process. However, at times in the process lifecycle it will lead the design process, cutting off possible avenues which could be taken. At others it will trail, being used to determine if the a design is adequate. An example of this type of activity can be extracted from the recommended development process for aviation SAE (1996) where FTA is used at the start of the process to allocate reliability requirements and during the design where it is used to confirm that those requirements have been achieved.

It also contains knowledge of what techniques are appropriate for different tasks, their weaknesses and how they can be adapted to different situations and purposes. It also helps to identify what the weaknesses of the techniques are. Again using FTA as an example, it is primarily used as a technique for determining reliability. However stripped down to its basic form the tree is also capable of revealing multipoint failures with a clarity that is not always apparent with other commonly used techniques such as FMEA.

Along with experience comes a realisation of when the results are suspect. Too often a hazard analysis can be an exercise in showing why a system is safe rather than to discover what can possibly go wrong. The expectation that failure will occur and that it is the norm is for most people a learnt response.

One issue with domain knowledge in this area is that it is quite amorphous. The author is aware that he possibly has considerable domain knowledge in this area however actually defining its composition has been unexpectedly difficult.

2.2 Method

Experience by itself is useful, but not sufficient, as experience exits inside a persons mind and is not directly accessible by others. In addition any one individuals experience is also rather limited, random and often not that well organised. In this form it's of fairly limited use for determining whether a system is safe or not. Therefore there needs to be a way of organising and sharing experience so the analysis can take place. This is the purpose of the methods and technique.

The specific methods and techniques are primarily about organisation and communication. For example some methods organise information by forming it into a list or table: HAZOP and FMEA are both examples. Other techniques organise information by providing a graphical abstraction of the system. FTA gives an abstract view of how subsystems are logically related relative to a specific top level failure mode; for electronic hardware this is usually a refinement of another graphical approximation of the actual physical device, the schematic diagram.

Because information is organised in a consistent way, groups of people can work with the data and add meaning to it, such as identification of failure modes, consequences and effects. It also allows the information to be critiqued by other engineers who may have more experience and knowledge of sections of the analysis. Methods are not magic bullets, they are information exchange systems.

3 Examples

3.1 Systems

The first step in every safety analysis activity is determining what the system being analysed comprises. Immediately we have come to the first and possibly the worst of all the possible problems. What correctly defines the boundaries of the system that we are analysing? It is the one question that has, does, and will continue to plague the hazard analysis process. One man's system is another's component.

For example consider a simple system such as electronic control unit for an internal combustion (IC) engine. If we consider the engine to be the system then its failures and their effects on that system can be defined in a relatively straight forward manner for an experienced engineer (that is one who understands the effects of the controlled parameters in the engine and has perhaps plastered one or two across a test cell from time to time). The problem here is that engines are rarely used as an isolated unit and test cells don't count because the engine is not isolated but is connected to a quite complex load.

The bad news for defining the system boundary is that often there is not a solution unless an organisation is supplying a complete system. It takes experience to recognise and understand this simple fact, years of failing to do it helps. There are partial solutions, but again we have to recognise that they are partial. We can treat the engine purely as a component in a larger system and draw the boundary at the engine. Then we can provide documentation on how the engine will behave and can be operated and integrated safely to the group that builds the engine into the next higher level in the system hierarchy. In some situations this is both allowed and required, for example an industrial engine is considered a machine under the European Machinery Directive (EUD 1998) and machines must be supplied with such documentation. In a similar way the FAA (2003) produce guidance on how an IC engine can be treated as a single component to be integrated with an airframe.

While this is in many cases a practical means of moving forward, and one that is often forced on the analysis process, it is not completely satisfactory. To some extent this can be mitigated by considering "typical" uses. However fairly robust system domain knowledge is required to be able to do this.

To illustrate how this can play out in real situations consider the use of internal combustion engines in passenger vehicles. Here one can reasonably expect that for an engine the boundary of the system is the vehicle itself and the hazards that arise are directly derived by how the vehicle is affected by a failure. At the moment this does not need to directly involve all the other vehicles on the road as there is currently no direct connection between vehicles.

In this case the boundary is reasonably clear. For want of a better expression it's where the rubber meets the road. There are two ways in which we can change the boundary. The first is to add electronics to the vehicle and while this doesn't change the system boundary of the vehicle, it may change the sub-system boundaries within the vehicle. The second is that we can look at similar systems, but change the context and observe how the situation changes.

For engines that are used in heavy good vehicles (HGV's) we find that while the majority of applications are road vehicles, a significant proportion of those vehicles can be considered "unusual". Vehicles such as fire appliances are capable of powering both the vehicle itself and its auxiliary equipment at the same time. Also a significant number of applications, though still vehicles, are a primarily for off-road use such as tractors and combine harvesters. This type of engine is also used in completely different application areas such as marine vessels of various sizes, generator sets and in the pumping of gas and liquids. All of these different applications increase the number of failure modes that may have to be taken into account and the consequences that that have to be considered.

How does experience come into play here? Some system domain knowledge will cross over directly as the mechanics and thermodynamics of the engine are very similar, so is much of the domain knowledge related to engine components and is directly applicable. In a similar way some of application knowledge can be readily adapted. But note the use of the qualifiers "much" and "some". Experience with passenger vehicles is of no use when performing the hazard analysis of maritime vessels.

If we extend the discussion to stationary industrial engines we discover that these are almost as bad, for while they are stationary, this only removes one set of possible failure mode. This doesn't necessarily help as they are used in almost as many different applications. The sheer size of the engines also makes their failure effects worse in that the systems they are incorporated into which potentially have effects over far wider areas. Large engines of this type can supply power to entire towns not just single buildings.

As with the engines used in HGV's some engine specific domain knowledge carries over, however the thermodynamics are slightly different as some of the engines are lean burn units but domain knowledge related to applications such as electric power generation and pumping is directly applicable. At least as the engines are stationary we can discount failures associated with moving vehicles. As an aside, that assumption was of course wrong. There is a railway shunting engine in New Zealand using one of these engines where we assume that fuel is supplied from cylinders of compressed gas (it seems infeasible that a pipeline could be used).

We should now consider what has occurred with our expertise. Domain knowledge with respect to the methods we use to perform the hazard analysis remains intact. However the system domain knowledge has becomes diluted. While our knowledge of how the engine itself performs and fails remains largely intact, the domain knowledge associate with the effects of those failures is now is in large parts redundant.

As domain knowledge is diluted two things need to happen. First it needs to be recognised that knowledge has become diluted. Second the dilution needs to be countered in some manner. Of the two problems the first is the more critical. Failure to recognise the dilution could cascade into flaws with the hazard analysis and further into a failure in the system. Once the first has been recognised the second can be auctioned. Being able to recognise the first requires the experience with the domain knowledge associated with performing the hazard analysis. An inexperienced engineer will often try to perform an analysis regardless of the lack of domain knowledge (guilty). An experienced engineer will be more likely to recognise their own weakness and seek the advice of others.

3.2 HAZOP and FMEA

Once the system boundary has be defined (either by analysis or presented as a fait accompli) we are presented with the task of performing an analysis. At the top level the analysis usually considers the system that comprises of subsystems which in turn need to be considered as systems in their own right. In this section I examine two of the more common techniques for performing this analysis Hazard and Operability analyses (HAZOP) and failure modes and effects analysis (FMEA) and its variants such as the design FMEA (DFMEA).

Both techniques use a tabular format to allow information to be organised. In the classic FMEA the items to be considered are individual components which in an electronic system would be resistors, capacitors etc. However current usage of the term FMEA applies a different interpretation and it is common in practice these days to consider system functions rather than components as the building blocks of the FMEA. Strictly this is a DFMEA, but in practice the use of terminology is rather lose. FMEA also has a facility for ranking failure modes and their effects however for the discussion here this shall be ignored.

Both HAZOP and DFMEA can be used as tools for discovering possible failure modes and enumerating their effects in the system under analysis. However in detail the approach used in the two techniques is somewhat different.

The primary difference to be considered here is the use by HAZOP of a defined set of keywords, the various interpretations that can be applied to them and the literature, primarily Redmill, Chudleigh, and Catmur (1999), that supports the practical application of the technique.

In contrast FMEA is relatively weak in this area with no standard set of keywords, leaving it up to the practitioner to decide what to consider. In some cases help may be provided, for example the Byteworx (2007) tool suggest the following "starter concepts"; no function, function degraded over time, partial function, over function, intermittent function and unintended function. While these can be matched closely with the set of HAZOP keywords, the lack of a standard set means that FMEA lacks the implicate forcing function provided by the keyword list.

Why describe the HAZOP keyword list as a forcing function? First, it can take quite some skill to determine what the meaning of keywords such as "as well as", "other than" and "part of" can take on in the context of the function being examined. The techniques strength is that you are forced to consider how they may apply. Second, it's just that bit harder to be lazy, because the list is standard the omission of a keywords use is glaringly obvious – even to the inexperienced and especially to reviewers. As may have been correctly surmised, I've been recently caught out in this department.

The standard literature for HAZOP also provides a good range of examples of how keywords may be interpreted in different contexts and situations. However the same level of support is not available in standard texts coving FMEA. For example both Palady (1995) and McDermott, Mikulak and Veauregard (1996) provide only a single detailed worked example.

In the terms of our discussion of the importance of domain knowledge it requires of the practitioners performing the analysis to have a relatively high level of skill in both domains.

The fact that the established set of keywords does provide the forcing function is key to my preference for using HAZOP over FMEA. While it may be personally embarrassing to have failed to find an in-context meaning for a keyword. We can take comfort from the fact that someone will normally suggest something to fill the rather obvious hole in the table. It may seem slightly bizarre but when supervising inexperienced engineers tasked with performing FMEA activities I normally point them at the examples section of the HAZOP literature.

Aside from this, the two techniques are otherwise functionally very similar. For some function determine and document how it can fail, what effects this could have and what mitigation is or can be put in place. Both also suffer from very similar weaknesses.

Both techniques are supposed to be applied in a team context, this is as part of a meeting or similar gathering with all the interested parties. While this ideal is possible to for a high level, broad picture analysis, a detailed analysis will occupy significantly more time and hence a meeting based approach is not usually feasible. For example, a recently completed preliminary HAZOP analysis for a FADEC unit extends over 147 pages (and another 77 for the FTA). Getting all the necessary people together in a room sufficiently often to actually complete a work of this size would be extremely expensive and time consuming. Especially so if the interested parties are on different sides of the Atlantic, spread over a number of sites and actually have their day job to do.

What effect this has on the finished product is not totally clear, however it is not likely to be critical (Porter and Johnson 1997) and might even be advantageous as a means of avoiding group-think. One big disadvantage is that the meeting as a venue for training has been lost.

Another problem posed for any hazard analysis of this size is how to organise it. If one followed the guidelines set out in for HAZOP then we would have a 140 page table and by any standard an object of that size is unreadable and probably not that amenable to review. As an alternative its proved feasible to split the analysis up into various tables where each looks at a specific item of the functionality (fuel injection, spark generation, channel synchronisation etc.). Additional adaptation of the process was achieved by applying keywords to sub-system components that affect the functionality. Actually the end result looks rather like a FMEA in some regards. Other authors have performed similar modifications, Trammell and Davis (2001) combining aspects of both methods, so this type of adaptation is perhaps not that unusual.

Does a modification of the technique in this way matter? Possibly not, if you understand the purpose of the adaptation and how it can affect the result. For example the system as a whole is probably too large to deal with as a single item and the division mirrors the actual hierarchical decomposition of the system used to organise the software and hardware design. The weakness here is the potential to miss failures that cross functional boundaries, such as a sensor that impacts both fuelling and turbocharger control which may only be included in one table but must account for failures in both sections. To counter this we of course rely on our domain knowledge of applying the techniques.

3.3 FTA

Fault tree analysis (FTA) is a primarily intended as a technique for evaluating reliability rather than safety. Although as noted above it's actually quite good when used for that purpose provided that we know the top level failure modes. However despite the truism that a reliable system is not necessarily safe (and vice versa), reliability can be a requirement for safety. Engine loss on take-off is dangerous in a single engine aircraft especially if the end of the runway has trees (Craig 2001).

Fault tree analysis is primarily about determining the probability of a specific failure in a specific hardware system and as such is hugely dependant on a number of things being known about the system before the analysis can take place. The primary considerations are;

- knowledge of the top level failure modes,
- knowledge of the system/hardware organisation,
- knowledge of failure modes,
- knowledge of failure rates.

The first of these should be known from a hazard analysis (e.g. HAZOP/FMEA). The second can and probably will be a moveable feast as it will change as the system evolves in response to numerous factors such as component availability[4] and the FTA analysis itself.

Even if we consider *only* the last two points we can encounter significant difficulties. There are several sources of publicly available information on both failure rates; NPRD-95 from the Reliability Analysis Center (1995) and the FRADIP.THREE database from Technis (2006). Failure modes, for example, can be sourced from NPRD-97 from the Reliability Analysis Center (1997). However these data sources suffer from a number of shortcomings. For example the data in both NPRD-95 and NPRD-97 is somewhat dated and does not cover a significant number of components that can be present in a more modern system.

Where the data has been sourced is also an issue. The NPRD data is almost universally derived from military experience and may possibly represent the worst case usage for the components, or it may not. Similar problems exist with data given in FARADIP.THREE in that it is not known whether the data is derived from dishwashers or defibrillators.

Other issues exist with using these data sources. For example O'Connor (2002) explicitly warns against using generic data sources, instead recommending that industry specific data is used. However much field data is confidential to the companies that collect the information and obtaining data directly from manufactures can be problematic, especially if you aren't in a position to order hardware in significant quantities.

Can we deal with these problems in any meaningful manner?

The reality of performing a full blown FTA is actually rather depressing. If a

---

[4] Parts can be come unavailable during development, shortening electronic lifecycles are making this problem more acute.

system contains items that are included in the standard data sources and they used the same terminology to describe it as you do (which they often don't), then one is left with deciding on the appropriate failure rate from the several that are normally presented.

Too illustrate the above, in NPRD-95 what is the difference between an "injector", and an "injector assembly, fuel"? I assume that if you have access to the military procurement numbers then you could work this out, but I don't, which is frustrating. Another issue is that these are diesel[5] injectors but no entry for petrol injectors. Failure rate data is just as frustrating, wiring harness failure rates in NPRD-95 range from 2 to 54 per million hour which forces the use of summary data in more cases than not.

Just as bad is data on the provenance of the failure rate information, NPRD-95 is quite good at supplying some information but a statement on sources such as "Mfr:Various,Pop:5" doesn't inspire huge amounts of confidence and nether does "No Details".

If the components you're seeking information on are not in the data bases then either you have to seek information from the manufacture or find a close equivalent. Manufacturer's data is gold dust, and lets you construct something better than a first order approximation. If this is not available then "engineering judgement" comes into play. For example you may not have detailed information on electronic diesel injectors however some aspects of there construction is similar, but not identical to petrol injectors. Therefore if you have knowledge of failures modes and rates for one then it *may* be possible to reuse some of that knowledge.

For example if we assume that both devices use coils to move a shuttle then it *might* be reasonable to assume that the coils will have similar failure modes and failure rates if the two types of injectors are used in vehicles with similar operating profiles and lifetimes. In the same way failures that affect the connectors will be similar as often the same (or similar) designs are used.

This process of extrapolating from a petrol to a diesel injector can't be carried much further. For example a stuck on failure in a diesel injector is very different from that in a petrol injector. A indirect petrol injector positioned near the inlet values in the manifold will spend a high proportion of its life operating at high duty cycles. It is it designed to operate at or near full capacity. Coping with a stuck on failure is therefore a matter of ensuring that the injector is sized so that a combustible mixture is always obtained.

However this approach doesn't work with a diesel injector as the pressures used are so much higher, as are the flow rates. In this case a stuck on injector could lead to either hydraulic lock or to a loss of pressure in fuel rail resulting in a loss of injection on the other cylinders[6]. If either event occurs the engine stops.

In the same way, a leak on a petrol injector is annoying, it increases fuel consumption, ruins the emissions, but won't (usually) destroy the engine. Petrol is highly volatile and evaporates and burns. A leak on a diesel injector in contrast can potentially dribble into the oil sump, contaminating the oil and eventually cause the engine to seize because of the loss of lubrication.

---

[5] At least I *assume* they are diesel as they are sourced from Cummins.
[6] I don't know, please feel free to perform the necessary hydraulic modelling.

This is an extreme example of the necessity of systems domain knowledge, and down to an extremely low level. If the practitioner isn't in possession of the information required it is going to be terrifically difficult to obtain the knowledge from any other source (I have tried).

The discussion above has concentrated on the problems associated with systems domain. We haven't even touched on issues directly associated with applying the technique.

Firstly, as with HAZOP and FMEA, there are issues associated with the sheer scale of the diagrams that make up the trees and how they are organised. Consider a two channel full authority digital engine control unit (FADEC). If the sensor set for each channel is symmetric, with full duplication then failure of the FADEC channels can be accounted for at a high level in the tree.

However, even in aerospace there exist cost sensitive applications and there are situations where hardware (e.g. sensors) redundancy can be traded off against algorithmic redundancy. That is using different sets of sensors to infer values for non-redundant sensors. However we now have an asymmetric situation where the loss of one channel will affect the tree in a different manner to the loss of the other. In this case the placement of nodes representing channel failures is far less obvious.

4 Discussion

The argument as presented so far presents the three necessary factors for a successful hazard analysis. These form a triangle composed of systems domain knowledge, analysis domain knowledge and the techniques that are applied when actually performing the analysis.

What happens when the analysis is perform when one of these is missing, weak or wrong?

If the application of the techniques is weak then at best we will have a failure to communicate and can suffer all the problems that any failure to communicate can inflict on a system. This failure mode can be found with each of the specific techniques that we have examined.

The situation with a numerical FTA is slightly different. The FTA tree represents an actual equation, the calculation of the expected failure rate. Substituting an AND gate for an OR gate (and vice versa) can make large differences to the values calculated and make the system appear ether far more or less reliable than it in fact is. However the fact that in general a tool is required to perform this type of calculation provides some defence. If there is an *a priori* expectation of the actual reliability should be, then the calculation process itself provides a cross check. Numbers that look wrong probably are. But this again is a learnt response, to question the results that automated tools supply is itself an example of analysis domain knowledge.

An excellent example of the type of result comes from performing analysis according to the MIL-HDBK-217F (1991) standard, as specified by a customer. The analysis provided a predicted failure rate over an order of magnitude larger than the known field failure rate for hardware which operates both in a more demanding environment and has a high parts count. To be aware of this it was necessary to have the relevant system domain knowledge, i.e. actual hardware failure rates. To understand the discrepancy requires knowledge in the analysis domain. There is a significant amount of doubt about the validity of the approach used in MIL-HDBK-217F and that the standard itself is prohibited from use in all new US Army programs. O'Connor (2002) suggests an over emphasis on the effect of high temperature as the main issue. For the grim details both Pecht, Fink and Wyler (1997) and Pecht, et al (1998) are enlightening. However 217F is enshrined in tool sets and customer requirements so its application will probably be perpetual.

We have now slid effortlessly into the area of application domain knowledge, a large part of which is associated with having the ability to determine when the analysis is delivering rubbish. One of the main problems with hazard analysis is the it is often conducted in a superficial manner and locates only the obvious failure modes. There is also a tendency to understate how bad failures can be, often because the systems in which the system is embedded has not been taken into account. A recent example that springs to mind involves the analysis of regeneration on a particulate filter trap for a diesel engine. This had the failure mode "gets hot". This, while technically correct, ignores the possible effects on the vehicle as a whole and brings us neatly into the absolute necessity for systems domain knowledge.

The lack of systems domain knowledge is interesting as in general you don't know what you don't know (I shall resist the temptation to quote a certain US politician). If you don't know about diesel regeneration systems function then you're not going to be able to perform a complete analysis and you're certainly not going to get all the possible consequences right. A trawl of the VOSA recall data finds at least one case where the top level hazard is a risk of the vehicle catching fire. The heat has to go somewhere.

In a similar vein the previous example of an engine seizing in a car and its consequences compared with the case of a motorcycle engine seizing may not be obvious if the person performing the analysis has no experience of motorcycles. Another example is that the hazard analysis of engine failure in passenger cars normally assumes that in a vehicle fitted with power steering the driver will retain residual directional control. This has been tested out on the track by staff at Pi-Shurlok and found to be the case. However with the author's current vehicle, a somewhat boxy, tank-like saloon from the late 1980's, this wasn't the case when it happened *unexpectedly* on a winding country road due to failure of the mechanical idle control. However the driver's normal reaction, to hit the brake hard prevented anything worse that a memorable event to be related in papers on safety critical systems.

5 Conclusions

This paper has presented a case for three necessary elements when undertaking hazard and safety analysis tasks in a robust manner, knowledge in the systems domain, knowledge in the analysis domain and the techniques themselves.

I believe that the order stated above also correctly indicates the relative importance of the three arms of the triangle (ranking order). If you don't understand the system and its application then you are going nowhere. If you don't understand how the techniques should be applied then you have a higher probability of making an error. The technique or techniques used to perform the analysis have an essential supporting role. However it needs to be make clear that no one of these things is sufficient on its own, they are all complementary.

The argument put forward in this paper is not especially rigorous and represents the personal view of the author. However I hope that if not totally convincing it will at least stimulate further discussion on the topic.

Acknowledgements

The author would like to thank Felix Redmill for the invitation to present a paper in this area and allowing the author a wide scope to explore his own ideas. Great thanks is also due to Graham Tebby of Pi-Shurlok for his useful review comments and related discussions and to James Stone and Theresa Ellims for additional comment.

References

Byteworx (2007). http://www.byteworx.com,accessed August 2007

Craig, P.A (2001). The Killing Zone: How and Why Pilots Die. McGraw-Hill, New York, 2001 pp. 96-98

EUD (1998). Directive 98/37/EC of the European Parliament and of the Council, Official Journal of the European Communities,1998

FAA (2003). Aviation Administration, Advisory Circular 33.28-2, Guidance material for 14 CFR 33.28, Reciprocating Engines, Electrical and Electronic Engine Control Systems.

FAA (2005). System Safety Handbook, http://www.faa.gov/library/manuals/aviation/risk_management/ss_handbook/, accessed November 2006

Health and Safety Executive (2007). Managing competence for safety-related systems Part 1: Key guidance. 2007

IEC 61508 (2002). Functional Safety of Electrical/Electronic/Programmable electronic safety-related systems, Part 1: General Requirements, BS EN 61508-1:2002. British Standards, 2002.

O'Connor, P.D.T. (2002). Practical Reliability Engineering, Fourth Ed. John Wily & Sons. Chichester, 2002

McCammon, I. (2000). The Role of Training in Recreational Avalanche Accidents in the United States, Proc. Intl. Snow Science Workshop, Oct 2000, Big Sky Montanna, 37-45.

McDermott, R.E. Mikulak, R.J. Veauregard, M.R. (1996). The Basics of FMEA. Productivity, Portland, 1996

MIL-HDBK-217F (1991). Military Handbook: Reliability Prediction of Electronic Equipment. United States Department of Defence, 1991

Palady, P. (1995). FMEA Failure Modes and Effects Analysis: Predicting and Preventing Problems Before they Occur. PT Publications, Palm Beach, 1995.

Pecht, M.G. Fink, J. Wyler, J. (1997). An Assessment of the Qualified Manufacturer List (QML), IEEE AES Systems Magazine, July 1997

Pecht, M. Boullie, J. Hakim, E.Army Jain, A.K. Jackson, M. Knowles, I. Schroeder, R. Strange, A.D. Wyler, J. (1998). The Realism of FAA Reliability-Safety Requirements and Alternatives, IEEE AES Systems Magazine, February 1998

Porter, A.A. Johnson, P.M. (1997). Assessing software review meetings: results of a comparative analysis of two experimental studies. IEEE Trans. Softw. Eng. 1997; 23:3, 129-145

Redmill, F. Chudleigh, M. and Catmur, J. (1999). System Safety: HAZOP and Software HAZOP. John Wiley & Sons, Chichester, 1999

Reliability Analysis Center (1995). Automated Data Book: Electronic Part Reliability Data, Version 2.20, 1994-1999

Reliability Analysis Center (1997). Automated Data Book: Failure Mode/Mechanism Distributions, Version 2.20, 1994-1999

SAE (1996). Guidelines and Methods for Conducting the Safety Assessment Process on Civil Airborne Systems and Equipment: Aerospace Recommended Practice ARP476, SAE International, Warrendale, 1996

Technis (2006). FARADIP.THREE, Technis 2006

Trammell, S.R. Davis, B.J. (2001). Using a Modified Hazop/FMEA Methodology for Assessing System Risk. Proc. 2nd Int'l Workshop on Engineering Management for Applied Technology 2001

VOAS (2007). Recalls Bulletin, Vehicle Safety Recalls, Vehicle and Operator Services Agency

Simplifying the Creation and Use of the Risk Matrix

Robin Cook
RPS Health, Safety and Environment
Alton, UK

Please note that the views expressed in this paper are the author's own and do not necessarily reflect the views of RPS Health, Safety and Environment

1 Introduction

Likelihood	Severity			
	catastrophic	critical	marginal	negligible
frequent	A	A	A	A
probable	A	A	A	B
occasional	A	A	B	C
remote	A	B	C	C
improbable	B	C	C	D
incredible	C	C	D	D

Table 1: Example risk matrix

A risk matrix, in the context of safety management, is a technique for assigning a risk class to a potential accident[1] or to a hazard in accordance with the predicted severity[2] and absolute likelihood of the potential accident or hazard. This technique involves the construction and application of a two dimensional matrix of the form illustrated in Table 1. The resulting risk class defines how that accident or hazard will be managed throughout the life of the system with which it is associated. This should be defined in a system's safety management system (SMS).

The technique is well established in safety management but suffers from several issues. These include:

---

[1] Section 2.1 addresses the role and application in more detail.

[2] The use of the terms severity and likelihood is discussed in more detail in sections 2.2, 4.2, 4.3 & 4.4.

- Equivalent levels of safety are not delivered by different SMS;
- There are several approaches to 'tailoring the risk matrix'[3] and these deliver different results;
- 'Tailoring the risk matrix' is a little understood process;
- The likelihoods being considered are often so small that it is difficult to consider them meaningfully; and
- The severity and likelihood categories are very broad.

The risk matrix technique itself is not solely to blame for these issues. They relate to the categorisation used and the lack of coherent ways of addressing the requirement in different parts of the overall process. However the risk matrix forms a central focus for these issues.

Effective use of the risk matrix requires a consistent and coherent approach to the process of risk assessment and the processes around it. It also requires knowledge of various techniques for addressing safety requirements and discussing the concepts meaningfully.

To take the safety community, particularly the safety practioners and the safety-related system users and managers, forward towards better use of the risk matrix and the resolution of the current issues requires a general discussion of the use of the technique. The discussion was recently rekindled by Glen Wilkinson (Wilkinson 2007). It is very much needed so that we can make forward progress; this paper is intended to promote that discussion and form a foundation for it. In order to progress a discussion on this subject, this paper aims:

- To summarise and identify the underlying principles of the main processes and techniques involved in evaluating risk, setting risk criteria and their incorporation into the risk matrix and the onward use of the result (risk classes), identifying and explaining some of the concepts and techniques around the successful creation and use of the risk matrix; and
- To make constructive suggestions for simplifying the setting up of a coherent system that is consistent with other systems, suggesting an approach that reduces the number and magnitude of the problems many people encounter with the risk matrix at the current time.

To achieve this, the paper looks at: the role, application and context of use of the risk matrix; the use of the resulting risk class; the evaluation of accidents and hazard in terms of their severity and likelihood; the safety requirements from which the risk matrix is set; and finally the setting up (tailoring) of the risk matrix itself. The result will introduce many to new concepts and give others a platform from which to advance.

Some readers may consider that I have been too free with the concepts and others that I have missed key aspects. I have deliberately sought to reinterpret the

---

[3] See Section 6.1.

principles in the light of more recent supporting techniques, as I believe that this is necessary to overcome the issues being experienced. Alternative definitions have often been used, rather then repeat those that are familiar, to stimulate thought. While I may have interpreted concepts freely, I have aimed to ensure that my usage and any extension of the concepts are mathematically sound. If I have missed key aspects then I apologise. I have tried to be comprehensive but this is a paper, not a book and some selection is necessary. The aim is not to write the ultimate paper on the risk matrix but to address many of the underlying concepts and stimulate the wider discussion.

This paper specifically addresses UK practice although the principles are more widely applicable.

2 The Risk Matrix

2.1 Role and application

As stated in the introduction, the role of the risk matrix is to assign a risk class to a potential accident or a hazard in accordance with the predicted severity[4] and absolute likelihood[5], or frequency, of the potential accident. This can be seen in the example given in Table 1, above. The risk classes (A to D in Table 1) are assigned in accordance with the likelihood and severity determined by the evaluation. The application of these attributes is considered in more detail in section 3, below.

The risk matrix can be applied to hazards, hazardous events or potential accidents. The SMS should define which. An accident is an unintended event during which harm occurs. Accidents (variously termed "accident", "consequence of the hazard" and "mishap") are used by the UK MoD [in 00-56 issue 2 (MoD 1996) but currently moving standards], the UK HSE, and the US DoD [Mil Std 882D(US DoD 2000) and 882E (US DoD 2005)]. Hazardous events are events at the boundary of the system under consideration that may lead to an accident. Risk matrices used for air traffic management by Eurocontrol, the CAA in CAP 728 (CAA 2003) and the UK MoD refer to hazardous events. Other SMS apply the severity to the hazard, defined as a state or condition that contributes to an accident. The US DoD used to work this way [Mil Std 882C (US DoD 1993) and previous versions]. In this paper "accident" is used inclusively for simplicity; the principles apply to all three.

---

[4] The term "severity" as used here includes the concept of the number of harmed people as well as the level of harm to each. Similarly, if environmental harm is being considered, it includes the scope affected. The term is addressed in more detail in section 4.2.

[5] The term "likelihood" is an absolute measure of the frequency with which an event occurs or the probability of an event occurring, once or more than once, in a given period of time. The term is addressed in more detail in sections 4.3 & 4.4.

The risk matrix has no direct role in the evaluation of ALARP[6], its only role being indirectly to affect the rigour of ALARP justification required. The risk matrix uses similar terms as an ALARP justification and the aim of the ALARP principle can be illustrated in terms of the risk matrix when the severity categories are ordered and cumulative. However ALARP is a relative requirement while the tolerability requirement addressed by the risk matrix is an absolute requirement.

The risk matrix technique addresses safety requirements that are essentially quantitative in nature. The risk matrix addresses the level of risk under each severity category. This level of risk can be expressed as a probability of a harmful event occurring one or more times in a given time period, as a mean frequency of such events occurring or as a mean time between such events. Often the probability is categorised (see Section 4.3). Many consider this to result in a qualitative approach. It is however still quantitative. What has been done in generating probability categories is that a small set of discrete levels have been identified and all probabilities rounded to the nearest. It is still possible to perform arithmetic on the categories but the resolution is lowered. Thus "quantitative" remains the appropriate adjective.

Where use of the term "qualitative" arises from may be confusion with the term "subjective". The aspect that is more subjective is how a probability is allocated to an event. Often a subject matter expert, a user or a maintainer, is asked how often they expect to certain events to occur. The safety committee then discusses the situation and allocates a category. This is subjective but still quantitative.

Truly qualitative requirements are not addressed by the risk matrix and are only touched on in this paper. There is, however, much less contention in their setting and evaluation.

2.2 Context of Use

The evaluation and assessment of safety risks is a key process in most SMS. The risk matrix is one technique that supports this process. It is not the only way of performing the evaluation but, in the author's experience, it is the most common. It assigns a risk class according to the severity of the harm resulting from an accident and the likelihood of that harm occurring derived in an evaluation of an accident. The risk class is then used to identify the ongoing level of safety management to be applied to that accident or to the system/equipment as a whole.

Figure 1 provides an example of an SMS that can use a risk matrix. The risk matrix addresses part of the "assess compliance" process within the whole process.

---

[6] ALARP is the UK legal test that requires all possible safety improvements to be implemented until the predicted cost of any further safety improvement is grossly disproportionate to the predicted safety benefits. ALARP is a UK specific requirement that requires the highest realistic level of safety to be delivered. While this approach may seem less exacting than an absolute requirement, it is the most stringent definition possible that can always be complied with.

It provides a simple table (the matrix), set up in accordance with the identified quantified risk criteria, for assessing the results of the evaluation process. An 'acceptable' result is expanded on in section 5.2. Please note that the risk reduction measures are augmented to achieve an acceptable risk, not the risk criteria modified.

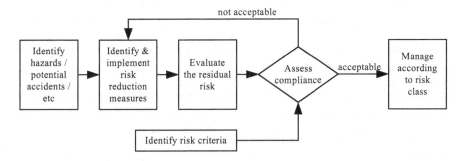

Figure 1: Example part of an SMS that can use a risk matrix

The important aspects of this SMS (in order that a risk matrix can be part of it) are that:

- The risk of harm from the accidents, as reduced by the control measures and mitigating factors, is evaluated in terms of the severity of the harm expected from the accident and the likelihood of the accident happening;
- The system, in part or in whole, is given a safety risk classification based on the residual severity and likelihood, or frequency, of harm and that safety risk classification is then used to define the ongoing safety management regime.

However the risk matrix is not the only means of assessing compliance. On some small simple systems, the likelihood of the harm occurring is so small that it is difficult to consider with meaningful categories. In this case it may be more appropriate for the safety committee to allocate a risk class directly. This is more likely for the lower risk classes (C and D).

It also has to be possible to override the risk matrix. On various occasions people have told me that they have a system in service with one or more risk class As (intolerable) remaining. I contend that these risks have normally been analysed in far more detail than most risks, good ALARP justifications made and considered by relevant authorities. These authorities have then declared the risk to be tolerable, although very undesirable and maybe only for a given time. The A/B boundary has then effectively been moved for that accident and the risk is strictly a class B. This doesn't need to be shown in the risk matrix. Whether the hazard log management system can cope with the situation is a different issue.

3 Risk class and its use

3.1 What is a risk class?

Accidents (or hazardous events or hazards as appropriate, see section 2) and
systems are categorised with a risk class that denotes how they will be managed.

Table 2 shows an example of a set of risk classes. This set is deliberately uses
definitions that are different from those commonly seen. Four risk classes have
been shown as this works well in practice. It is important that people think about
how they are using risk classes in their SMS or the whole approach becomes
meaningless. Also classes C and D have been renamed to address the issue that
where class C is often entitled "tolerable", this gives the incorrect impression that
risk class B is intolerable. Table 3 is a continuation of Table 2 and defines the
action required for systems or accidents according to their risk class.

Class	Title	Definition with respect to a system	Definition with respect to an individual accident
A	intolerable	The system is unfit to enter or remain in service until the associated safety risk has been reduced to a lower risk class	The individual accident renders the system risk class A. Hence the system is unfit to enter or remain in service until this accident has been reduced to a lower risk class.
B	undesirable	The level of safety risk associated with the system is tolerable but without a significant margin for error.	The individual accident is tolerable but without a significant margin for error. Several such accidents may accumulate to render the system risk class A.
C	medium	The level of safety risk associated with the system is tolerable with a reasonable margin for error.	The individual accident is tolerable. The risk is significant but not uncomfortably so. Several such accidents may accumulate to a risk class B.
D	low	The level of safety risk associated with the system is readily tolerable. This class is sometimes referred to as "broadly acceptable".	The individual accident is readily tolerable. The risk is not significant. However, several such accidents may accumulate to form a risk class C. This class is sometimes referred to as "broadly acceptable".

Table 2: Example risk class scheme (definition)

There are two points of view on whether risk class C and D can be allocated to the
higher severities. Logically, there is no reason why not. Risk class B acts as a
buffer below the limit of tolerability. However safety requirements have a sense of
society's expectation about them as well as logical correlation with other safety
requirements. One aspect for the safety committee on any programme to consider

is whether assigning risk class C and the attendant management scheme to the risk of a fatality is acceptable to society. Hence the three Cs in the catastrophic and critical columns of Table 1 could be changed to Bs. It is not a matter of absolute class labels but of the level of management applied to the risks.

Class	Title	Application to a system	Application to an individual risk
A	intolerable	The system is not permitted to enter or remain in service until the associated safety risk has been reduced to a lower risk class.	The individual accident renders the system risk class A. Hence the system action applies.
B	undesirable	If the risk increases, the system is likely to have to be removed from service. Therefore significant effort will be needed to: • Strive to reduce the risk; • Rigorously monitor the risk to identify any deterioration (possibly quarterly reporting); and • Making a rigorous ALARP argument at system level.	Each individual accident at risk class B will need significant effort to: • Strive to reduce the risk; • Rigorously monitor the risk to identify if it deteriorates (possibly quarterly reporting); and • Making a rigorous ALARP argument for the individual risk.
C	medium	Effort will be required to: • Try to reduce the risk; • Monitor the risk to identify any deterioration (annual review); and • Make an ALARP argument at system level.	Each individual risk at risk class C will need effort to: • Try to reduce the risk; • Monitor the risk to identify if it deteriorates (annual review); and • Make an ALARP argument for the risk.
D	low	Some effort but not much will be required to: • Try to reduce the risk; • Monitoring the situation to identify any deterioration (five yearly review); and • Make an ALARP argument at system level.	Each individual risk at risk class D will need some but not much effort to: • Try to reduce the risk; • Monitor the risk to identify if it deteriorates; and • Make an ALARP argument for the risk.

Table 3: Example risk class scheme (action required)

Note that several individual accidents at any risk class may accumulate to form a risk at the next higher level. The splitting of an accident into several lower risk accidents in the analysis has been referred to as "salami slicing" and does not reduce the overall risk. The SMS should ensure that the overall risk is addressed for every system.

3.2 Allocation of risk class to an accident

A risk class is allocated to an accident through applying the risk matrix.

3.3 Allocation of risk class to a system

There are two approaches to the allocation of risk class to a system.

Where the system level likelihood requirement has been numerically divided between the accidents, the maximum risk class of the individual accidents is the system risk class.   This simple method also works where each likelihood requirement relates to only one accident. It can also work where the likelihood of a given severity of harm to a hypothetical individual is recorded as one accident.

Where the risk class is defined by the requirement at system level (not divided by the number of accidents) and more than one accident applies to each requirement, it is necessary to sum the likelihoods of a number of accidents before correct comparison against the system requirement and hence the risk matrix boundaries at system level, can be made. This requires a further step, beyond the functionality of current software hazard log management systems.   However it is important to ensure that the summation is carried out and the basis of risk assessment matches that of the risk requirement.

4 Evaluating potential accidents

4.1 General

For the purposes of providing input to the risk matrix, accidents (or hazardous events or hazards) need to be evaluated in terms of the severity of the resulting harm and the likelihood of that harm occurring.   The risk matrix is tabular (although a continuous version is considered later) and therefore categories must be generated.

4.2 Severity

Severity is a measure of the extent of harm.   In system or functional safety management, the severity normally incorporates the number of victims as well as the level of harm to them.   In health and safety management the number of victims can be considered separately to the level of harm.   This paper is written with a functional safety bias and adopts the combined measure.

In theory it should be possible to have a continuous measure of severity. This is approached by some techniques such as the F/N curve[7]. In practice discrete measures of severity are much more common. When considering harm to an individual, death is a very discrete step as can be levels of disability.

There are two schools of thought on whether the discrete severity categories addressed by the risk matrix are related. It is possible to relate them, particularly if the term "or more" or equivalent is used. This is not normally found to be effective. Alternatively the severity classes can be unrelated. I recommend this latter approach in this paper due to its simplifying effect. There is no one-right-answer. What is important when using the risk matrix is that it is known which of these alternatives is being used.

A traditional example set of severities is provided in Table 4. This set of categories, with slightly longer definitions, has been in use for many years and many people are very comfortable with it and its application to system events.

Category	Brief definition (all apply to an event)
catastrophic	Multiple deaths
critical	Single death and/or multiple severe[8] injuries
marginal	Single severe injury and/or multiple non-severe injuries
negligible	At most a single non-severe injury

Table 4: A traditional example of severity categories

There are three issues with this that underlie the issues raised in the introduction. Firstly, the difference between "single" and "multiple" is small. The terms "few" (for example a car load of people) and "many" (a bus load) might be more appropriate. Secondly, the application to system events makes a translation process necessary. This translation is one of the most contentious items in safety engineering when it is being undertaken and reviewed and is open to varying results. Lastly, the definitions include no mention of the victims. Attempts have been made to address the different requirements for different classes of victim by moving the definitions to different classes to allow for this but the result is a poor compromise.

To resolve these issues requires a change in approach. This change is subtler than the author originally thought. The definitions need a slight rephrasing to match the quantified safety requirements, changing the application of the definitions to "risk to people" not "risk of system events". Safety is not about systems and equipment, it is about people and the environment.

---

[7] The F/N curve addresses the frequency of incidents with n or more fatalities and is more applicable to more severe situations than the risk matrix is normally applied to.

[8] In the UK, a severe injury is normally defined as one that is reportable under the Reporting of Injuries, Diseases and Dangerous Occurrences Regulations 1995 (RIDDOR) (UK Government 1995). This list was originally created for measuring injury at work but forms a practical boundary for defining severity categories.

Table 7, in section4.3, lists a set of quantified safety requirements. The first three of these are taken from R2P2 (HSE 2001). The next two reflect the levels of harm addressed above but are rephrased to address harm to the individual rather than system events. The last is an example drawn from an industry. This is included to show that the approach can address such requirements although it is not the approach in current general use.

Each of the severity categories in Table 7 has an independent quantified requirement. As they are independent, there is no sideways relationship in the risk matrix. This simplifies the process.

4.3 Likelihood of accidents and hazardous events

Likelihood is a measure of how often an event[9] occurs (its frequency) or the probability of it occurring in a given time period. The use of frequency or probability in unit time is arbitrary. Indeed both can be used in the same analysis. The example set of likelihood categories in Table 5 varies the form of definition to the most appropriate for the category (frequency for the categories where an event occurs many times and probability for categories where the event is unlikely to actually occur). The aim of this is to present a definition that makes the most sense to the user of the table. It is notable that probability in unit time and frequency are interchangeable measures provided the frequency is constant with respect to time.

Category	Brief definition (with respect to the operational lifetime of the fleet)
frequent	1000 times in the lifetime of all instances of the system
probable	100 times in the lifetime of all instances of the system
occasional	10 times in the lifetime of all instances of the system
remote	63% chance in the lifetime of all instances of the system
improbable	10% chance in the lifetime of all instances of the system
incredible	1% chance in the lifetime of all instances of the system

Table 5: Example frequency categorisation scheme

The relationship between frequency (f) and probability (P) in time (t) is:

$$P = 1 - e^{-ft} \qquad (1)$$

Other related measures such as mean time between events can also be used.

In the example, factors of ten have been used between the frequency in each category[10] although this can be varied. Many big systems use factors of 100 here.

---

[9] An accident is an event.

[10] The percentages 63, 10 and 1 relate to the frequencies 1, 0,1 and 0.01 in the lifetime of all instances of the system. Equation 1 has been used to derive these values. Using the Poisson

Often a factor in between ten and 100 is optimum but this is rarely seen, as the numbers are not so easy to work with. It is not essential to use a consistent factor but it is simpler to do so.

The definitions in Table 5 are descriptive with respect to the system. These can then be related to actual frequencies and probabilities in unit time. This is normally added to the table as a further column. There are three values to be noted for each category: upper limit, nominal and lower limit. Values are best allocated to provide boundaries at the optimum points to match the quantified safety requirements. This is addressed further in sections 6.3.5 and6.4.5.

4.4 Likelihood of hazards

The likelihood of hazards is different to that of accidents. True hazards [as defined strictly, the UK Defence Standards (MoD 2006) for one source] are states, not events. States can be referred to as conditions. One example is "the vehicle is on a public road". The likelihood of this is measured in terms of the probability of being true at any instant in time. The probability might be 0.1, a number with no units. The probability would be true whether the vehicle went onto the public road once an hour and remained there for six minutes or once every ten days (240 hours) and remained for 24 hours each time. Accidents are events, they cannot be reversed, and have time in their likelihood. An analogy would be reliability (related to time, like an accident) and availability (a simple probability at any instant, like a hazard).

Common hazard log management systems record a likelihood for each hazard using the same likelihood definitions as for accidents. This forces a fudge such as recording the frequency of the onset of the hazard state or the frequency of arriving at the following stage of the accident sequence. Where the frequency of the onset of the hazard state is recorded, then the frequency of leaving the hazard state should also be recorded. The reliability and availability analogy holds well here: a reliability engineer would expect to record mean time to restore (MTTR) as well as mean time between failures (MTBF) if determining availability. Why does a safety engineer expect to work on half the information?

Category	Brief definition	Probability range
always	The hazard is always present	=1
likely	The hazard will often be present, nominally 1 in 3	≥0.1 to <1
rare	The hazard is possible but unlikely, 1 in 30	≥0.01 to <0.1
improbable	Very little chance of encountering the hazard, 1 in 300	≥0.001 to <0.01
incredible	Virtually no chance of encountering the hazard, 1 in 3,000	<0.001

Table 6: Example hazard likelihood categorisation scheme

distribution and summing for the number of events being greater than or equal to 1 gives the same result.

Where time related categories are applied to hazards then the process is either fudged or mathematically incorrect. This issue has persisted for many years and causes difficulty in the process of allocating of likelihoods.

A good solution would be to use a separate set of category definitions. Consider the situation where there is a hazard, say the low visibility of a vehicle when on the public road. The safety committee considers this and finds that "frequent" is a poor descriptor since it fails to address the concept of "always". Table 6 provides an example of a set of hazard likelihood categories. These relate to the instantaneous probability of the hazard existing when another event occurs[11].

4.5 The virtual or hypothetical individual

The concept of the virtual individual is a powerful tool in assessing safety. When we talk of risk to the individual, we have issues with what else that individual does for the rest of the time. If however I consider a virtual or hypothetical maintainer, I can think of this individual maintaining the specific equipment all their working year whether or not any real person would do that. If I provide for this virtual individual's safety then I have addressed the requirement effectively.

As an example, consider a fleet of five vehicles, each expected to be used for 900 hours each year. There might be twenty trained drivers but that is irrelevant (provided there are no issues with currency of experience). What is relevant is how many virtual drivers there are. Now each driver works for around 1800 hours each year. Therefore we have 2.5 virtual drivers (900 x 5 ÷ 1800) and hence 2.5 portions of individual risk budget since no individual can drive two vehicles at once.

As another example, consider a virtual bystander. The virtual bystander is subject to the non-involved risk criterion. They stand by a virtual fence some distance from the system, 24 hours a day. They may experience more risk from other systems; not our problem. This virtual bystander experiences the worst risk that we can subject one uninvolved person to. They may run around the perimeter but they can only be in one place at once; if the perimeter is 100m long and the virtual bystander is 1m wide then there is a 1 in 100 chance of being hit by a single randomly directed projectile. With a virtual individual we can put our blinkers on during the analysis and consider the effect of the system on that one virtual individual not the whole world. Thus the analysis is significantly simplified.

---

[11] By definition an event occurs at an instant. If an event takes time then the time resolution of the analysis needs to be modified. For example: the opening of a door can be described as "the door opens" or alternatively as "the door starts to open", "the door is opening" and "the door finishes opening". If the increased definition is relevant to the analysis then it should be used, otherwise the simpler form suffices.

4.6 Low likelihoods

An issue with evaluating small systems is the low likelihood required for accidents. Many people have difficulty in working with small likelihoods. Consider a special unit that is to be used for eight hours a day, 220 days a year. This matches the working year of the operator/maintainer. Therefore, using R2P2, the tolerability limit for causing a fatality is once in 1,000 years. Too many people this is a meaning less number. However the analysis should look to 100 times less frequent and it is important that this is done. Amending the requirement to make the numbers easier is not a solution.

Two approaches are suggested. One is to analyse the system as if it where much more plentiful, as if there were 1000 units rather than one. The other is to consider a much longer period of use. It may be a counter-intuitive result but as long as the risk matrix is set for number of units and life that is used for the evaluation, the results of the process hold when the life or the fleet size is changed.

5 Identifying Safety Requirements

5.1 Safety Requirements / Safety Targets

In some industries people refer to "safety targets" when they mean "safety requirements". They are different (see the discussion below for definitions). Why is this? Cynically, it began as a contractual trade requested by suppliers to reduce their risk. However the customer can then end up with a system that cannot be put into use! We need both safety requirements and safety targets in order to conduct safety engineering.

A "safety requirement" level needs to be met before the system goes into use; a "safety target" level is an input to the design process and is the level that will be achieved if the design process works well. These terms can relate to quantitative or qualitative measures of the system. With qualitative measures (for example: the end of the train shall be coloured yellow for visibility) there may be no difference between the requirement and the target. However for quantitative measures (such as the level of risk, with which we are more concerned in this paper) the two should differ. The target is normally between ten and a thousand times safer than the requirement. The target must be demonstrably ALARP[12] (this is a good check at the design review before detailed design takes place) while the requirement is an absolute level. The target is then used to set design guidelines and choose appropriate techniques, of which safety integrity levels (SILs) are one example.

The general safety engineering concept is simple and illustrates the difference:

---

[12] Although this paper does not address ALARP, it is relevant here. Unless the target is at least as safe as the ALARP level, the design is unlikely to achieve ALARP status.

1. Understand the **required** maximum risk levels (there may be several for different aspects);
2. Set target maximum risk levels such that meeting the required maximum risk levels (and ALARP) can be demonstrated; and
3. Implement control measures to achieve the target maximum risk levels.

However we need a large education programme to get suppliers to work this way in safety even though it maps what would be done in other areas. This issue is not only related to safety. It is found in reliability and maintainability too. Hence it may relate to all so-called "non-functional requirements".

The risk matrix addresses the requirement, not the target. The boundaries in between risk classes in the risk matrix are based on the A/B boundary being the requirement. The target will normally be located in risk class C or D. Very occasionally a risk class B target may be justified.

It is also important not to over-tighten safety requirements. Over-tightening of safety requirements can result in resource being spent on safety in one area where it would be more effectively spent in another. Safety targets however must be tightened in order that the system meets the ALARP principle.

5.2 Overall requirements

The actual safety requirements will vary from system to system. In the UK (particularly in the UK MoD but not restricted thereto) the general safety requirement can be expressed as:

- All relevant legal safety requirements (acts, regulations and approved codes of practice) have been complied with;
- All safety requirements set by an overarching system or system of systems, if one exists, have been met;
- The risk of harm is as low as reasonably practicable (ALARP);
- The risk is less than any relevant tolerability standards that have been set [the Health and Safety Executive (HSE) and the Civil Aviation Authority (CAA) are examples of bodies that define such standards];
- A safety management system that supports the above four requirements, both initially and for the foreseeable future, is in place and is working; and
- Evidence that the above five requirements have been, and will continue to be, achieved has been collected and collated in a documented safety argument, often known as a "safety case" or in some areas the "health and safety file".

This paper concentrates on the fourth bullet: the risk is less than any relevant tolerability standards that have been set. This is the aspect that the risk matrix addresses. However the requirements are not independent and the fourth may inherit requirements from the others.

For some systems the safety requirements from an overarching system may define the risk matrix. This replaces the generation of a risk matrix for the aspects of the system that it addresses. One example is the situation with air traffic management (ATM) in the UK. Eurocontrol have now issued a risk matrix for the functional risks associated with an ATM system. This can be used with only some interpretation of the accident likelihoods for the functional hazards of any ATM system. However a second risk matrix (or an enlargement) is still required for the physical hazards.

5.3 Tolerability requirements

There is no legal definition of the required maximum tolerability of safety risk, in absolute terms, in the UK. What has happened is that the Health and Safety Executive (the HSE, a body set up by the Health and Safety at Work etc Act 1974) has been authorised as a safety regulator in certain industries. Over a number of years the HSE has determined criteria against which it regulates these industries. These criteria have been published in a document known as R2P2 (HSE 2001) and address societal harm plus the death of involved[13] and uninvolved individuals. The HSE surround all three definitions in R2P2 with caveats and the suggestion that these are initial figures. However they are based on serious work on the level of risk that is just tolerable.

Sources of requirements for the less severe severity categories, non-fatal harm, are more difficult to find. Work carried out by HVR for the Defence Logistics Organisation in 2002 (Giles 2002) established requirements of 12,600 RIDDOR-reportable injuries per 100,000 employees per year and 210,000 non-RIDDOR-reportable injuries per 100,000 employees per year. This work was based on statistics collected and a labour force survey carried out by the UK Health and Safety Commission.

Some industries have other tolerability requirements. As an example of these, the aviation industry has a tolerability requirement for technical faults and failures. This has been used as an example of the type in this paper since it is one of the more established. It is unusual to treat the aircraft example in this manner, possibly because it addresses fatal accidents in an industry where risk class C and D are not applied to fatal accidents. The requirement is still useful to this discussion as it provides a good example and would work if relevant.

This gives subjects and values of the tolerability requirements defined in the UK as listed in Table 7. The table also serves to provide examples of tolerability requirements. All define a maximum acceptable probability of risk.

Some comment is appropriate on the societal figure and its relationship to that for an uninvolved individual. The societal figure applies to a single major industrial activity or equivalent. The uninvolved figure applies to each person individually. There is therefore a large disparity in the application of the two

---

[13] See Section 5.4 for discussion of involved and uninvolved people.

limits. The HSE also introduce a figure to be used when giving advice to planning authorities on new major industrial activities near to housing or housing development near to major industrial activities of $1x10^{-5}$ /year for the limit risk to an individual living in the houses. This can be seen as a variation on the uninvolved individual limit.

Title	Source – Paraphrased definition	Maximum tolerability
societal	R2P2 (HSE 2001) The death of a significant number of people (of the order of 50 or more) from a single event.	$2x10^{-4}$ /yr /system
uninvolved	R2P2 The death of a person caused by a system that they are not working on or with.	$1x10^{-4}$ /yr /person
involved	R2P2 The death of a person working on or with a given system.	$1x10^{-3}$ /yr /person
severe	Giles 2002 A RIDDOR reportable injury.	$1.3x10^{-1}$ /yr /person
marginal	Giles 2002 A non-RIDDOR reportable injury but where working time or equivalent is lost.	2.1 /yr /person
technical	Joint Airworthiness Requirements (JARs), etc reflected in JSP 553 (MoD 2006) as an example of an industry specific requirement. Loss of an aircraft or death of any aircrew or passengers due to a technical failure on a civil aircraft or aircraft derived from a civil type.	$1x10^{-7}$ /flight hour

Table 7: UK Tolerability requirements

5.4 Involved and uninvolved individuals

The HSE has identified a distinction between involved and uninvolved individuals. This appears in Table 7. In simple terms:

- A person who is involved with a given system or item of equipment is one who is working on that system, normally as crew or a maintainer, and derives most of their current safety risk from that system;
- A person is uninvolved when they are working on other equipment (from which they derive their main risk) or observing from a distance.

There are borderline cases, for example riding as a passenger; these are for the appropriate safety committees to discuss. A corollary to the definition is that involved individuals are at risk for only the working day while uninvolved individuals are at risk for 24 hours each day. A maritime example might be a ship navigator who is involved with the navigation equipment while on watch (and at risk from using the equipment) but is uninvolved while off watch (not at direct risk but still at risk from poor navigation).

5.5 Victim-based requirements versus system-based requirements

Traditionally the risk matrix has been set against the likelihood of system events. The safety requirements (Table 7) are generally set in terms of risk to the individual. This has resulted in difficult and often poorly justified manipulation of the victim-based requirement into a system-based requirement in order to achieve this. This is probably the main cause of the problems experienced with setting the risk matrix. It is entirely feasible to leave the requirements in their original terms and allocate a column of the risk matrix to each one.

The main advantage of leaving the requirements in their original terms is that there is no manipulation to be carried out and justified. There is also a second advantage in that, generally, when more examples of a system are put into use, the usage pattern changes or the life of a system is shortened or extended, the risk matrix remains the same. If you are operating a fleet of vehicles and double the number of vehicles then you also double the number of drivers. Each new driver brings additional risk budget. Using the traditional system based approach, the risk matrix changes every time a change is made. A third advantage of victim-based requirements is that the analysis can address less scope at one time. One victim can be considered in one environment, evaluated and the analysis move on. There are more individual analyses to carry out but each one is easier. The approach also removes the paradox associated with the number of passengers in a vehicle (or the number of crew in an aircraft etc). I remember a gentleman from the RAF raising a point at a meeting on safety management in the early 1990s. His issue was that the emerging safety management standard required the safety requirement for a Tornado aeroplane to be ten times safer that that for a Jaguar aeroplane. This was due to the former being a two-crewmember aeroplane while the latter was a single-seater. With victim-based requirements, the requirement becomes the same. The same effect occurs with the number of traveller in a vehicle when changing from driver only to driver and passenger.

The disadvantage of victim-based safety requirements is that many people are very system oriented. Many will want to address the rate of dangerous occurrences on a given platform (be it an aircraft a ship, a telephone or any other item). This can form a good focus for the analysis but if the requirement does not address the item it should remain as a focal point not drive the risk matrix.

6 Tailoring of the Risk Matrix

6.1 General

The role, form and context of use of the risk matrix are addressed in the introduction (Sections 2.1 and 2.2). Table 1, shows the general form. Each column has an A at top and proceeds through B and C to D as the likelihood reduces. However the matrix may only show the middle portion.

'Tailoring the risk matrix' is the process of setting the risk class for each severity/likelihood combination with reference to the safety criteria. It is important that the A/B boundaries reflect the level of risk above which the system would not enter or remain in service and the other boundaries follow appropriately.

6.2 Qualitative Tailoring

While the bulk of this paper addresses the quantitative tailoring of the risk matrix, it is quite feasible to allocate risk classes to severity-likelihood pairs through discussion of the acceptability of pairs by the safety committee. This does have connotations of the "smoke filled room" as a method but can be sound when the practitioners have sufficient experience. The auditor would normally expect to see good minutes including supporting justifications of suitably qualified and experienced people (SQEP) being present. However this method will never achieve the required consistency between differing systems.

6.3 Traditional Tailoring

6.3.1 Introduction

One of the issues with the risk matrix is the large variety of approaches to tailoring the risk matrix. This is one and presents themes that are common to many approaches.

6.3.2 Step 1 - Identify the severity categories

Traditionally, programmes have adopted the severity categories in Figure 1 without further thought.

6.3.3 Step 2 - Identify the requirement for the single death column

The single death column is addressed first. This relates to the R2P2 figures (risk to an individual of fatality at work to be not more than 0.001 in any calendar year etc). Before the HSE produced R2P2 (HSE 2001), the aircraft figure of one accident per 1×10^7 operational hours (or 1×10^6 for military equipment) was used as the basis for this column (including many non-aircraft programmes). Both of these require the figures to be converted to appropriate system events.

Many approaches to this conversion have been attempted but very few are justified to a good standard. The question is "What frequency of system events, where a single death is likely (f_{max}), equates to the risk of 0.001 per calendar year of death to each involved individual?" One of the simplest forms is:

$$f_{max} = n.p.R \qquad (2)$$

where:

 n is the number of people directly at risk from the system;

 p is the proportion of their time that they spend with the system;

 (n.p is then the number of hypothetical people at risk from this system all year)

 R is the limiting risk probability for tolerability.

For example: if 200 operators (n) are directly at risk from the system under analysis, each for 50% of the time (p), then this constitutes 100 hypothetical operators (n.p). This figure is multiplied by the limit (0.001 per calendar year) giving 0.1 per calendar year or one such event every ten years. If the life of the system (t) is 25 years then the tolerability limit is 2.5 fatal events (f_{max}.t) in the life of the system. Note that it at this late stage that the system life has entered the considerations.

This seems relatively simple but is confused by the presence of different classes of individuals, risks from other systems and the low numbers that emerge. The two main classes of involved individuals are operators and maintainers. The number of maintainers is normally lower than the number of operators and they work on the system for a lower proportion of the year. Therefore a lower f_{max} is applicable for maintainers. A complication for the operators is that they may be operating several systems at once. Their risk budget must therefore be divided between these systems. These aspects are rarely well addressed and assumptions are made in order to simplify the evaluation process. The hidden nature of the assumptions, given the practitioners' familiarity with them, and the gross nature of the simplifications gives rise to some of the issues raised with the risk matrix process.

In many programmes the limiting value is apportioned to the various (independent) accidents. This avoids the need to consider the accumulation of accidents but again reduces the figure. In the example given we are now down to 0.25 or 0.1 of an event in the lifetime of the system and some system experts see this as zero and need to be guided into thinking of it as a probability.

This tolerability requirement defines the A/B boundary in the single death column. The B/C boundary is placed a factor of ten (normally one category) lower and the C/D boundary a factor of a thousand (in line with the ratio between the R2P2 quantitative definitions the limiting risk of death for an involved individual and "broadly acceptable") below the A/B boundary. Class C therefore relates to one or two likelihood categories depending on the size of the categories (see section 4.3.

6.3.4 Step 3 - Identify the requirement for the other columns

Ideally, the working in the previous section should be repeated for each column based on an original safety requirement that related to that column.

In practice, this is rarely done. The quantified requirements are stepped from the single death column: one category more onerous for multiple deaths, one less onerous for severe injuries and two less onerous for non-severe injuries. This produces the diagonal lines visible in Table 1. As a process this makes assumptions on the size of each category and that one step is appropriate. It is however simple although difficult to justify.

6.3.5   Step 4 - Identify suitable likelihood categories

Typical likelihood category definitions are listed in Table 5. It is now necessary to identify the boundaries in quantified terms. One approach to this is to start with the remote-improbable boundary. The 63% and 10% values were derived using frequencies of 1 and 0.1 in the lifetime and equation 1. The initial value for the boundary is set to the geometric mean of the two frequencies (0.32). This equates to 27%.

Note that if converting years to hours then care must be taken to select calendar hours or working hours as appropriate.

Defence Standard 00-56 (MoD 2006) identifies that where the requirement lies in a specific likelihood category then the boundary shall be placed at the bottom of this category. This very correctly allocates either the ideal boundary or a more onerous one. In order to minimise the onus on safety management, the boundaries should be set so that a minimal level of requirement increase arises out of this digitisation process. As the boundary is adjusted, so that required limiting frequency is on or just above the nearest boundary, so the probability of the event happening at the nominal (midpoint[14]) frequency in each category reduces. A quick check on the reasonableness of the result can be obtained by calculating the probability of an event in the lifetime of the system and checking that "likely" is interpreted as >50% and "unlikely" as <50%.

The other categories are then defined by applying factors as discussed under likelihood in Section 4.3. A check can be made on the size of the categories by checking that the nominal value of the frequent category equates to the definition.

6.3.6   Step 5 - Populate the risk matrix

In each column, identify the next frequency boundary (Section 6.3.5) below the tolerability limit (Sections 6.3.3 and 6.3.4). Make each entry above this point risk class A. Make the one entry below, in each column, risk class B. Make the two entries below that risk class C and any more risk class D.

Now consider whether the result makes sense. If, as considered in Section 3.1, it is decided that risk class C and D are inappropriate where fatalities are involved then any Cs and Ds in that area must be replaced with Bs.

---

[14] Note that the midpoint in a geometric sequence is obtained by applying the square root of the multiplying factor. In the sequence 1, 10, 100 the midpoints are 3 and 30, not 5 and 50.

6.4 Revised approach to the risk matrix

6.4.1 Introduction

The following presents a method of tailoring the risk matrix that I regard as easier, more correct and more effective than the other approaches that I have seen. It avoids the conversion from individual risk to system risk; it is the method that I would prefer to use; and it illustrates several issues to be considered in formulating a good common approach. It has been published previously (Cook 2007). This description incorporates a number of improvements.

The two key differences of this from the method normally used are that:

- The severity category definitions change to directly reflect the issues addressed by the top-level quantified safety requirements; and
- The definition of likelihood/frequency categories becomes the last stage and can vary between severities when that aids understanding.

6.4.2 Step 1 – Identify the safety issues subject to quantified safety requirements

The severity categories should be defined in a manner that directly addresses the issues addressed by these requirements. Table 7 identifies the three areas addressed by R2P2 (HSE 2001), the two injury requirements and an example single industry requirement. These have quantified requirements associated with them and are the general requirements in the UK today. For any specific application, the existence of other requirements will need to be investigated.

6.4.3 Step 2 – Quantified requirements

Table 7 also provides the values associated with the severity definitions. These are used as the A/B boundary points. R2P2 also talks about the level of risk that can be considered "broadly acceptable". This is taken to relate to the C/D boundary. Both sets of values are listed in Table 8 (note that the values for severe and marginal have been rounded) in a format ready for expansion to address the risk class boundaries.

	Severity					
	societal	uninvolved	involved	severe	marginal	technical
A/B boundary	2×10^{-4} /yr /system	1×10^{-4} /yr /person	1×10^{-3} /yr /person	1×10^{-1} /yr /person	2 /yr /person	1×10^{-7} /flying hour
C/D boundary		1×10^{-6} /yr	1×10^{-6} /yr			

Table 8: Quantified safety requirements

The reference to years looks simple until the conversion to hours is carried out. This shows an underlying issue that can be addressed with thought. The conversions are included in Table 9. The number of hours at risk in a year has been added to aid understanding (8760 for a calendar year and 1800 for a working year). It is recommended that years or hours be used according to which most applicable to the assessment being made. Traditionally hours have been used. It may be that years are generally the better option.

Having carried out the change to hours, this can be seen to be the start of the conversion that was being avoided in this revised approach. Therefore, after using the conversion to illustrate the point, it is recommended that the original units be retained.

The completed set of boundary values is given in Table 9. Values for the B/C boundaries have been added a factor of ten below the A/B boundary. Where the system is such that C and D are not used, the B/C and C/D boundaries will not appear. Unless otherwise directed (the uninvolved column) the C/D boundary has been placed a factor of a thousand below the A/B boundary, in line with the involved column and older practice.

	Severity					
	societal	uninvolved	involved	severe	marginal	technical
Hours at risk /yr	8760	8760	1800	1800	1800	Not applicable
A/B boundary	2×10^{-4} /yr /system	1×10^{-4} /yr /person	1×10^{-3} /yr /person	1×10^{-1} /yr /person	2 /yr /person	-
	2×10^{-9} /calendar h /system	1×10^{-8} /calendar h /person	5×10^{-7} /working h /person	5×10^{-5} /working h /person	1×10^{-3} /working h /person	1×10^{-7} /flying hour
B/C boundary	2×10^{-5} /yr /system	1×10^{-5} /yr /person	1×10^{-4} /yr /person	1×10^{-2} /yr /person	2×10^{-1} /yr /person	-
	2×10^{-10} /calendar h /system	1×10^{-9} /calendar h /person	5×10^{-6} /working h /person	5×10^{-6} /working h /person	2×10^{-4} /working h /person	1×10^{-8} /flying hour
C/D boundary	2×10^{-7} /yr /system	1×10^{-6} /yr /person	1×10^{-6} /yr /person	1×10^{-4} /yr /person	2×10^{-3} /yr /person	-
	2×10^{-12} /calendar h /system	1×10^{-10} /calendar h /person	5×10^{-10} /working h /person	5×10^{-9} /working h /person	1×10^{-6} /working h /person	1×10^{-10} /flying hour

Table 9: Quantified risk class boundaries (no categorisation)

6.4.4 Step 3 – A columnar chart

These quantitative boundaries (Table 9) can be plotted on a chart. Multiple scales can be used as required. The chart based on Table 9 is shown in Figure 2. Note that there is a break between the marginal and the technical columns as the likelihood scale changes from years to flying hours. Also note that the chart is continuous vertically, not categorised.

This is sufficient to allow each risk to be allocated a risk class. It allows risk to be accumulated in each column where that is appropriate. It is also constant across all systems (subject to removing or replacing any columns in addition to the first five) and holds when a system's life is extended or the fleet size is increased! However it does require people to work with numbers.

The severity columns apply to individuals or systems as per the units in Table 9.

frequency (/year, societal to marginal)	severity						frequency (/flying hour, for technical)
	societal	uninvolved	involved	severe	marginal	technical	
10							1×10^{-3}
					A		
1				A	B		1×10^{-4}
0.1	A	A	A		C	A	1×10^{-5}
				B			
1×10^{-2}							1×10^{-6}
1×10^{-3}				C			1×10^{-7}
			B			B	
1×10^{-4}	B	B					1×10^{-8}
1×10^{-5}			C	C	D	C	1×10^{-9}
1×10^{-6}	C	C		D			1×10^{-10}
1×10^{-7}	D	D	D			D	1×10^{-11}

Figure 2: Columnar chart of continuous frequency/likelihood for each discrete severity

6.4.5   Step 4 – Create likelihood categories

Likelihood categories enable people to work with frequency and likelihood concepts rather than numbers.

Note that:

- Category boundaries do not have to be separated by a consistent factor (but it helps);
- The factor between boundaries does not have to be 10 or 100; and
- Different definitions can be used for different severities if that helps.

The continuous likelihood version of the risk matrix in Figure 2 shows the ideal category boundaries. The actual boundaries between risk classes will decrease in risk from the ideal to the next likelihood category boundary below. Hence it is desirable to set the likelihood boundaries on or just below the ideal to minimise this decrease, as discussed in section 6.3.5. Options for likelihood categories can be tried and the best fit selected. .

Table 10 shows numbered categories defined by frequency ranges that are reasonably compatible with the ideal in Figure 2. In Figure 2 (which is the general case in the UK) the boundaries are all on values of $1x10^n$ or $2x10^n$. If categories are set up based on boundaries at $1x10^n$ per year, and $1x10^n$ per flying hour, then a few boundaries will be rounded down from $2x10^n$ to $1x10^n$, which is generally not too significant

Category titles and definitions are then created from the frequency definitions. A verbal definition is required for each category and it often helps to change from frequency definitions to likelihood definitions as the risk decreases (this makes the definitions more meaningful). Likelihood/frequency category definition is where the relationship to the size of the fleet and numbers of people using the system becomes relevant. For example if the safety committee is used to the concept of "remote" relating to one incident in the life of the system as being unlikely, then this can be used as the definition of the most relevant category. The definition interprets the category for a given severity and can be clearer and more relevant than the traditional approach given its generation late in the process.

6.4.6 Step 5 – Convert the chart to a matrix

Finally the complete risk matrix can be drawn by converting the chart of Figure 2 to form the risk matrix in Table 10. In this example the category titles and definitions have been omitted. They should take the form illustrated in Table 5.

Category	Frequency /year	Severity						Frequency /flying hour
		societal	uninvolved	involved	severe	marginal	technical	
1	≥ 1	A	A	A	A	A	A	$\geq 1 \times 10^{-4}$
2	1 to 0.1	A	A	A	A	B	A	1×10^{-4} to 1×10^{-5}
3	0.1 to 1×10^{-2}	A	A	A	B	C	A	1×10^{-5} to 1×10^{-6}
4	1×10^{-2} to 1×10^{-3}	A	A	A	C	C	A	1×10^{-6} to 1×10^{-7}
5	1×10^{-3} to 1×10^{-4}	A	A	B	C	D	B	1×10^{-7} to 1×10^{-8}
6	1×10^{-4} to 1×10^{-5}	B	B	C	D	D	C	1×10^{-8} to 1×10^{-9}
7	1×10^{-5} to 1×10^{-6}	C	C	C	D	D	C	1×10^{-9} to 1×10^{-10}
8	1×10^{-6} to 1×10^{-7}	C	D	D	D	D	D	1×10^{-10} to 1×10^{-11}
9	1×10^{-7} to 1×10^{-8}	D	D	D	D	D	D	$< 1 \times 10^{-11}$

Table 10: Example risk matrix

Some hazard log management systems have a limited number of severity and likelihood categories available. This should be extended for flexibility. However if there are insufficient severity categories then two hazard logs will be required. This approach has often been used for functional and physical hazards with their different risk matrices. If there are insufficient likelihood categories then categories will need to be combined or end categories omitted. In the example in Table 10, categories 1, 8 and 9 can reasonably be removed. This prevents a risk class A being assigned to the risk of chopping a finger at the knuckle weekly but the standard example in Defence Standard 00-56 for many years has had risk class B at the top of this column. Columns 7, 8 and 9 address the low risk classes with the more severe accidents where assigning risk class D is controversial anyway. Also in this example, it can be seen that, with changes on each boundary, combining categories would cause significant increase in the assignment of a higher than necessary risk class.

6.5 Using the suggested risk matrix

The suggested risk matrix is very generic. Therefore it remains constant through changes in system lifespan and the size of the system.

It also addresses risk to the individual. Therefore each scenario can be evaluated separately, considering two or three hypothetical people who are at risk all year. Is the person standing by the fence all year during activity X tolerably safe? If the answer is yes then the evaluation can pass on to activity Y, the operator or the maintainer. It is feasible to evaluate each class of person at each activity – a handle turning exercise.

7 Conclusion

This paper has presented a rapid description of the risk matrix, the processes around it and several techniques that support its use. It has also presented a new approach to the risk matrix that highlights just what can change to make its setting up and use easier and more understandable. Indeed the suggested approach leaves the definition of the likelihood severities to the end and makes it unnecessary.

In particular:

- We need to think more broadly to resolve the issues with the risk matrix techniques and be prepared to challenge the initial steps and dogma that surrounds it;
- Techniques such as considering hypothetical people and risk to the individual have much to offer in setting requirements and analysing their satisfaction;

I hope that readers find the suggested alternative risk matrix of interest. I believe that it is conceptually and practically easier to apply and understand. I also believe that it is inherently more correct. Please try the ideas and see how they work.

Let us continue this debate and move towards the goal of consistent safety requirements addressed in a consistent manner. As the overall discussion progresses it should itself be evaluated. Its effectiveness can be assessed by the extent of:

- The identification and resolution of the issues with safety criteria and their application; and
- The convergence of the safety management and assurance industry to safety criteria that are increasingly consistent and justifiable.

References

Wilkinson G (2007). Safety criteria – getting it right. Safety Systems, The Safety-Critical Systems Club Newsletter. Volume 16, Number 3, May 2007.

MoD (1996). Safety Management Requirements for Defence Systems, Def Stan 00-56. Issue 2, 13 December 1996 (note that, while superseded, this standard is often quoted as it contains information on techniques that has not yet been incorporated elsewhere)

US DoD (2000). Department of Defense, Standard Practice for System Safety, Mil Std 882D, 10 February 2000

US DoD (2005). Department of Defense, Standard Practice for System Safety, Mil Std 882E draft 2, January 2005

CAA (2003), CAP 728, Management of Safety, Issue 1, 28 March 2003, ISBN 0 86039 9 12 5

US DoD (1993). Military Standard, System Safety Programme Requirements, Mil Std 882C, 19 January 1993 (note that, while superseded, this standard is still often quoted in preference to 882D due to the latter's minimalist nature)

UK Government (1995). Reporting of Injuries, Diseases and Dangerous Occurrences Regulations 1995 (SI 1995/3163)

HSE (2001). Reducing risks protecting people, The HSE's decision-making process. HSE, London, C100, December 2001. ISBN 0 7176 2151 0

Giles P (2002). Safety Criteria Calculator for Land Systems (Explanatory Note), LR01z/002 Issue 1, October 2002, produced by HVR-CSL for the Defence Logistics Organisation

MoD (2006). Military Airworthiness Regulations, JSP 553, 1st Edition, Change 4, 1 November 2006

MoD (2006). Ministry of Defence, Defence Standard 00-56, Safety Management Requirements for Defence Systems, DS0056 iss 4

Cook R (2007). A novel approach to tailoring the risk matrix. Safety Systems, The Safety-Critical Systems Club Newsletter. Volume 16, Number 4, September 2007.

AUTHOR INDEX